VisualAge for C++

Visual Programmer's Guide

The VisualAge Series

Bitterer, Brassard, Nadal, and Wong
VisualAge and Transaction Processing in a Client/Server Environment

Bitterer, Hamada, Oosthuizen, Porciello, and Rambek
AS/400 Application Development with VisualAge for Smalltalk

Bitterer, Carrel-Billiard, Bianco, Bosman-Clark, Georges, and Tsang
World Wide Web Server Development with VisualAge for C++ and Smalltalk

Carrel-Billiard, Jakab, Mauny, and Vetter
Object-Oriented Application Development with VisualAge for C++ for OS/2

Carrel-Billiard, Friess, and Mauny
Programming with VisualAge for C++ for Windows

Fang, Chu, and Weyerhäuser
VisualAge for Smalltalk and SOMobjects: Developing Distributed Object Applications

Fang, Guyet, Haven, Vilmi, and Eckmann
VisualAge for Smalltalk Distributed: Developing Distributed Object Applications

Nilsson, Jakab
VisualAge for C++: Visual Programmer's Handbook

VisualAge for C++
Visual Programmer's Handbook

Dale R. Nilsson
Peter M. Jakab

PRENTICE HALL PTR
UPPER SADDLE RIVER, NEW JERSEY 07458
http://www.prenhall.com

To join a Prentice Hall PTR Internet mailing list, point to:
http://www.prenhall.com/register

Library of Congress Cataloging-in-Publication Data

Nilsson, Dale.
    VisualAge for C++: Visual programmer's handbook / Dale Nilsson and Peter Jakab.
        p.   cm.
    Includes index.
    ISBN 0-13-614322-9
        1. Visual programming (Computer science) 2. VisualAge.
    3. C++ (Computer program language)   I. Jakab, Peter. II. Title.
QA76.65.N55   1996
005.1'18--dc21   96-41953
                                                           CIP

Editorial/production supervision and Interior Design: *Joanne Anzalone*
Manufacturing manager: *Alexis R. Heydt*
Acquisitions editor: *Mike Meehan*
Marketing Manager: *Stephen Soloman*
Editorial assistant: *Kate Hargett*
Cover design: *Design Source*
Cover design director: *Jerry Votta*

© 1997 by Prentice Hall PTR
Prentice-Hall, Inc.
A Simon & Schuster Company
Upper Saddle River, New Jersey 07458

The publisher offers discounts on this book when ordered in bulk quantities.
For more information, contact:
Corporate Sales Department
Prentice Hall PTR
1 Lake Street
Upper Saddle River, NJ 07458

Phone: 800-382-3419, Fax: 201-236-7141
E-mail: corpsales@prenhall.com

Printed in the United States of America
10 9 8 7 6 5 4 3 2

ISBN 0-13-614322-9

Prentice-Hall International (UK) Limited, *London*
Prentice-Hall of Australia Pty. Limited, *Sydney*
Prentice-Hall Canada Inc., *Toronto*
Prentice-Hall Hispanoamericana, S.A., *Mexico*
Prentice-Hall of India Private Limited, *New Delhi*
Prentice-Hall of Japan, Inc., *Tokyo*
Simon & Schuster Asia Pte. Ltd., *Singapore*
Editora Prentice-Hall do Brasil, Ltda., *Rio de Janeiro*

To my three sons Karl, Erik, and Nikolaus who I miss when traveling on business and who can't wait for Dad to finish writing the book. And to my loving wife, Jacqueline, for her patience, understanding, and endless support.

—Dale Nilsson

To my wife Mabel, my daughter Jessie and my son Justin. Without their support and encouragement this book would not have been written. And lastly, to Goldie, our Golden Retriever, who always kept me company during the long days and nights writing this book.

—Peter Jakab

Table of Contents

List of Figures

List of Tables

List of Code Segments

Foreword

The need for a new breed of application development tools has never been greater. Today's developer is faced with increasing complexity, cross platform requirements, client server requirements, and the need for increased productivity. IBM's VisualAge for C++ product on OS/2 and Windows (95 and NT) was developed with the objective of helping developers deal with these challenges. It consists of a very robust set of class libraries, application builder tools, and an integrated development environment. VisualAge for C++ represents a state of the art C++ development environment.

VisualAge for C++ has been recognized with numerous external awards.

- ❏ In March of 1995 at the Object World Conference in Boston it won 2 awards:
- ❏ Attendees Choice Award for "Best New Object Technology Product"
- ❏ Judges Choice Award for "Best New Application Development Tool".
- ❏ In October of 1995 OS/2 Professional Magazine named it the— "Best New Development Tool".
- ❏ In March of 1996 at Object World Conference in Boston the Compound Document Framework shipped as part of IBM Open Class was awarded—"Best New Component."

There are so many powerful tools and capabilities in these two products that I feel we must have a comprehensive book to articulate the capabilities to you. I am very pleased that Dale Nilsson and Peter Jakab have taken on this challenge. Both Dale and Peter are experienced C++ programmers and both have taught, demoed, and extensively interacted with a great number of customers on these products. Their practical style leads the reader through a series of application development exercises, adding on new functions as the application becomes more complicated. You will find the material easy-to-learn and easy-to-reference.

Welcome to the world of VisualAge for C++. You will be glad you are part of it.

Robert LeBlanc
Director, Object Oriented Application Development
IBM, Software Solution Division

Preface

What's in this Book

This book is adapted from a one week intensive class developed to provide Proof-of-Concept Prototyping education to software services providers. This course was taught, by the authors, to customers and IBM developers to jump start the introduction of VisualAge for C++. The attendees provided feedback each time the course was conducted. This feedback was used to improve the course content. The course was taught to developers all over the world, including the United States, Canada, France, Taiwan, Australia, Brazil, and Japan.

We had many requests for the course material from people wanting to learn VisualAge for C++. We decided to convert the course to a book that could be used for the course and by individuals for self-study. To make the book we combined the course presentation material, the lab scripts, and lecture content into this book.

While making the book we improved all the sample applications. We improved their design, used better controls, and adapted them for the Windows version.

This book helps you learn VisualAge for C++ with step-by-step instructions. The book assumes you already understand the basics of the C/C++ programming language and Object Oriented programming concepts. Additional books that can help you with these areas are listed in the Related Publications section.

This book helps prepare you for IBM VisualAge for C++ Certification. There are currently two levels of certification:

Certified VisualAge for C++ Object-Oriented Associate Developer

Certified VisualAge for C++ Object-Oriented Developer

This book is the result of a truly a collaborative effort. Both authors contributed equally to the entire book with their writing and technical skills. The result of this effort is an easy to follow, comprehensive handbook for learning VisualAge for C++ Visual Programming.

Congratulations to Dale Nilsson for winning the coin toss which determined whose name went first on the cover of the book.

How the Book is Organized

Every chapter in this book starts with a brief description of what will be covered in the chapter and ends with a summary. The book has a number of small applications to illustrate a broad range of application development topics. The applications in the following list start with the very simple and progress to more complex as you proceed through the book:

- ❑ Hello World
- ❑ Adding Machine
- ❑ Calculator
- ❑ Reminder List
- ❑ Car Lease Calculator
- ❑ Flat file Reader
- ❑ Car Lease Notebook
- ❑ Database Viewer
- ❑ Database Viewer with Add record

Conventions used in this book

The screen captures displayed in the pages of this book are from the Windows version of the VisualAge for C++ product. The OS/2 screens are virtually identical with the exception of the frame window icons.

When procedures or concepts are different between Windows and OS/2 versions of VisualAge for C++, they are marked with either a Windows or OS/2 icon. For example:

Windows specific instructions

OS/2 specific

The words **enter** and **type** are used interchangeably. A courier monospaced font is used to show code segments. Anything typed in this font should be taken literally and entered exactly as shown.

Names of fields in a dialog box are bolded, for example, enter John Smith in the **Name** entry field. Bolding is also used throughout the book to improve readability of VisualAge for C++ terms.

Terms Used in the Book

Some terms in this book use the C++ language statements and Open Class Library terms and these are not necessarily standard English words. For example, the Open Class Library provides the classes IFrameWindow and IMultiCellCanvas. The first time this class name is used in the book, it is mentioned by its formal name. In later sections of the book the more informal term is used, for example: frame window or multicell canvas.

In the VisualAge for C++ product documentation there are some terms that are not commonly used between developers. For example, some on-line books use the term Visual Application Builder and in other places Visual Builder is used. For simplicity, instructions in this book use the shorter term Visual Builder.

Disclaimer

The agreement between the authors and IBM requires the following disclaimer:

The opinions expressed herein are those of the authors and do not represent those of their employer.

Related Publications

The C++ Programming Language, 2nd Edition by Bjarne Stroustrup, 1993.

C++ Primer, 2nd Edition by Stanley P. Lipman, 1993.

C++ FAQs Frequently Asked Questions by Marshall Cline and Greg Lomow, 1995.

Developing C/C++ Software in the OS/2 Environment by V.Mitra Gopaul, 1994.

Power GUI Programming with VisualAge for C++ by Kevin Leong, William Law, Robert Love, Hiroshi Tsuji, and Bruce Olson, 1996. ISBN 0-471-16482-8

Object Oriented Application Development with VisualAge C++ for OS/2 by Marc Carrel-Billard, Peter Jakab, Isabelle Mauny, Rainer Vetter, 1996. ISBN 0-13-242447-9

Object Oriented Programming Using SOM and DSOM by Christina Lau, 1994.

Getting Support

Telephone support for VisualAge for C++ is provided in the USA and Canada by calling (800) 992-4777. Outside the USA and Canada you can call (416) 448-4363. On the Internet send email to va_cpp@-vnet.ibm.com. Help is available through Compuserve via GO VACPP.

About the Authors

Dale Nilsson received a B.S. in Computer Science from California State University Long Beach in 1982. He has been programming for over 20 years and has worked for the State of California, McDonnell Douglas, IBM, and as an independent consultant. Dale Nilsson has held various development, management, and planning positions in IBM and has worked with customers and vendors throughout the United States, Europe, and Asia.

Dale is currently on the VisualAge C++ team developing and deploying VisualAge C++ worldwide. He is a certified C++ instructor and presents to audiences at trade shows, technical interchanges, and customer locations. Dale Nilsson works with C++ developers providing software development consulting.

Peter Jakab has been working with IBM since 1969. He has spent the last 16 years in software development. In the past eight years he has held a variety of positions at the Software Solutions Division Laboratory in Toronto, Canada, ranging from developer to team leader and project management.

Peter has been involved in developing Object-Oriented software solutions for the last six years. He has been working with VisualAge C++ since October 1994. Peter is currently working for SWS Software Product Services providing consulting and education to customers developing real world C++ applications.

Both Dale Nilsson and Peter Jakab are part of the team that developed and deployed the VisualAge C++ Proof-of-Concept Prototyping workshop and the VisualAge for C++ Certification Program. Their experience from these projects and their background in Object-Oriented application development form the foundation for this book.

Dale Nilsson is at DRNilsson@vnet.ibm.com
Peter Jakab is at PJakab@vnet. ibm.com

Acknowledgments

A number of dedicated professionals helped us with this book. Our managers Peter Spung, Michael Ha, Oma Sewhdat, and Allan Friedman provided their support, encouragement, and most importantly the permission to write this book. Our legal eagles, Arnie Rosen and Ed Duffield, for their wisdom, colorful stories, and contract approval. Sheila Richardson who helped with the book proposal and agreement. Maria Kwok who provided administrative support. Karen Kluttz who printed the review drafts of this tree killer. Steve Goldwasser for his DB2 expertise. Peter Brandt for volunteering his machine to test the various installation programs and Bob Russin for letting us include his OS/2 INI file editor on the CD-ROM.

The technical reviewers John Akerley, Bill Sarantakos, and Mike Polan were very helpful in ensuring the accuracy of this book. The reviews by Bryon Kataoka, Sanjeevan Pujji, Jerry Stuckle, Geza Szivos. Mike Meehan and Joanne Anzalone of Prentice Hall was great to work with. Also thanks to the many people in the VisualAge for C++ team who assisted us with information and support.

What's in Chapter 1

The CD-ROMs included with this book have evaluation copies of both the OS/2 and Windows versions of VisualAge for C++, DB2, the completed applications covered in this book, and the data required for the exercises. This is a lot of software, and this chapter covers some of the considerations when installing these components. This chapter covers:

❑ Reviewing hardware requirements

❑ Reviewing software requirements

❑ Using the on-line documentation

❑ Starting the VisualAge for C++ tools

1

Breaking Open the Box

Welcome to the VisualAge C++ Visual Programming Handbook! The instructions for installing the software on the CD-ROM included with this book are in the section **Installing the Necessary Software.** If you have not read this section, you will need to complete it before you start building the sample applications. The sample applications in this book require VisualAge for C++, and some utilities on the CD-ROM. The samples in Chapters 12 and 13 require that you also install DB2. The next sections cover specific information on the development and runtime environments for VisualAge for C++.

What Hardware and Software Do You Need?

When using application development tools you need to consider the hardware and software requirements of both the development environment and the target application runtime environment. This section describes the factors you should consider in the development environment. VisualAge for C++ is a robust application development system, and you will need sufficient hardware and the required software to be productive while using VisualAge for C++.

1

There are a lot of other considerations for the target runtime systems which run your applications. Throughout the book there is information on these considerations along with a wide number of options available when you build application executable files. You can usually assume that users of your applications will not have the same level of hardware resources that you use when developing an application.

Tuning applications for increased performance is special for each application. Using the iterative development process is a good way to insure adequate application performance. Throughout this book you will use iterative development, and you should continue to use this process when developing applications.

Hardware Requirements

C Programming Requirements

VisualAge for C++ provides a complete development environment to develop applications in both the C and C++ languages. The average C developer can use a computer with a 486 processor running at a clock speed of 33 megahertz (MHz) and 8 megabytes (MB) of RAM installed. This is because C development only requires a text editor, some basic libraries, a compiler, a linker, and a debugger. The debugger is only needed if you make programming errors.

C++ Programming Requirements

Development in the C++ programming language introduces additional overhead, especially when the target application will run in an operating system that supports a graphical user interface. C++ development in this environment uses the standard class libraries, the Open Class Library, the Class Browser, the Debugger, on-line help, Visual Builders, and other tools. All of these tools and services make you more productive and allow you to construct applications with a lot of function. However, these tools and services use a lot of system resources when used at the same time.

In layered and more complex applications, compiling and linking requires more memory. You can make this work on a computer with a 486 processor running at a clock speed of 66 MHz and 16 MB of RAM installed, but if you have more memory or a faster processor you will see performance improvements. Strangely enough, adding memory seems to provide better performance improvements than increasing the processor speed.

When using visual development tools like the Visual Builder, the Class Browser, and the Data Access builder, you will frequently run multiple tools at the same time. For example, you can run the visual tools, text editors, and help system sessions simultaneously. You will also probably be LAN attached and have multiple device drivers loaded for the various hardware devices on your system. With the extensive use of the Internet, you may also have a web session open. All this function is not free. It takes computer resources to run all of this software.

Professional developers and those who need to achieve high output and productivity should use a computer with a minimum 486 processor running at 100 MHz or a Pentium processor running at 90 MHz and 32 MB of memory. The amount of free RAM directly affects the amount of paging the operating system must perform to keep all of the applications running.

For fixed disk requirements, you need a minimum of 130 MB for the OS/2 version and 300 MB for the Windows version. Both versions support a minimal installation where the majority of the files are left on the CD-ROM and fetched as required. This installation requires very little disk space but the performance of the product is impacted as the CD will be accessed frequently. If you install all the components on one system you need a maximum of 250 MB for the OS/2 version and 400 MB for the Windows version. These are pretty big numbers, but the maximum is required only if you install all the components, samples, on-line documentation, and documentation Post-

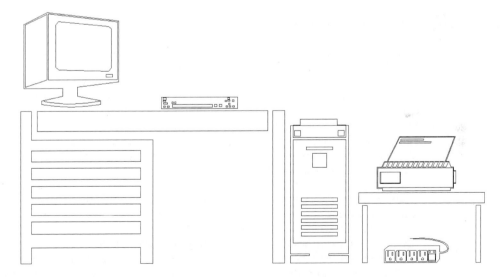

Figure 1: Development Environment

Script files. The Windows version also includes the source code for the Open Class Library. The best guideline is to install only the components which you will use most frequently.

All the components and tools run on a VGA (640 × 480) resolution display, but an SVGA (1024 × 768) or higher (1240 × 1024) resolution display is recommended, especially when designing graphical user interfaces using the Visual Builder. For very high resolutions to be usable you will need a large screen monitor. Typically a 17 inch monitor is the minimum size for 1240 × 1024. When you are using multiple tools like the Visual Builder, Editor, and WorkFrame, you will be able to use as much screen real estate as these higher resolution displays allow.

Software Requirements

The VisualAge for C++ product, at the time of publishing, is available the following operating environments. The product names are:

- ❑ VisualAge for C++ for OS/2 Version 3.0 runs on OS/2 Version 2.11 and OS/2 Warp.
- ❑ VisualAge for C++ for Windows Version 3.5 runs on Windows NT Version 3.51 and Windows 95.

VisualAge for C++ for Windows supplies a 32 bit compiler which supports the Win32s V1.30 API. The VisualAge for C++ for Windows tools will not run on Windows V3.1, but you can develop applications on Windows 95 or Windows NT, and run the applications on Windows 3.1. You will need to keep in mind that most Windows 3.1 systems have slower processors and less memory than Windows 95 or Windows NT systems.

There is an IBM C++ compiler product for AIX, OS/400, and MVS. These products are older versions of the CSet product and do not have the visual tools. There are plans to include the visual tools on AIX.

A 60 day trial version of the VisualAge for C++ product is included on the CD-ROM with this book. In order to run the exercises and compile the C++ code you will need to have VisualAge for C++ installed. If you already have the commercial version of the product installed, all you need to do is install the Corrective Service Diskettes (CSDs), also called FixPaks.

You may already have installed some CSDs on your system. In OS/2 you can verify the service levels currently on your machine by typing `syslevel` and comparing the service level with Table 1. The syslevel command reports the current level for all the software on your system, so be patient as the screen fill with messages.

Table 1: Minimum service levels

Component	OS/2 Service Level
Compiler	CTC303
Class Library	CTO303
Visual Builder	CTV303
Data Access Builder	CTV003
Debugger	CTU002
WorkFrame/2	CTW302
Documentation	CTD001

Please note that the exercises in this book have been created and tested using the products at the level found in the CD-ROM. It is very unlikely that higher level of Fixpak will introduce problems. If the software installed in your machine is not at the level in Table 1 and you experience problems running or building the exercises you should regenerate and recompile all of the exercises source code provided in the ANSWERS directory of each exercise.

The latest VisualAge for C++ Fixpaks can be found at the following FTP site: ftp.software.ibm.com in sub-directories

❑ for version 3.0 (OS/2):
   /ps/products/visualagecpp/fixes/v30os2/english-us

❑ for version 3.5 (Windows):
   /ps/products/visualagecpp/fixes/v35win/english-us

Note: Fixpaks for the products cannot be applied to the software in the CD-ROMs. They are only for the commercially available versions of the product.

Database Considerations

There is a very useful component in VisualAge for C++ called the **Data Access Builder** which helps you write programs that access relational databases. The Data Access Builder maps database tables and views into C++ classes and generates the C++ code for parts. These parts can then be used in the Visual Builder to connect to relational databases and manipulate the database tables. You must have DB2 installed on your workstation to use the Data Access Builder. A 60 day trial version of DB2 is included on the CD-ROM with this book. If you already have DB2 installed, you do not need to install it again.

Even if you are not a database expert you will be able to learn how to use the Data Access Builder. You will construct an application, using step-by-step instructions, which manages a sample database. The database definition is supplied on the CD-ROM and includes sample data.

Development vs. Runtime Requirements

It is important to take into consideration both the development and runtime environments when you develop an application. The applications you develop on your 200 MHz Pentium with a 20 inch SVGA display and 4 gigabytes of disk space will not have the same performance level running on a 33 MHz 486 system with a low resolution 12 inch VGA display and 100 MB of disk space (see Figure 2). Throughout this book there are suggestions and pointers which cover some of the many build decisions that need to be made for an application to run well in a given environment. It also covers the trade-offs required to build an application which is flexible enough to run in many environments. Not many books cover this mysterious part of application development.

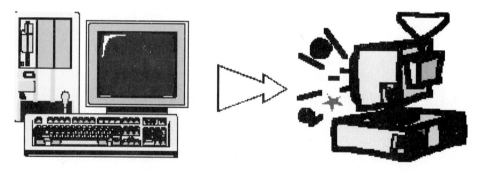

Figure 2: Applications must run in the client machine

Installing the Necessary Software

There are two CD-ROM disks included with this book, one for OS/2 and one for Windows. The Windows version can be installed on Windows NT or Windows '95.

Even though programs created with VisualAge for C++ for Windows will run on Windows 3.1 machines, the development environment does not run on Windows 3.1. You should not attempt to install these CD-ROM on a machine running Windows 3.1.

Place the CD-ROM for the operating system you are running in the CD-ROM drive, switch to the root directory of the CD-ROM and in a command prompt window type: **install.**

You should install the Sample Applications and Tools and the trial version of VisualAge for C++. For the exercises in chapters 12 and 13 you will also need to install the trial version of DB2. If you chose to install DB2 make sure you install it before you run VisualAge for C++.

Please read the information presented in the **Installation and last minute information** window of the installation program, for detailed instructions on how to install the different components available in the CD-ROM and any other important information which did not make the press deadline for this book. This same information is available for printing in the file called **READ.ME,** also found in the root directory of the CD-ROM.

For the very latest information and possible fixes for the exercises in the book you may access the IBM Object Technology Certification home page at: http://www.software.ibm.com/spslibrary and select the following links:

❏ Object Technology References

❏ VisualAge for C++ Reference list

❏ IBM Publications

Find the entry for this book and select the link to the Latest updates.

Installation notes

Windows NT:

If you installed on Windows NT you will have to edit the User Environment listed below to include the corresponding System Environment variables in the User Environment.

❏ INCLUDE

❏ LIB

❏ BOOKSHELF

❏ HELP

Add %**nameofvariable**%; in front of each of the above User Environment variables. For example to fix the INCLUDE environment variable add %INCLUDE%; in front of the current INCLUDE User Environment variable.

If you installed DB2 on Windows NT version 4.0 you will notice that no shortcuts or folders have been created on your desktop. This is a known problem with DB2 installation on NT 4.0. To get the latest fix for this problem please call IBM DB2 Service and Support.

The exercises are packed in a self-extracting file in the \VABOOK directory of the CD-ROM. This file will be extracted by the installation program to the correct subdirectory on the chosen installation drive. You should not have to install this file manually. To refresh the exercises on your disk or reinstall to a different drive, just run the installation program from the CD-ROM again.

What's in the VisualAge for C++ folder

After installing VisualAge for C++, the VisualAge icon appears on your desktop. In Windows the icon is a plain folder, in OS/2 the icon is the VisualAge logo. This icon is a folder which contains the various VisualAge for C++ components.

❏ **Open VisualAge for C++ by double-clicking the mouse on this icon.**

The current OS/2 version and the current Windows version have different icons for the components. The Windows components are shown in Figure 3 and the OS/2 components are shown in Figure 4. Only the installed components appear in these folders. You can add or remove a component at any time. You can reorganize these folders, move the components, or combine them in other folders using drag and drop. Now let's look at the VisualAge for C++ Help System.

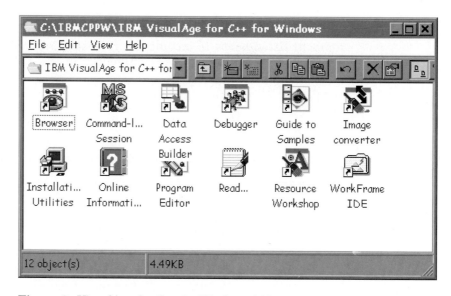

Figure 3: VisualAge for C++ for Windows folder

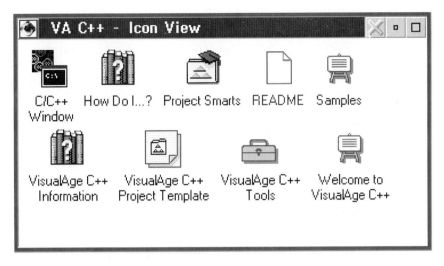

Figure 4: VisualAge for C++ for OS/2 folder

The folder shown in Figure 4, gives you access to the Help, Samples, Project Smarts, Project Template and How do I...? items. The actual program products are in the Tools folder. Double-click on the Visual-Age C++ icon to see the actual programs included with the OS/2 product shown in Figure 5.

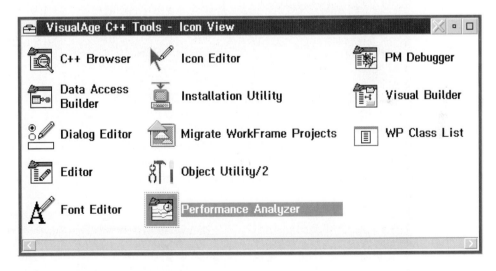

Figure 5: OS/2 VisualAge program in Tools folder

Using VisualAge C++ Documentation

The information folder has the reference books and user guides for C/C++, the Open Class Library, and the components currently installed. In the Windows version the documentation is all in the Online Information folder. In the OS/2 version there are two folders, the documentation is in the **VisualAge C++ Information** folder and the tutorials are in the **How do I..?** folder.

❏ *Double-click the mouse on the information folder.*

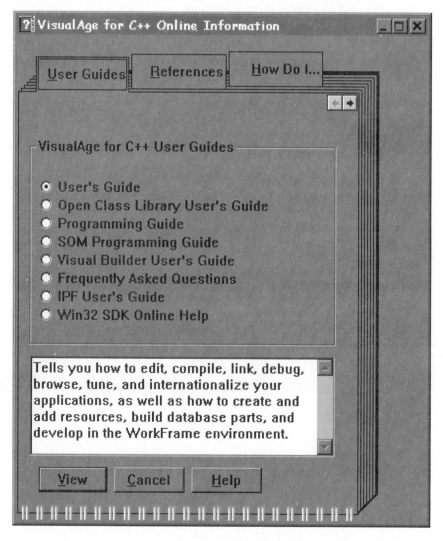

Figure 6: VisualAge C++ for Windows documentation notebook

This displays all the documentation supplied with the product. The Windows version looks like Figure 6 which has the different types of documentation separated on three pages of the notebook This notebook gives a convenient way to quickly find the book you need.

The OS/2 version looks like Figure 7 with separate book icons for each book. You can quickly and easily get to any book you choose from this folder. You can also make a shadow of any frequently used books in the Tools folder or on the desktop.

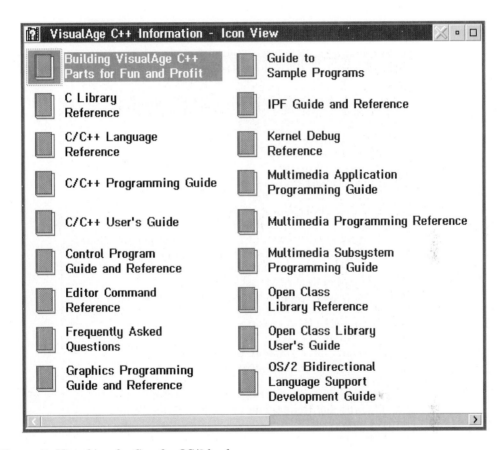

Figure 7: VisualAge for C++ for OS/2 books

The on-line documentation is preferred over the hard copy because the search engine in the Help subsystem is very useful. If you need to find some information, you can easily select **Search** from the **Services** menu of any book, enter a key word, and a list of all the occurrences of that term displays. You can locate any of the items in the list by a simple mouse double-click. For example, if you look up **date** in the Open Class Library Reference document:

In the Windows version,

- ❑ Select the **References** page of the notebook.
- ❑ Select the **Open Class Library Reference** radio button.
- ❑ Select the **View** push button, which display like Figure 8.
- ❑ Select the **Search...** push button at the bottom of the window.
- ❑ Enter **date** in the **Search for** entry field.
- ❑ Select the Enter key.

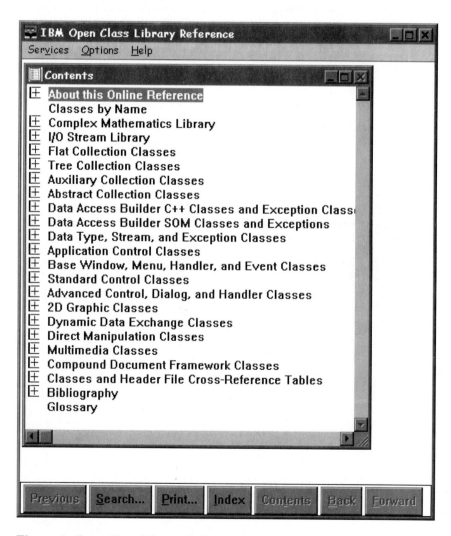

Figure 8: Open Class Library Reference

In the OS/2 version:

❏ Double-click on the **Open Class Library Reference** book.

❏ Select the **Search...** push button at the bottom of the window.

❏ Enter **date** in the **Search for** entry field.

❏ Make sure the **All sections** radio button is checked.

❏ Select the Enter key.

The system will search for all occurrences of **date** in this document. Be careful about choosing the **All libraries** for the search. The Search system will search all the books on the system. The search

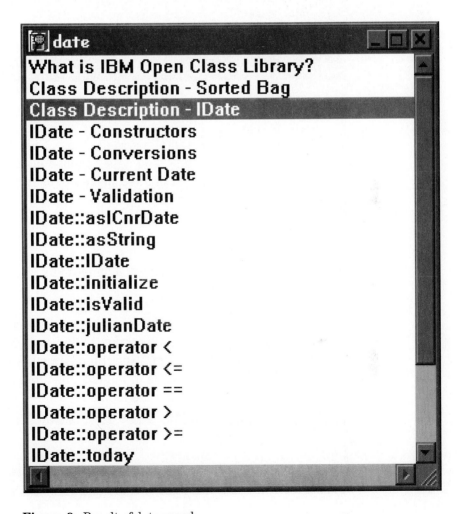

Figure 9: Result of date search

will take a long time and will probably yield a very long list of unrelated topics.

When the search is complete, the search results are displayed in the window as seen in Figure 9.

❑ Now scroll to the **Class Description - IDate** item in the list box
❑ Select this item by double-clicking the left mouse button.

This opens a window with the class declaration of the IDate class, as shown in Figure 10. This description of the IDate class is adequate for most purposes. If you need detailed information on the class interface, you can view the header file directly from this window.

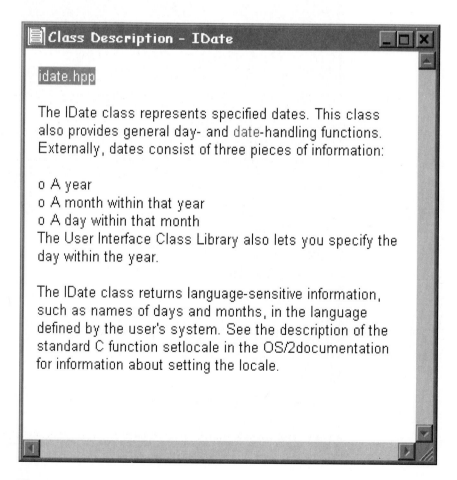

Figure 10: Class Description - IDate

□ Move the mouse to the **idate.hpp** text highlighted at the top of the window.

□ View the header file by double-clicking this text.

The header file for IDate displays in the Editor as shown in Figure 11. You can see all the public data types and public member functions in the class. From this window you can view the header file for the IDate class. Header files are the public interface for the class. You also have access to the clipboard, so you can select text with the mouse and use the copy/cut/paste feature to use a description or piece of code.

When you are finished with help, you need to close all the open help windows to save system resources. If you have a high powered system, you may want to keep the Open Class Library Reference or the Visual Builder Reference open.

If you need the details of a class, for example you need to find the public member functions of the IString class, you can quickly go to

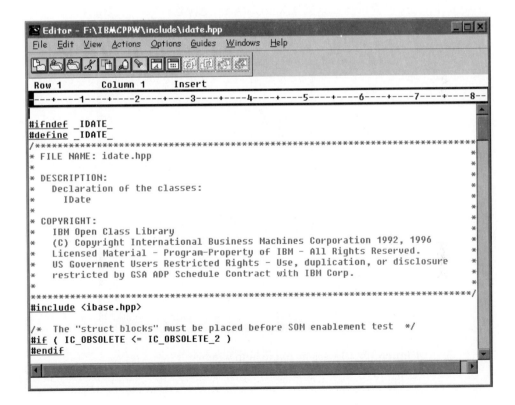

Figure 11: IDate header file

the page containing the details by double-clicking the **Classes by name** help item. This brings up a separate help window listing all the classes in the library. From there you can select IString to see the details of the class, see Figure 12: Classes by name help window.

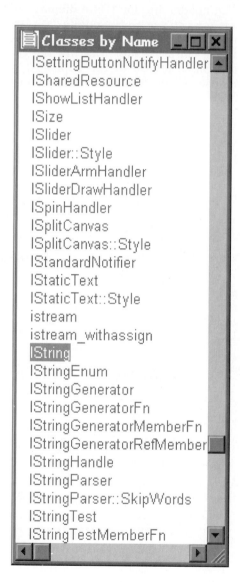

Figure 12: Classes by name help window

Starting VisualAge for C++ Tools

You can start all of the tools from a command prompt, but for this book most of the instructions will use the icons to open folders or start applications. In this book, the instructions work with the tools individually. This helps you learn the basics much quicker.

This book does not cover developing an application using the tools within a WorkFame project. Developing in a project is a bit complex and you will appreciate its benefits after you have a good understanding of the basics. So start the Visual Builder.

In the Windows Version:

❏ Double-click the **Visual Builder** icon.

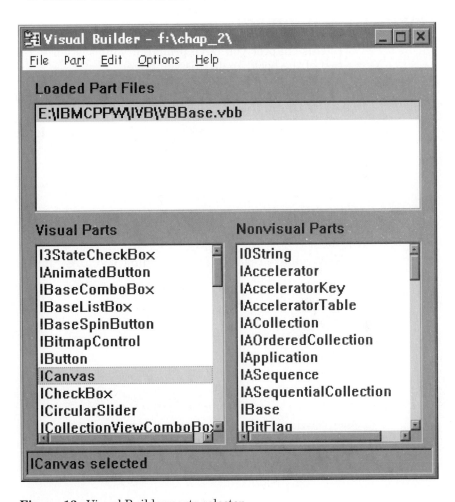

Figure 13: Visual Builder parts selector

In the OS/2 Version:

❏ Double-click the **VisualAge for C++ Tools** icon.

❏ Double-click the **Visual Builder** icon.

Make sure the Visual Builder comes up correctly. The Visual Builder Parts Selector should display on your screen, as shown in Figure 13.

Now that VisualAge C++ is installed and working, you are ready to start building applications! The instructions in this book rarely direct you to look in the documentation. If at any time while developing the applications in this book, you need more information, you should consult the on-line documentation.

Chapter 1—Summary

In this chapter you have prepared your system to continue with the rest of the book. To do this you have:

❏ Reviewed the hardware and software requirements for running VisualAge for C++.

❏ Seen how to find information in the on-line documentation. This will be very helpful when using VisualAge C++ and the Open Class Library.

❏ Learned about what components are included with VisualAge for C++.

❏ Started the Visual Application Builder and everything is working properly.

Now you are ready to start building VisualAge for C++ applications.

What's in Chapter 2

Now that you have all the necessary software installed, you are ready to start visual programming. In this chapter you build your first VisualAge C++ application which is a simple Hello World window. Building this application covers the basic elements of visual programming that you will continue to use throughout this book. In this chapter you will learn how to:

❑ Start the Visual Builder

❑ Use the Parts Selector

❑ Work in the Composition Editor

❑ Use simple controls to design a screen

❑ Generate C++ code

❑ Build and run an application

2

Building
Hello World

Starting the Visual Builder

Let's get started making your first application with VisualAge for C++ using the Visual Builder. The process for building the application will use the iterative development method. You develop the user interface, generate the C++ code, make an executable file, and then run the application. You will iterate by adding additional function and user interface elements, generating more code, and then recompiling the application. This allows you to see the results of your work a lot quicker than waiting until you have finished all the application development. Iterating also allows you to catch problems or mistakes before you have created an uncorrectable mess and lost track of what caused the problem.

The simplest way to start the Visual Builder is to select the Visual Builder icon in the VisualAge folder. In the current VisualAge for OS/2 version all the tools, including the Visual Builder are, in the VisualAge C++ Tools folder which is inside the VisualAge for C++ folder.

If you use the Visual Builder a lot you may want to create a *shortcut* or a *shadow* of its icon. You can place the *shortcut* icon directly on the desktop.

To do this in Windows:

❑ Open the IBMCPPW folder.

❑ Open the IBM VisualAge for C++ for Windows folder.

❑ Select the Visual Builder icon, Press and hold the left mouse button and drag the icon to the desktop.

To do this in OS/2:

❑ Open the IBM VisualAge for C++ folder.

❑ Open the Tools folder.

❑ Press and hold Shift and Ctrl.

❑ Select the Visual Builder icon with the right mouse button and drag onto the desktop.

When you start the Visual Builder all the visual and nonvisual parts in the Open Class Library are automatically loaded from the VB BASE.VBB file. Files with the extension of **.VBB** contain the binary image of parts and classes which can be used by the Visual Builder. VisualAge for C++ is a file based system. The VisualAge part files and specialized C++ classes you use to build an application must be loaded into the Visual Builder before they can be used.

Using the Parts Selector

The first window that appears when you start the Visual Builder is the Parts Selector also called the Parts Bin, see Figure 14. The list box at the top of this window lists all the .VBB files that are loaded in the Visual Builder. The Visual Builder can only use parts that have been loaded. Since C++ is a type specific language, the Visual Builder works on defined part types. Also, it is important to remember that parts are C++ classes and need to have unique valid C++ names.

Parts Selector Options

There are a number of options you can set in the Parts Selector. You can load .VBB files from different directories and different disk drives. For example, you may have two part files with the same name but in different directories. One part file is working fine and the other is being modified. For this reason and many others it is a good practice to see the full path names for the loaded .VBB files. To see the full path of the loaded part files complete the following:

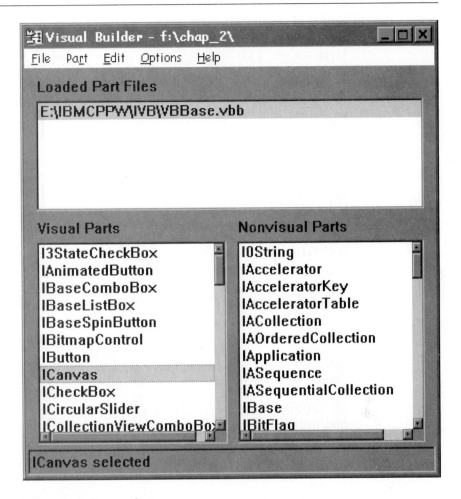

Figure 14: Parts selector

❑ Select **Options** on the menu bar and select **Show full file names**. See Figure 15.

❑ On the Options menu, **Default to FAT files names** is checked.

This forces an eight character file naming convention used by the FAT (File Allocation Table) file management system which originated in DOS. In OS/2 some people prefer to use the HPFS (High Performance File System), which allows file names longer than eight characters and is more efficient at managing disk space and other disk related operations. In order to use long file names you need to deselect this option. This book uses the eight character file naming convention for FAT file names.

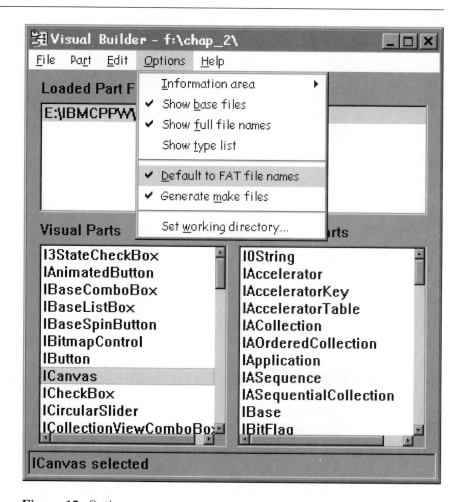

Figure 15: Options

OS/2 supports long file and short file names using two different file management systems. Some systems only have the FAT file management system and are limited to short file names. If there is any possibility that your parts will be used to develop applications on a machine with only the FAT file system, you should only use short eight character file names.

When you install VisualAge C++ for Windows, the working directory is set to **x:\ibmcppw\working** where **x:** is the drive you installed VisualAge for C++. The OS/2 version uses **x:\ibmcpp\working** as the default working directory. You need to set the working directory where VisualAge C++ generates code for this application.

❑ From the **Options** menu item, Select **Set working directory...**

❑ Enter **x:\VABOOK\HELLO** where **x:** is drive where you installed the lab exercises, see Figure 16.

Making a New Visual Part

You might have skipped some of the introductory information at the beginning of this book, but it is good to follow these first few chapters very closely to begin understanding the VisualAge for C++ development environment as you go along. Now you will construct a simple application which is a graphical window with the words **Hello World** in it. It is probably the simplest application you can build, but you will use all the steps involved in building a more complex application. In fact you use these same steps throughout this book to visually build all the applications. Start building the **Hello World** application by following these steps:

❑ From the parts bin, select the **Part** item on the menu bar at the top of the panel.

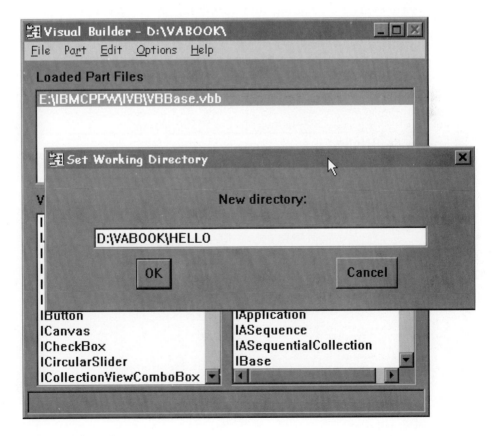

Figure 16: Working directory

❑ Select **New** and the panel to specify a part new is displayed. See Figure 17.

❑ In the **Class name** field enter **Hello**.

❑ In the **Description** field enter **Hello World - My first VA C++ Application.**

The **File name** is the .VBB file where the part information is stored and this defaults to the class name. The HELLO.VBB part file is written to your disk when you save the part. The default **Part type** is **Visual part** and the default Base class part is **IFrameWindow.** These defaults are exactly what you need for your first application. Select the **Open** button to start designing the **Hello World** application. This opens a new window called the **Composition Editor**.

Getting Acquainted with the Composition Editor

The Composition Editor is one of three views of a part. It is the default view when you open a visual part, and it provides a lot of functions for creating and modifying parts. You design the entire graphical user interface (GUI) for an application in the Composition Editor. The Composition Editor is where you combine parts with con-

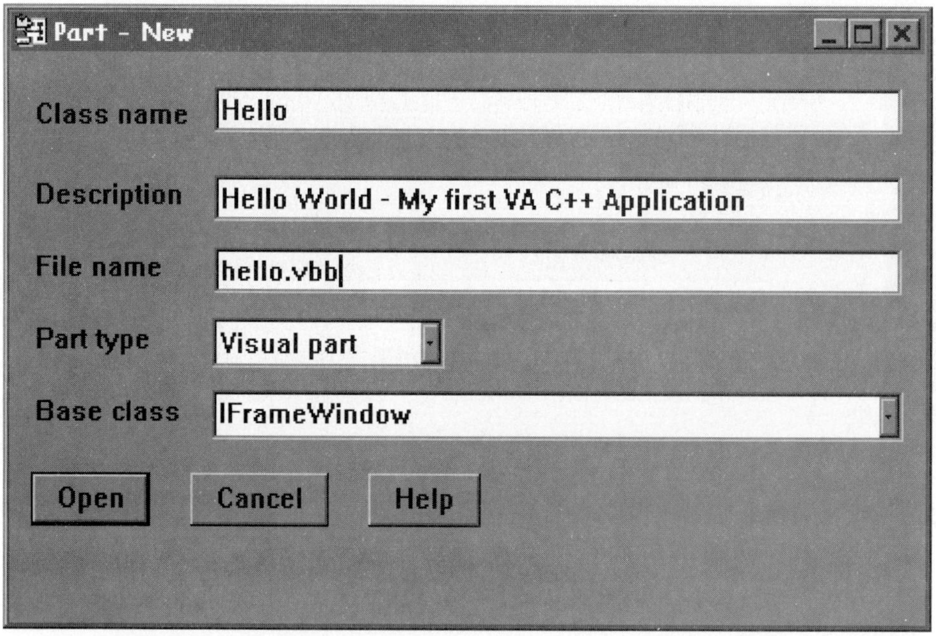

Figure 17: New visual part

nections to make composite parts and applications. The areas of the Composition Editor are shown in Figure 18.

Categories and Controls

On the left of the Composition Editor are two columns of icons. The left column is a scrollable list of folders called **Categories**. These categories hold parts grouped by common types. The right column holds the controls or parts which are contained in the currently selected category. Pressing the arrows at the top and bottom of category and control lists allows you to scroll through the lists.

In the Windows version bubble help displays when you place the mouse pointer over a category or control. The bubble help makes it a lot easier to find the part you need. In the current OS/2 version you need to select a category or icon to see its description in the information area at the bottom of the screen. This is a bit awkward, but at least you can find out what the part icons represent. A complete list of the default categories and parts is shown in Figure 19. It would be

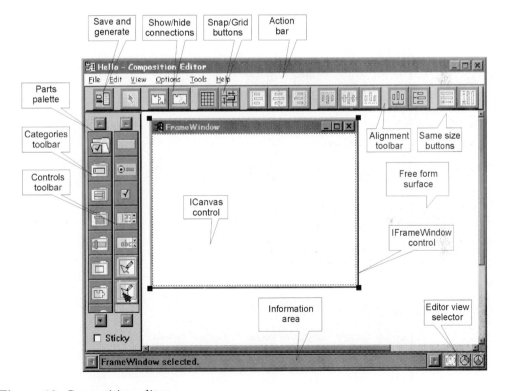

Figure 18: Composition editor

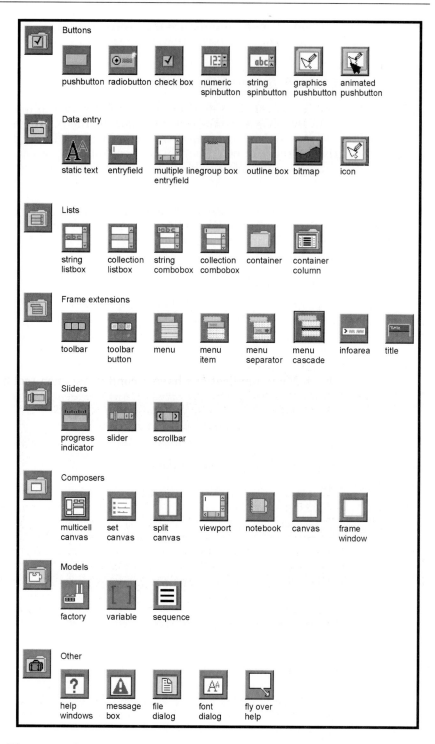

Figure 19: Visual Builder parts palette

a good idea for you to copy Figure 19 to have it handy as a reference until you become familiar with the available categories and controls.

Free-form Surface

The large blank area in the center of the panel is called the free-form surface. This is where you construct the user interface for the application. This is a virtual area because as you add more parts to the free-form surface it will grow to accommodate them. You may have to scroll the free-form surface to reach parts that are not in the current work area.

The Composition Editor free-form surface shows windows exactly as they appear at runtime. Even the startup position of your frame window is the same as the position of the window in the free-form surface.

Using a Tool Bar

Just like many of the applications available today, the Composition Editor has tool bars to make it easier for you to select functions. These are first generation tool bars with very basic functions like showing a group of icons and allowing the user to cause actions by pressing the icons. The user can also choose to hide or show the tool bars. Many applications have second generation tool bars which support drag and drop, have multiple views, and can be modified by the user at runtime. The applications you build using the Visual Builder can implement these advanced functions.

Visual Builder Menu Bar

The menu bar has items for all the icons on the tool bar except the generate button on the left end. If you need more screen real estate in the Composition Editor you can hide the tool bar. You can do this by selecting **Options**, then unchecking the **Show pallet** menu item. When you save the part this setting is saved with the part. When you open the part the Composition Editor will not show the tool bar. Unfortunately there is not global setting to make this the default setting for all Composition Editors. In this book the tool bar will stay in view. You can also hide the part pallet using the **Options** menu which will provide even more screen real estate.

Using Controls—IFrameWindow

Since you are creating a new visual part and you selected **IFrameWindow** as the Base class, the Composition Editor opened with an **IFrameWindow** object in the free-form surface, as seen in Figure 20. **IFrameWindow** is a C++ class in the Open Class Library

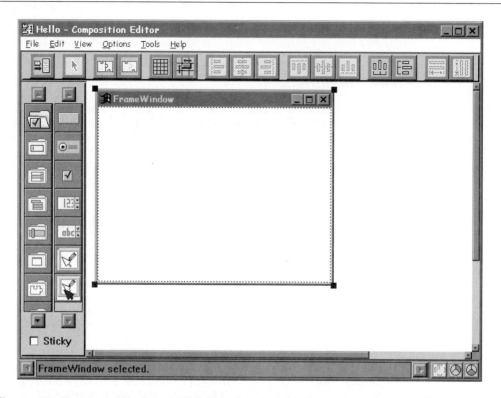

Figure 20: Canvas inside frame window

that provides very rich default behavior. The **IFrameWindow** control can be resized and repositioned at runtime, can be minimized or maximized, and has a default system menu. All of these attributes can be changed in the Visual Builder.

A frame window alone is useless, so a default **ICanvas** control is placed as the client of the frame window. Place the mouse pointer in the middle of the frame window and press the left mouse button. The name of the selected Canvas is displayed in the info area at the bottom of the Composition Editor. User interface controls are placed and positioned on canvases, the Open Class library provides several varieties of canvases which you will use later in this book. For this first application you use the **ICanvas** control because it is the simplest control of this type. If you place a button or other control on a frame window without a canvas, the control expands to fill the entire client area. This looks pretty funny and is not very practical. You need to have some kind of canvas to hold user interface controls.

The Hello World application needs a control that will display text. The proper control to use is the **IStaticText** control. Add an IStaticText control with the following steps:

❑ Select the second category, called **Data entry**, which has the **IStaticText** control.

❑ Place the mouse pointer on the **IStaticText** icon, press and release the left mouse button.

You have loaded the mouse pointer with an **IStaticText** control to paste on the Composition Editor. You can tell it is loaded because the mouse appears as a cross hair as it is moved to the free-form surface. If you picked the wrong control, just go to the correct icon on the palette and select that icon. You can unload the pointer by selecting the arrow icon on the tool bar.

❑ Move the mouse to the canvas and press the left mouse button to place the static text control on the canvas.

You now have an **IStaticText** control which should look like Figure 21.

The text **StaticText1** is not very descriptive by itself, but it identifies the control on the canvas. Enter the desired text by *directly editing* the static text with the following steps:

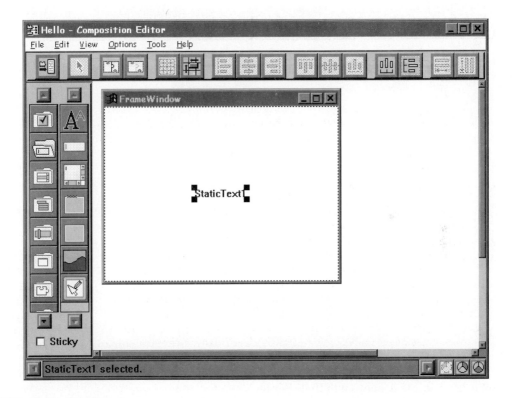

Figure 21: Static text

□ Edit the text by placing the tip of the mouse pointer on the static text, press and hold the Alt-key and then the left mouse button. This allows you to directly edit the text of the control.

□ Enter Hello World.

□ Click outside the text you are editing to complete the operation, and your screen looks like Figure 22.

Changing Fonts

Now, that looks a little bit better, but it is still pretty plain. Change the font size and color to make it look even better.

□ Select the static text field by clicking once on the words **Hello World.**

□ Open the settings notebook for the static text field by either pressing the right mouse button and selecting **Open settings,** or by double-clicking the left mouse button.

Figure 22: Static text changed to Hello World

❏ Select the **Font** page of the settings notebook, see Figure 23.

❏ Press the **Edit** button which displays the Font dialog as seen in Figure 24.

❏ Select a font type, size, and style that looks good to you. For example you could use a Times New Roman font with a Bold Italic style and a size of 24 points.

❏ Select **OK** on the font dialog box and select **OK** again on the settings notebook. Your text should look like Figure 25. If the words Hello World appear clipped when the new font is applied, you have two choices:

1. Select the text control and manually size it until all of the text is displayed.

2. Select the text control, bring up its pop-up menu and select **Reset to default size**. This is the preferred method.

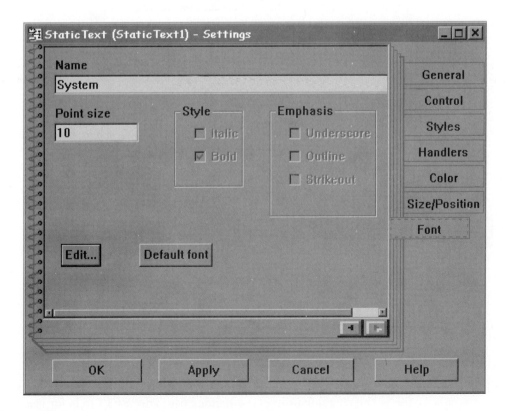

Figure 23: Setting notebook for IStaticText

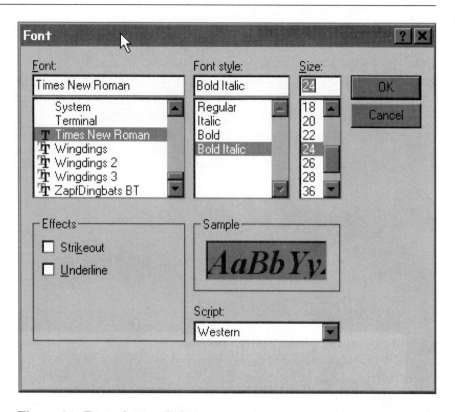

Figure 24: Font selection dialog

Generating C++ Code

The next step is to generate the C++ code.

❏ Select the Save and generate button on the tool bar.

The Visual Builder saves the part definition in the HELLO.VBB file and then generates the following files:

1. HELLO.CPP

2. HELLO.HPP

3. HELLO.H

4. HELLO.RCI

The .CPP file extension is standard for C++ source files and the .HPP file is the corresponding C++ header file. The .RCI file is for resource information and the .H file is for the definitions of the resource file.

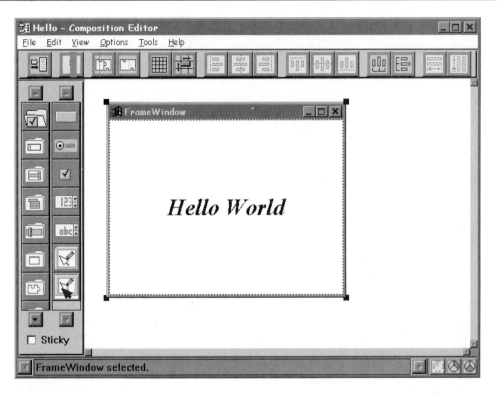

Figure 25: Hello World with formatting applied

In order to compile this code into an application you need two more things. First an entry point for the executable file, which is the C++ main() function. Second, you need a **make** file to help you compile the application's components. Fortunately, you do not need to write the code for either of these files. Instead, the Visual Builder will generate them for you. Execute the next step which is shown on Figure 26.

❏ On the menu bar select File, Save and generate...,main() for part.

This generates the following files

1. HELLO.APP
2. HELLO.RCX
3. HELLO.MAK

The HELLO.APP contains the main() function for the application and looks like Code segment 1.

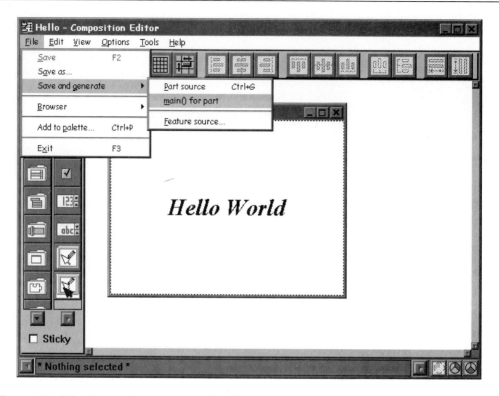

Figure 26: File, Save and generate, main() for part

As you can see, after all the include files, the main() function starts the application. A new Hello part is allocated in memory by the **new** operator, the Hello class constructor runs and returns to main(). The next step is execute the **initializePart**() function.

If anything goes wrong during these two operations an exception will be throw. The allocation of the Hello object and initializePart() functions are executed in a try/catch block, so that any exceptions can be caught. If an exception is thrown, it is caught, and a message box displaying an appropriate message is shown. These operations are tried again until there is no exception or the user selects the Cancel button.

The Visual Builder generated all the C++ code necessary to compile and run the Hello application. Having a separate .APP file is a con-

```
/*****************************************************************
 * FILE NAME: Hello.app
 * DESCRIPTION:
 *   Main program stub for class:
 *     Hello- This is the Hello World Application
 * ----------------------
 * Warning: This file was generated by the VisualAge C++
 * Visual Builder.
 * Modifications to this source file will be lost when the part is
 regenerated.
 *
 *****************************************************************/
#ifndef _IWINDOW_
#include <iwindow.hpp>
#endif

#ifndef _IAPP_
#include <iapp.hpp>
#endif

#ifndef _IMSGBOX_
#include <imsgbox.hpp>
#endif

#ifndef _HELLO_
#include "Hello.hpp"
#endif
//--------------------------------------------------------------
// main
//--------------------------------------------------------------
int main(int argc, char ** argv)
{
   IApplication::current().setArgs(argc, argv);
   Hello *iPart;
   IMessageBox::Response resp = IMessageBox::unknown;
   do {
      try {
         iPart = new Hello();
         iPart->initializePart();
         }
      catch (IException& exc) {
         resp = IMessageBox(IWindow::desktopWindow()).
                  show(exc);
         }
      }
   while (resp == IMessageBox::retry);
   if (resp == IMessageBox::cancel)
    IApplication::current().exit();

   iPart->setAutoDeleteObject();
   iPart->show();
   IApplication::current().run();
   return 0;
}   //end main
```

Code segment 1: main() for application

venient method which allows you to compile the HELLO.CPP file as an application or use it as a secondary window in another application. The next step is to use the make file to build the application.

Building and Running the Hello World Application

Open a command prompt session and switch to the working directory you set at the beginning of this chapter. You could start the VisualAge C++ compiler by typing **icc** followed by any parameters needed for compiling and then the .CPP file. This creates object files (.OBJ) which are linked with the Open Class Library files (.LIB) to create an executable file (.EXE). This method takes far too much typing and time for anything but the most trivial application. The applications you build in this book rely on the **nmake** utility, which comes with VisualAge for C++, to execute the compiler steps. The nmake facility only compiles the modules required to update the executable program. This is most important when an application consists of several source files. Using nmake insures that no time is wasted. It only compiles the source files which have changed since the last compilation.

Start the build process by entering at the command prompt:

nmake hello.mak

As the make file executes, it performs the following steps:

1. HELLO.APP is compiled with the C++ compiler and makes HELLO.O.
2. HELLO.CPP is compiled with the C++ compiler and makes HELLO.OBJ.
3. HELLO.RCX is compiled using the resource compiler and makes HELLO.RES.
4. HELLO.O and HELLO.OBJ are linked, making HELLO.EXE.
5. HELLO.RES is bound to HELLO.EXE by the resource compiler.

The steps to compile an application are shown in Figure 27 for OS/2 and Figure 28 for Windows.

Steps to Compiling an Application

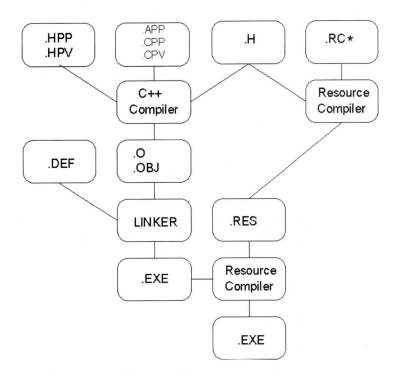

Figure 27: Compilation steps for OS/2

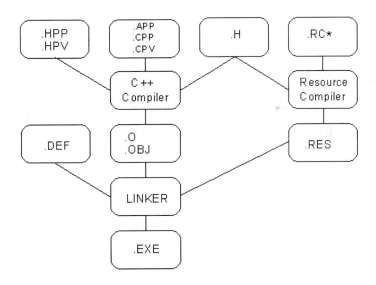

Figure 28: Compilation steps in Windows

Run the application file HELLO.EXE by entering **hello** at a command prompt. The operating system loads the HELLO.EXE file into memory and displays the Hello window as shown in Figure 29.

The Hello World window can be repositioned on the screen by pointing to the title bar, holding down the left mouse button and moving the window. You can also change the size of the Hello window by selecting one of the window edges with the left mouse button and moving the mouse. As the window resizes the **Hello World** text stays in the same relative position in the window because the window has an ICanvas control which does not adjust its contents as it is resized. In a later chapter you will learn how to use an IMultiCellCanvas to improve this behavior.

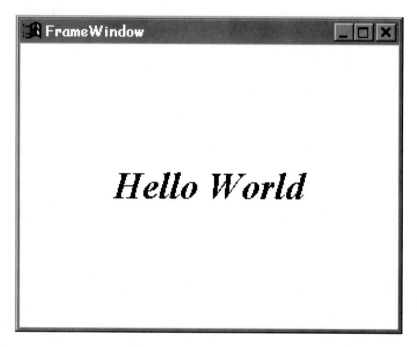

Figure 29: Running Hello World application

You can also minimize or maximize the window by selecting the icons at the upper right part of the window. When you are done with the Hello World window, select the system icon in the upper left corner of the Hello World window and select **Close** to end this application. This is a simple graphical window, but you developed it without writing any C++ code. The window has a lot of function that comes free from the built in behavior of the IFrameWindow control.

Adding More Function to Hello World

Now that you have constructed a very simple application, you can add more function and iterate on the Hello program. Return to the Hello window definition by selecting the Composition Editor in the Visual Builder.

Now you will add a push button which causes the program to exit when it is selected. This is accomplished without writing any code with the following steps:.

- ❏ Select the first category which is the Buttons category.
- ❏ Use the mouse to select the first icon which is the **IPushButton** control.
- ❏ Move the mouse pointer to the canvas below the **Hello World** text, and press the left mouse button to drop the **IPushButton** control on to the canvas.

Now the canvas has a push button. To change the default text of **PushButton1** directly edit the text on the control:

- ❏ Press and hold Alt, then the left mouse button to directly edit the push button.
- ❏ Type **E~xit** and move the mouse off the push button control, and press the left mouse button.

The push button automatically resized to match the **Exit** text you entered as shown in Figure 30. Also, the tilde (~) character provides the key with a mnemonic, so you can press the **x** key to select the button when you run the application.

Subpart Names

In addition to changing the text of the push button, it is also good practice to change the name of the button. By default controls are named sequentially using the name of the control appended with a number. The first push button you add to a canvas is named **Push-Button1**. This is not really a good name, especially when you try to read the generated code, debug the application, or simply look at a

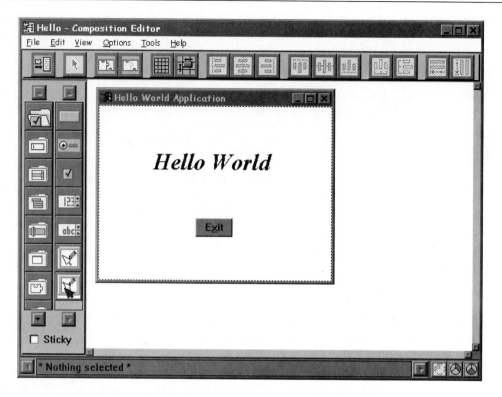

Figure 30: Hello World with the Exit push button

connection from this button. A name such as **pbExit** would be much better. You should name all your parts with meaningful names which describe the functions the controls perform. To change the name of a control you need to display the pop-up menu for the specific control:

❑ Position the mouse pointer over the push button.

❑ Press and release the right mouse button to bring up the pop-up menu.

❑ Select **Change Name...,** type **pbExit**, and press **OK**.

The title bar of the application also needs some meaningful text. Directly edit the text on the title bar of your application:

❑ Move the mouse pointer to the title bar of the **IFrameWindow** control.

❑ Press and hold Alt and press the left mouse button.

❑ Enter **Hello World Application,** move the mouse off the title bar, and press the left mouse button.

Selecting Parts

As you have seen, the left mouse button is used to select the controls. In OS/2, to select multiple adjacent controls, place the mouse pointer over the first control to be selected, hold down the left mouse button, and move the mouse over the other controls. While the mouse button is down you will continue to select controls. Release the mouse button when you are finished selecting controls. This is called marquee or swipe selection. This technique is currently not available in the Windows version of the product.

Selecting multiple nonadjacent controls is different in Windows and OS/2. In OS/2, select the first control, then press and hold the Ctrl key and click the left mouse button over the other control(s) you wish to select. In Windows, start by selecting one control by clicking the left mouse button, press and hold the Shift key and select the other control.

The controls on the canvas need to be aligned so that they are centered on the canvas.

❑ Select the **Hello World** text and the **Exit** button individually and press the horizontal center button.

❑ Select both the **Exit** push button and the **Hello World** static text. Both of the selected controls have boxes around them, and the last control selected has black boxes or handles. Press the vertical center icon.

 There are buttons to align to the left, right, top, bottom, and center.

There are also buttons to distribute the controls either vertically or horizontally within the frame window and also within a **box.** A box is defined as the area between the first and last control selected. This last feature is very useful, for example, if you are trying to space five entry fields vertically and evenly between the first and fifth entry fields.

Making Connections

Pressing the pbExit push button should make the **Hello** window close. To achieve this without VisualAge for C++ you would need to write some C++ code. VisualAge for C++ introduces Construction from Parts which allows you make connections that trigger events. Make a connection with pbExit as shown in Figure 31:

❑ Place the mouse over the pbExit push button, and press the right mouse button to get the context menu.

❑ Select **Connect** from this menu.

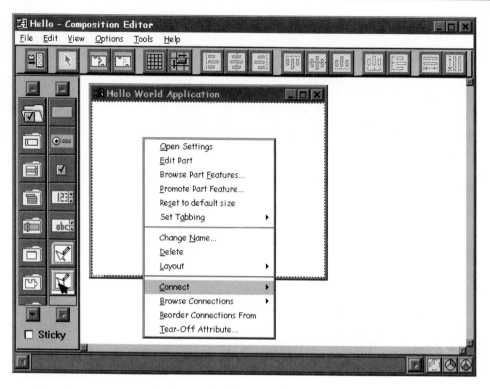

Figure 31: Context menu for the Exit push button

This displays the **Preferred** connections list as seen in Figure 32. This is a short list of the most commonly selected connection items. Some items on the preferred list can be disabled or gray. The Visual Builder prevents you from making some types of invalid connections by graying out improper options.

❑ Select the **buttonClickEvent** with the left mouse button.

The mouse pointer changes shape and looks like a spider, indicating you have started a connection and need to select a target for it.

❑ Move the mouse to the title bar of the Hello window and press the left mouse button to select the target for the connection.

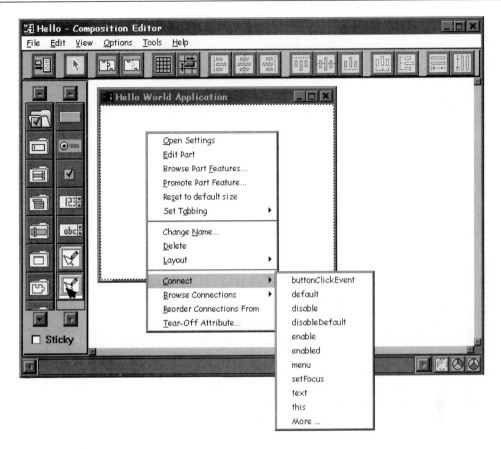

Figure 32: Preferred list for the Exit push button

This displays the preferred list of connections available for the frame window as shown in Figure 33.

❑ Select the **close** action on the menu and you see a line connecting the Exit button and the Hello frame window.

❑ Move the mouse pointer so its tip is on the line and press the left mouse button to select the connection.

This displays a description of the connection listed in the info area at the bottom of the Composition Editor as shown in Figure 34.

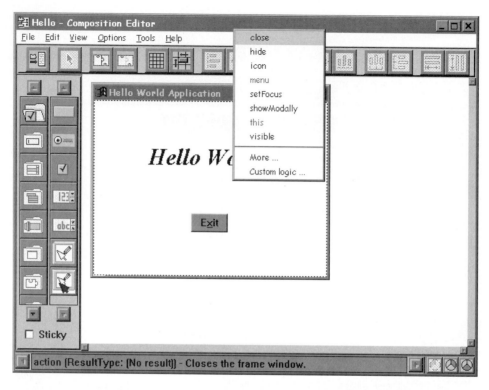

Figure 33: Preferred list for IFrameWindow

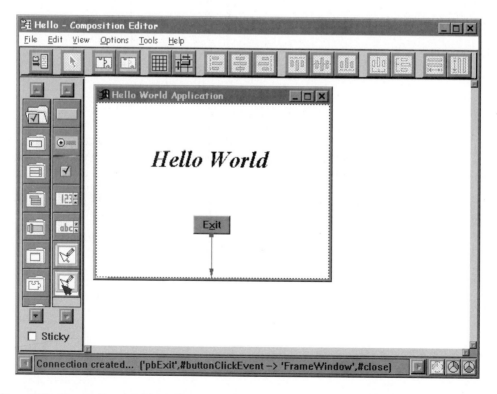

Figure 34: Connection to close a frame window

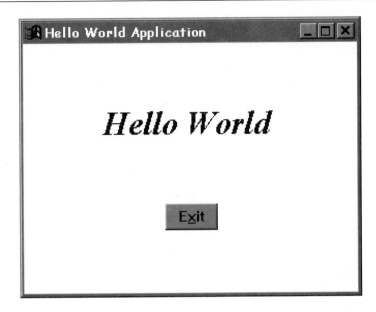

Figure 35: Running application

Save and Build the Improved Hello World

Repeat the steps for generating and compiling the application; this time, you do not need to generate the main() to get the **HELLO.APP** and **HELLO.MAK** files. You only need a new make file if you added new parts (usually nonvisual parts) which require changing the make file to include other **.OBJ** files or **.LIB** files. You can use the .APP and .MAK files generated previously. When you run the Hello application it looks like Figure 35.

All the old functions still work as they did before, when you select the **Exit** button the window closes. As you can see, it is very easy to make a graphical application with some basic function without writing any code!

Viewing the Generated Code

For this simple sample you can review the code generated by VisualAge C++. The Visual Builder generated 165 lines of code in the .CPP file. Let's look at **HELLO.CPP**, which is show in Code segment 2 through Code segment 6.

```
/************************************************
* FILE NAME: Hello.cpp
*
* DESCRIPTION:
*   Class implementation of the class:
* Hello- This is the Hello World
* Application
* -----------------------
* Warning: This file was generated by the
* VisualAge C++ Visual Builder.
* Modifications to this source file will be
* lost when the part is regenerated.
************************************************/
#ifndef _IFRAME_
#include <iframe.hpp>
#endif

#ifndef _ICANVAS_
#include <icanvas.hpp>
#endif

#ifndef _ISTATTXT_
#include <istattxt.hpp>
#endif

#ifndef _IFONT_
#include <ifont.hpp>
#endif

#ifndef _ICOLOR_
#include <icolor.hpp>
#endif

#ifndef _IRECT_
#include <irect.hpp>
#endif

#ifndef _IPOINT_
#include <ipoint.hpp>
#endif

#ifndef _IPUSHBUT_
#include <ipushbut.hpp>
#endif

#ifndef _INOTIFEV_
#include <inotifev.hpp>
#endif
```

```
#ifndef _IOBSERVR_
#include <iobservr.hpp>
#endif

#ifndef _ISTDNTFY_
#include <istdntfy.hpp>
#endif

#ifndef _HELLO_
#include "Hello.hpp"
#endif

#ifndef _IVBDEFS_
#include <ivbdefs.h>
#endif

#ifndef _ITRACE_
#include <itrace.hpp>
#endif
    .   .   .
```

Code segment 2: Include section of HELLO.CPP

The above code segment shows how the required include or header files are brought into the compiler. If you are not familiar C++ the **#ifndef** statements may look strange. In C++, just as in C, many files can include the same header files. In C++ header files contain code as well as declarations and can only be included once. The #ifndef precompiler statement prevents header files from being included and compiled more than once per compilation unit. In each of the header files you will see pre-compiler directives to define these flags. For example, the file **ITRACE.HPP** will start with the following code:

```
#ifndef ITRACE
#define ITRACE
...
...
#endif
```

The first time ITRACE.HPP is included, it will set the ITRACE flag and the file will be compiled. While the flag is set for this file it will not be included.

```
. . .
//************************************************
// Class definition for HelloConn0
//************************************************
class HelloConn0 : public IObserver, public IStandard
Notifier {
public:
virtual  ~HelloConn0(){};
//--------------------
// public member functions
//--------------------
void initialize(IPushButton * aSource, IFrameWindow *
aTarget)
{
source = aSource;
target = aTarget;
enableNotification();
};

protected:
//--------------------
// protected member functions
//--------------------
virtual IObserver & dispatchNotificationEvent(
const INotificationEvent & anEvent)
{
  if (anEvent.notificationId() ==
    IPushButton::buttonClickId)
  {
    IFUNCTRACE_DEVELOP();
    ITRACE_DEVELOP(" firing connection :
    pbExit(buttonClickEvent) to
    FrameWindow(close))");
    try {target->close();}
    catch (IException& exc) {};
  }
  return(*this);
};

private:
//--------------------
// private member data
//--------------------
IPushButton * source;
IFrameWindow * target;
};   //HelloConn0
. . .
```

Code segment 3: Code for connections for HELLO.CPP

Code segment 3 shows typical code for a connection; you only need to look at this code, which gets fairly complex, if you are interested in the inner workings of the generated code. You should never change this code because your changes will be lost every time you generate. Basically, connections are classes which derive from the IObserver and INotifier base classes. This provides the connections with the behavior necessary to use the notification framework which is the underlying support for the connections. If you are interested in understanding the notification framework, you should read the on-line book *Building Parts for Fun and Profit*, included with the VisualAge for C++ product. Also note that every connection has trace information added to it to facilitate debugging as necessary, see the statements containing **ITRACE_DEVELOP**. This book will cover how to add tracing information to your programs in a later chapter.

```
. . .
#pragma export (Hello::readyId)
const INotificationId Hello::readyId =
"Hello::readyId";

#pragma export (Hello::partWindowId)
      unsigned long Hello::partWindowId = 0;

//-----------------------
// Hello :: defaultFramingSpec
//-----------------------
#pragma export (Hello::defaultFramingSpec())
const IRectangle Hello::defaultFramingSpec()
{
  return(IRectangle(IPoint(30,
IWindow::desktopWindow()->size().height()
- 30 - 240),ISize(320, 240)));
}


//-----------------------
// Hello :: defaultTitle
//-----------------------
#pragma export (Hello::defaultTitle())
IString Hello::defaultTitle()
{
  return("Hello");
}

//-----------------------
// Hello :: Hello
//-----------------------
#pragma export (Hello::Hello(unsigned long, IWindow*,
IWindow*, const IRectangle&, const IFrameWindow::
```

```
 Style&, const char*))
 Hello::Hello(
       unsigned long id,
       IWindow* parent,
       IWindow* owner,
       const IRectangle& rect,
       const IFrameWindow::Style& style,
       const char* title)
     : IFrameWindow((partWindowId) ? partWindowId
 : id, parent, owner, rect, style, title)
 {
     partWindowId = (partWindowId) ? partWindowId : id;
     iCanvas = new ICanvas(
       IC_FRAME_CLIENT_ID,
       this,
       this,
       IRectangle());
     iStaticText1 = new IStaticText(
       partWindowId+WNDOFFSET_Hello_StaticText1,
       iCanvas,
       iCanvas,
       IRectangle(IPoint(70,97),ISize(170,
       44)));
     ipbExit = new IPushButton(
       partWindowId+WNDOFFSET_Hello_pbExit,
       iCanvas,
       iCanvas,
       IRectangle(IPoint(131,22),ISize(48,
       30)));

     conn0 = new HelloConn0();

     this->setFocus();
     this->setClient(iCanvas);
     iStaticText1->setFont(IFont("Times New Roman
 Bold Italic", 24, false,
       true).setBold(false)
       setItalic(false).setUnderscore(false)
       .setStrikeout(false).setOutline(false));

     iStaticText1->setText("Hello World");
     iStaticText1->setForegroundColor
       IColor(IColor::black));
     ipbExit->setText("E~xit");
 }     //end constructor
 . . .
```

Code segment 4: Constructor for HELLO.CPP

As you can see in Code segment 4, the constructor for the Hello part uses dynamic memory allocation to create the components in the frame window. In fact, the Hello class derives from IFrameWindow. Once the objects are created they are initialized to the user selected values by calling the appropriate member functions for each control. For example, see the line where the word **E~xit** is being used to set the text of the push button.

The destructor for the Hello application, in Code segment 5, cleans up the memory by deleting everything allocated in the constructor.

```
//-----------------------
// Hello :: ~Hello
//-----------------------
#pragma export (Hello::~Hello())
Hello::~Hello()
{
   conn0->stopHandlingNotificationsFor
    (*ipbExit);

   delete conn0;
   delete iCanvas;
   delete iStaticText1;
   delete ipbExit;
}
. . .
```

Code segment 5: Destructor for HELLO.CPP

```
. . .
//-----------------------
// Hello :: initializePart
//-----------------------
#pragma export (Hello::initializePart())
Hello & Hello::initializePart()
{
   makeConnections();
   notifyObservers(INotificationEvent(readyId,
    *this));
   return *this;
}

//-----------------------
// Hello :: makeConnections
//-----------------------
#pragma export (Hello::makeConnections())
Boolean Hello::makeConnections()
```

```
{
    this->enableNotification();
    iCanvas->enableNotification();
    iStaticText1->enableNotification();
    ipbExit->enableNotification();

    conn0->initialize(ipbExit, this);
    conn0->handleNotificationsFor(*ipbExit);
    return true;
}
```

Code segment 6: Using initializePart and makeConnections

If you remember when you looked at the main() function for the application in Code segment 1, the Hello object was allocated which runs the constructor for Hello. The next step calls **initializePart().** This function calls **makeConnections()** which enables the parts to handle notifications and initializes all connections. After all connections are completed the **ready** event is generated to indicate that the part has been constructed and initialized. You will use the **ready** event in many of the exercises in this book.

Chapter 2—Summary

Well, you are off to a good start. You built a very simple C++ application using VisualAge for C++. In this chapter you:

❑ Learned how to start the Visual Builder

❑ Became familiar with how to use the Visual Builder Parts Selector and add new parts.

❑ Learned the basic workings of the Composition Editor using simple controls to design a screen.

❑ Edited controls to change their default attributes.

❑ Saved the part definition and generated C++ code.

❑ Built an application using the generated make file with the NMAKE utility.

❑ Ran the compiled application and saw the many default features of the application by using the Open Class Library.

What's in Chapter 3

You have completed the Hello World application and you probably think this is very easy. Each chapter increases in difficulty and complexity and this chapter covers visual programming in more detail. You will build a nonvisual part and combine it with visual parts to make an adding machine. The following topics are covered:

Understanding VisualAge parts:

- ❑ Composite parts
- ❑ Visual parts
- ❑ Nonvisual parts

Building an adding machine:

- ❑ Building the user interface
- ❑ Adding the contents of two entry fields

Setting the Tab order

Creating nonvisual parts by:

- ❑ Defining attributes
- ❑ Defining actions
- ❑ Setting preferred features
- ❑ Working with the Class editor
- ❑ Adding user code to the generated files

Using nonvisual parts to make a composite part

3

Making an Adding Machine

As you go through this book, some Object-Oriented and visual development concepts are covered. There are many books that exhaustively cover a particular Object-Oriented methodology or specific design technique. Since this book focuses on implementation, it covers only those Object-Oriented design concepts necessary to understand the applications you are building.

Now that you have completed a simple application, Hello World, you can look back at the steps and understand how you built it. Before you go on to more complex applications, you need to understand the different types of VisualAge parts.

Understanding VisualAge Parts

There are different types of parts or classes used in the Visual Builder. There are *visual* parts, *nonvisual* parts, and *class* interface parts.

Visual parts and nonvisual parts are subclasses of the INotifier base class, and therefore inherit some special functions which support the notification framework in the Open Class Library. The notification framework provides the function which allows the parts to notify or send messages to other parts. This critical function is needed in the Open Class Library so you can build applications by making connections. Class parts are C++ classes used in the Visual Builder which are not subclasses of INotifier and therefore can not emit or send notification messages.

The most atomic or granular part is called a *primitive* part. Visual, nonvisual, and class parts can be primitive parts. Examples of primitive parts from the Open Class Library are IPushButton, which is a visual part, and IDatastore which is a nonvisual part. You can change the settings and default attributes of primitive parts in the Visual Builder.

Parts can be combined to create *composite* parts. When you combine two or more nonvisual parts you have a composite nonvisual part. For example, if you were building the nonvisual component of a Clock part, you would combine the ITime and IDate nonvisual parts in a composite nonvisual part named **Clock.** The Clock part would supply the services you would expect from such a part like setting and getting the time and date.

You create a composite visual part when you combine a visual part with one or more parts. For example, you can combine the previously discussed nonvisual Clock part with a user interface part that displays the time and date and has buttons to perform the various clock functions. You could call this part a **ClockView,** see Figure 36. In fact, the clock could have multiple views like digital, analog, or a combination where the date is shown in digital format and the time as a traditional clock with hands ticking.

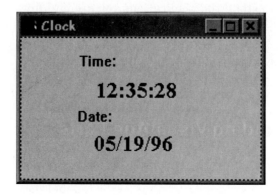

Figure 36: ClockView composite visual part

Visual Parts

Visual parts are user interface controls in the Open Class Library such as IPushButton, IEntryField, and IFrameWindow. The Visual Builder generates the C++ code for all the visual parts. Visual parts supplied with the Visual Builder are sometimes called *controls*. When talking about visual parts in this book we will refer to them as parts or controls interchangeably.

All visual parts are subclasses of IWindow which is an abstract base class in the Open Class Library. The IWindow class sets the base behavior for all user interface controls because IControl is a subclass of IWindow as shown in Figure 37.

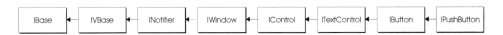

Figure 37: IPushButton inheritance hierarchy

Nonvisual Parts

Nonvisual parts are parts that contain business logic such as mathematical computations, data access functions, and application logic. The Open Class Library comes with a number of nonvisual parts that are very helpful in building applications. Most of these parts are designed for general purpose usage, and in many cases they need to be sub-classed to add application specific function. In Figure 38 you see the composition of the ClockView application combining both visual and nonvisual parts.

Building an Adding Machine

In this chapter you will build an Adding Machine application that combines visual and nonvisual parts. First you construct the Adding Machine application visual part **AdderView;** then you develop a nonvisual part, **Calc**, which you use in combination with the visual part to perform the calculations.

The Adding Machine allows you to enter two numbers, press a button to perform the addition of the contents of the two entry fields, and display the result in the output entry field. The application window has:

❑ Three entry fields which accept the two numbers to be added and display the result

❑ Three static text fields to label the entry fields

❑ Two push buttons for Add and Exit.

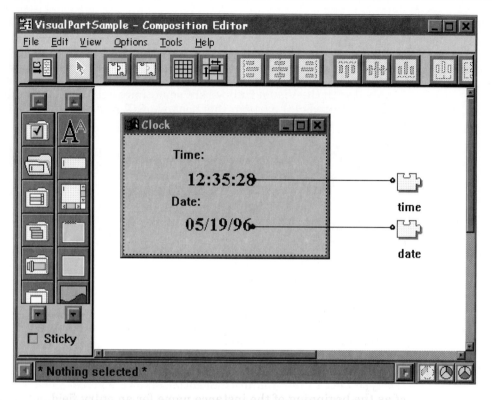

Figure 38: ClockView with nonvisual parts connected

There is also a nonvisual part which performs the addition operation and notifies the **result** entry field that the operation has been performed and the result attribute in the Calc part has changed.

Let's begin by starting the Visual Builder to build the view of the Adding Machine. You build and test the AdderView visual part before building the Calc nonvisual part. This is a new application, so you should change the *working directory* for the Visual Builder. By changing the working directory you keep the files for the different applications separate.

❑ In the Visual Builder Parts Selector, select the **Options** pull down menu.

❑ Select Set working directory.

❑ Enter x:\VABOOK\ADDER.

The new working directory is displayed in the title bar of the Parts Selector.

Naming Conventions

Before you begin building the application is a good time to have a short discussion on naming conventions. When developing applications it is very prudent to adopt some consistent naming conventions. C++ is a case sensitive type specific language. This means that each class, member function, and data element must have a unique name and a defined type. You should use descriptive names to make your parts more usable. A good guideline is to have a set of prefixes and suffixes which can be used to ensure consistent naming. For example, the Hello World application used the *pb* prefix for push buttons.

Most people have their own naming conventions as well as coding style conventions. In this book the names of classes and parts start with an upper case character. Each word in the name of a class or part also starts with an upper case character. For example, the view of the adding machine is called AdderView. Any attributes of a class or part start with a lower case character. Each subsequent word in the name of the attribute starts in upper case. For example, the attribute which holds the result of the calculation is called **result**. The convention for instances of a class is the same as that for attributes. For example, the instance of the entry field which displays the calculation result is called **efResult**.

When you create an instance of an object, you should try to identify the type of the class you are instantiating. For example, you can use *ef* as the beginning of the instance name for an entry field. Adhering to these simple suggestions makes it easier to follow and understand the generated code and the connection messages which are issued by the program at runtime. It also makes debugging easier, in the rare event that you make a programming error.

Constructing the AdderView

Start building the Adding Machine application as seen in Figure 39 by following these steps:

❏ From the Visual Builder Parts Selector, select **Part** then **New** from the menu bar.

❏ For the Class name enter AdderView.

❏ Enter a suitable description like This is the view for the adding machine application.

❏ In the File name field enter Adder. ADDER.VBB is the name of the file containing the binary image for this exercise.

❏ Select Visual part as the Part type. The default Base class for visual parts is IFrameWindow.

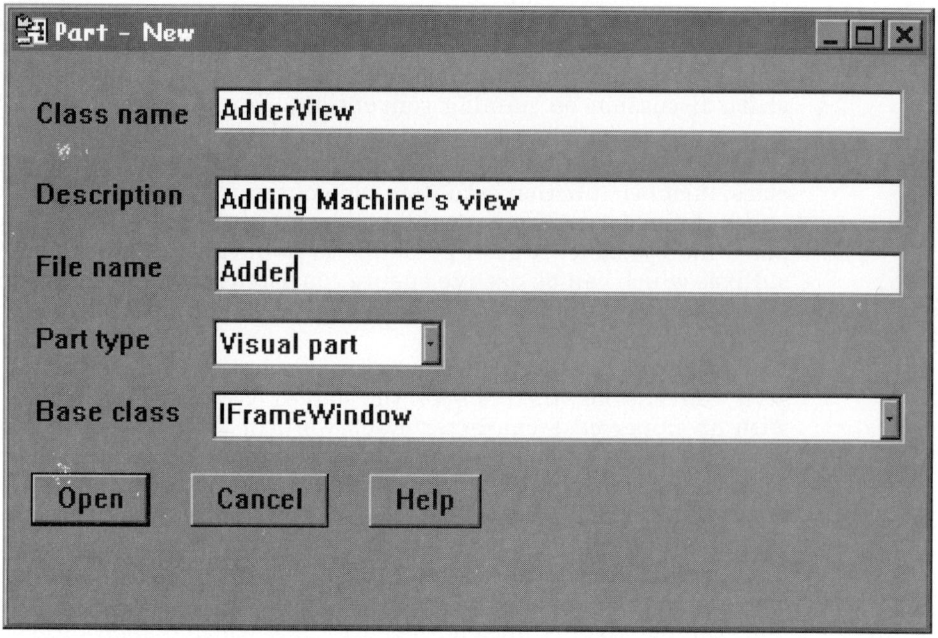

Figure 39: Creating a new visual part AdderView

> ❏ Press the **Open** button to open the Composition Editor for the **AdderView** visual part.

Adding Push Buttons

As in the Hello World sample, the Composition Editor opens with a frame window which has a default canvas control already placed as its client on the free-form surface. Now you start adding more user interface controls or primitive visual parts to create a composite visual part. The first control you use is the **IPushButton** control, which you already used in the Hello World application. Execute the following steps, which make the Composition Editor look like Figure 40:

> ❏ From the button category select the **IPushButton** control.
>
> ❏ Place two push buttons on the canvas of the frame window.

Make these push buttons the **Add** and **Exit** buttons by directly editing the text on the buttons.

> ❏ Place the mouse pointer on top of a button and press the left mouse button to directly edit the text of the button.

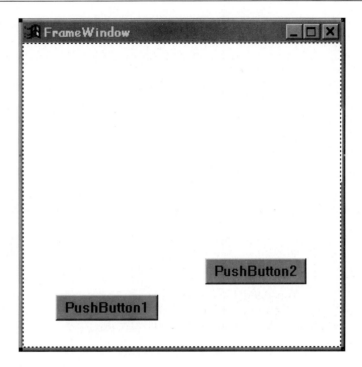

Figure 40: IFrameWindow with two IPushButton controls

❏ Change the text of the buttons so that one says **A~dd** and the other **E~xit**.

The tilde ~ character defines the character after it as the mnemonic for the button. For example, pressing **Alt+x** exits the program. To complete the direct editing mode, click the left mouse button outside the control you have edited.

Since it is very difficult to place the controls exactly where you want on the window canvas, your buttons probably look a little messy right now as they do in Figure 40. To clean this up you need to horizontally align the two push buttons, make them the same size and distribute them evenly on the frame window. Use the alignment buttons on the tool bar in the following steps:

❏ Select both push buttons on the canvas using either of the techniques described in the previous chapter.

❏ Use the **Same size** buttons to make the push buttons the same height and width.

❏ Press the *align at the bottom* alignment button.

❏ Press the vertical alignment button to distribute both buttons evenly across the width of the frame window.

The Composition Editor should now look like Figure 41. You can also use the **Grid** and **Snap** buttons to aid you with the placement of controls on the canvas.

Adding Entry Fields

The next control you use is the **IEntryField** control, which is used for entering data in a window. The entry field is widely used in forms-based applications. The entry field control is very rich in default behavior, but sometimes the default entry field is not well suited for a particular application. For the **Adder** you will set some settings to customize the default entry fields for the application. The entry field control is in the **Data entry** category along with other controls like IMultiLineEdit and IStaticText.

You need two entry fields to input the two numbers for the Adding Machine, and one entry field to hold the result of the operation. Let's add these controls to the canvas.

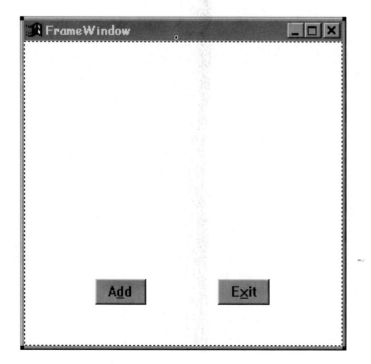

Figure 41: Push buttons aligned and renamed

❏ From the **Data entry** category, select the **IEntryField*** control and drop it on the canvas

❏ Repeat this step two more times so there are three entry fields on the screen as shown in Figure 42.

Adding Static Text

Next, add some text labels to the entry fields to identify them. To do this, use the **IStaticText** control which is also in the **Data entry** category as shown in Figure 43.

❏ Select the **IStaticText*** control, and place a static text control above each entry field.

You may want to use the **sticky** check box which makes it easier to drop multiple controls of the same type. To stop the sticky function, go back to the sticky check box and deselect it so there is no longer a

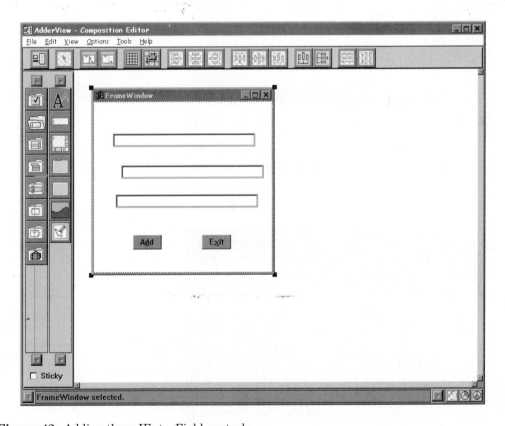

Figure 42: Adding three IEntryField controls

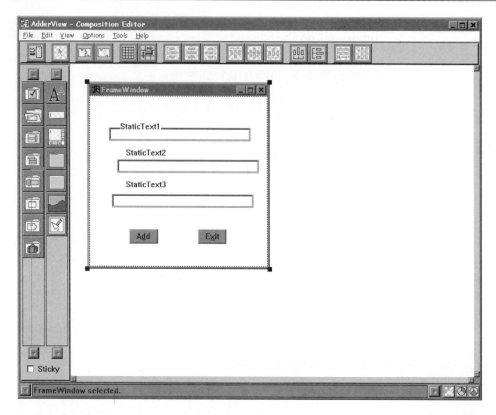

Figure 43: Adding three IStaticText controls

check mark. Another way to stop the sticky function is to press the **arrow** button on the Composition Editor tool bar.

The sticky function behavior is called *modal behavior* because you are in a specific mode. In general, modal behavior is not good for applications; it forces the user to figure out how to get into and out of a mode. However in some very special cases modal functions add some good function or actually improve application usability after the function is learned.

Aligning Controls

Next the entry fields and static text controls need to be aligned so they are evenly positioned on the canvas. You may have carefully placed the controls with good spacing on the canvas, but it is not necessary to spend a lot of time aligning the controls manually. With the alignment functions you can accomplish this task quickly and accurately. There must be at least two controls selected in order to use the alignment buttons on the tool bar. This is because the controls are aligned relative to the last control selected. Now align the controls:

❑ Select all six controls as described in the previous chapter. Once they are selected, the alignment buttons on the tool bar become enabled.

❑ Press the left align button.

❑ While all the controls are still selected, press the right mouse button with the mouse pointer on top of any of the selected controls. This brings up the context menu.

❑ Select **Layout**, **Distribute**, and **Vertically in bounding box** to obtain even spacing between the six controls as seen in Figure 44.

These simple steps aligned the user interface controls nicely; the Composition Editor should look like Figure 45.

❑ Directly edit the static text fields above each of the entry fields, and enter text to describe the entry fields. The labels should read **First number**, **Second number**, and **Result**.

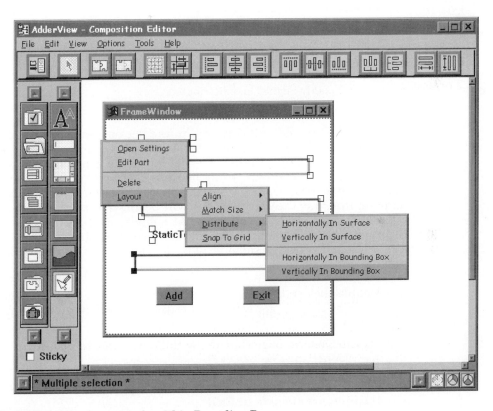

Figure 44: Aligning controls within Bounding Box

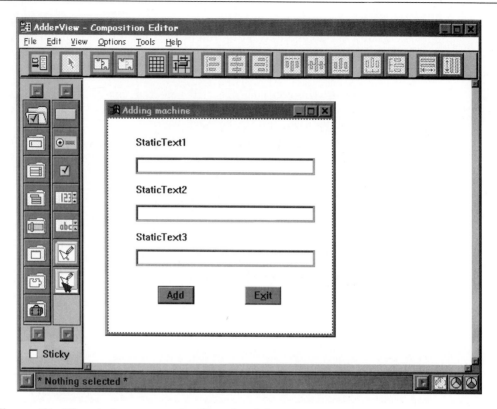

Figure 45: All controls are properly aligned and distributed

Each control has a default **Subpart name** because each control must have a unique name. The first entry field you dropped has a default subpart name of **EntryField1**. The default name is not very descriptive, but it is better than nothing because every control must have a subpart name. With many of the controls you use, the default subpart name is fine, but the controls that will be the source or target of a connection should have a meaningful subpart name. Changing the **Subpart name** to something meaningful helps you follow the generated code and provides some level of documentation to the application code.

❑ Double click on the **Add** button. This brings up a notebook where you can change the attributes of the **IPushButton** as seen in Figure 46.

❑ On the General page change the Subpart name to **pbAdd**.

❑ Press **OK** to save the settings.

❑ Open the settings notebook for the **Exit** push button and change the Subpart name to **pbExit**.

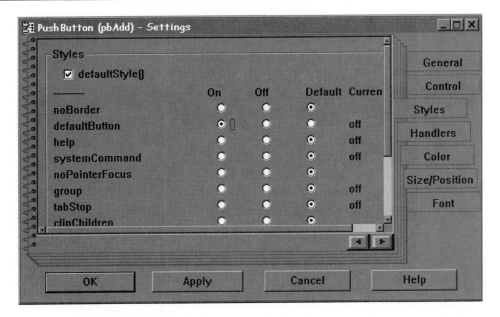

Figure 46: Settings notebook for pbAdd

❏ You do not need to change anything else on this control. Select the **OK** button to save the changes and close the notebook.

It is very common to use shortened words for variable names. The **pb** prefix is short for push button and helps identify this control. A quicker way to change the part name is to press the right mouse button while the mouse pointer is over the part you wish to rename. On the pop-up menu select **Change name**. Change the names of the entry fields to:

❏ efNum1

❏ efNum2

❏ efResult

Setting the Default Button

Each window can have a default button, which is selected when the user presses the enter key. A well designed panel will have a default push button which recognizes when the **enter** key is pressed. Make the **Add** push button the default for this screen as seen in Figure 46.

❏ In the settings notebook, click on the **Styles** notebook tab.

❏ Select the **On** radio button in the row labeled **defaultButton**.

The styles page is very helpful for customizing the default Open Class controls. The style page displays the specific style options for the different controls in the Open Class library.

❑ Select the **OK** button on the settings notebook to save the settings and close the notebook. If you look carefully, the **Add** push button now has a black outline, indicating that it is the default button.

If you ever make any changes to a control in the settings notebook and decide you do not like them, there is an easy way to go back to the old settings. After you close the settings notebook you can go to the **Edit** menu of the Composition Editor and select **Undo**. You can step back through the changes until you get the control back to how you want it.

Often you need to limit the number of characters which can be typed in the entry fields. The default length of an entry field control is 32 characters. This is too long for the numbers used in an adding machine.

❑ Select **efNum1** and open its settings notebook.

❑ On the General page, enter the number 5 in the limit entry field; this restricts the number of characters that can be typed to 5 as shown in Figure 47.

❑ Press the **OK** button to save the settings.

❑ Repeat for **efNum2**.

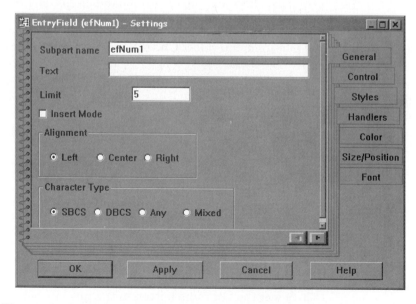

Figure 47: Restricting the number of characters in an entry field

The **efResult** entry field displays the result of adding the values in the other two entry fields. It is only used for displaying the result and input to it should be disabled. To achieve this behavior the **readOnly** style must be set.

❏ Select the entry field which holds the result and open its settings notebook by double-clicking the left mouse button.

❏ Select the Styles page of the notebook.

❏ In the row labeled **readOnly,** select the **On** radio button as shown in Figure 48.

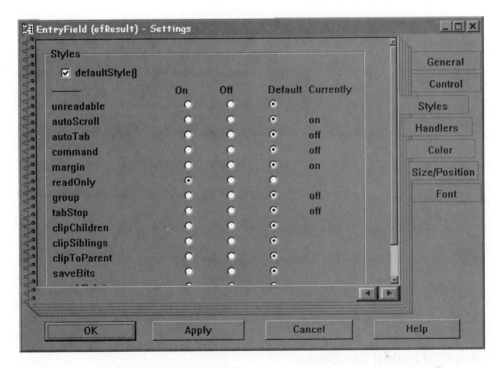

Figure 48: Settings notebook for efResult

What are Groups and Tab Stops?

Tabbing is a useful feature in user interfaces that improves screen navigation. There are two terms which need to be explained before you go on. These terms are:

• Tab stop

• Group

Each control placed on a canvas can be designated as a Tab stop, a Group, or both. This designation determines the position of the cursor after the user presses the arrow or tab keys.

Pressing the tab key moves the cursor from its current position to the next control, which has been designated as Tab stop. The sequence is determined by the order in which the controls were placed on the canvas. This order can be altered as explained below. Tabs can be used in both Windows and OS/2.

In OS/2 there is a second level of cursor control, the Group. Pressing the Up and Down cursor keys moves the cursor as described above with one exception. When the Down arrow key is pressed when the cursor is on the last control of a Group, the cursor returns to the first control on the same Group, not the next tab stop. This assumes the cursor movement is downward.

Thus, Groups designate logical association of controls from the keyboard navigation point of view. A Group begins with a control, which has been designated as Group and continues until the next control down the list, which has also been designated as Group.

In the Adding Machine example you have two groups which are the entry field group and the push button group. Pressing the Down arrow key cycles the cursor from the first entry field to the second entry field and then back to the first. While in the push button group, pressing the Right arrow key cycles the cursor from the **Add** button to the **Exit** button. The user pushes the Tab key to move between groups.

Designating a control as the beginning of a Group has no effect in Windows. If you want an application to behave the same in Windows and OS/2, you should not use the Group setting and mark all entry fields and buttons as Tab stops.

Setting Group and Tab Stops

Setting tab stops and tab order is different in the Windows and OS/2 products. If you are using VisualAge for C++ Version 3.0 for OS/2 skip the next section.

Setting Tab Order in Windows

If you are using VisualAge for C++ Version 3.5 for Windows, the following section describes how you can define tab stop and tab ordering.

By default Open Class controls have tabbing set to off. To set tabbing on for the **efNum1**:

1. Point to **efNum1** with the mouse.
2. Press the right mouse button to get the pop-up menu.
3. Select **Set tabbing**, **Tab stop** to set tabbing on, as shown in Figure 49.

Repeat these steps for **efNum2**.

Entry field **efNum1** and the push button you placed on the left should be marked as a Group and tab stop. Entry field **efNum2** and the other push button should be a tab stop.

There is a special dialog box to set the tabbing order of the controls on the part. First move the mouse pointer to a place on the title bar of the frame window and press the right mouse button; then select **View parts list ...** from the pop-up menu.

This window, as shown in Figure 50, provides a graphical tree view of all the subparts associated with this composite part. The subparts appear in the order in which you placed them on the canvas. If the entry fields and buttons do not appear in the proper order, you can drag and drop them into the proper sequence by:

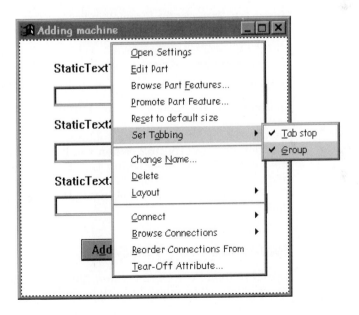

Figure 49: Setting tabs and groups

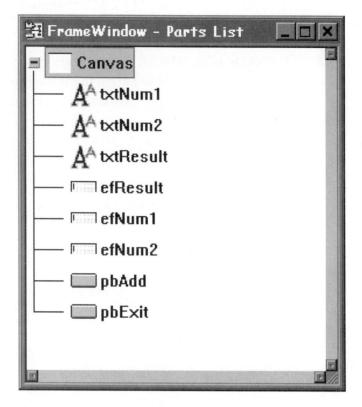

Figure 50: Parts list for IFrameWindow

1. Selecting one or more controls

2. Using the mouse and drag the control to the proper position

3. Releasing the mouse button to drop the control and set its position

Set the tabbing order so the tabbing sequence starts with **efNum1** and then goes to **efNum2**. When you have the tabbing order set, close the window by double-clicking the left mouse button on the system menu in the upper left corner on the dialog or pressing the close button. This saves the new tabbing order. Now go to the next section, *More Connections*.

Setting Tab Order in OS/2

If you are using the OS/2 version, the following section describes how you can define tab stops and tab ordering.

❏ Move the mouse pointer to a place on the canvas which has no controls and press the right mouse button.

❏ Then select Tabbing and Depth order from the pop-up menu.

In this window, seen in Figure 51, you define groups and tab stops for the whole part. Note that the headings for the columns of check boxes are **Group** for the left column and **Tab stop** for the right column. If the entry fields and buttons do not appear in the proper order, you can drag and drop them into the proper sequence by:

1. Selecting one or more controls

2. Using the mouse and drag the control to the proper position

3. Releasing the mouse button to drop the control and set its position

Continue dragging and dropping the controls until they are in the proper order. Once the controls are in the proper order, mark efNum1 as **Group and tab stop**. The push button you placed on the left

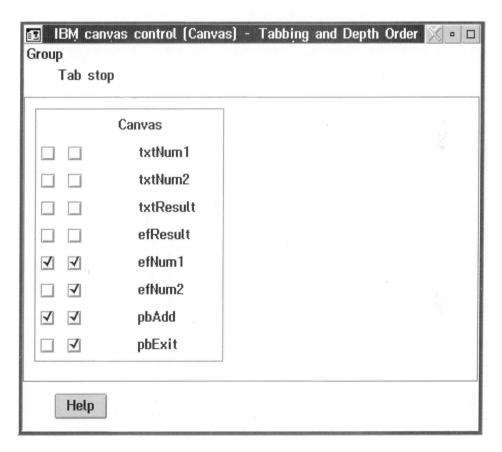

Figure 51: Tabbing and Depth order in OS/2

should be a Group and tab stop, and the other push button should be a tab stop.

❑ Double click on the system menu icon to close the dialog and save the settings.

Making More Connections

The **Exit** push button ends or closes the application. You can achieve this by making one connection:

❑ Point to the **Exit** push button and use the right mouse button to start a connection with the **buttonClickEvent**.

❑ Remember from the Hello World application that when making connections to a frame window, drag the end of the connection to any point over the title bar.

❑ Press the left mouse button and complete the connection to the frame window's **close** action as seen in Figure 52.

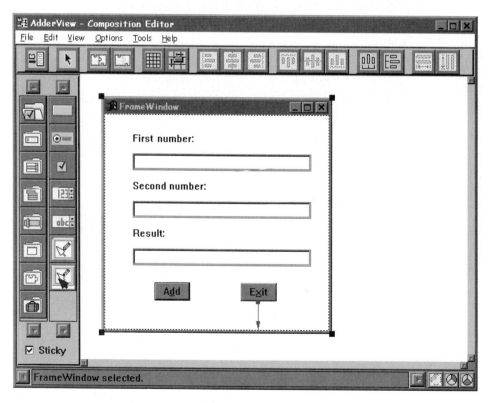

Figure 52: pbExit connected to IFrameWindow close

Generating C++ Code for the Adding Machine

Let's see what the Adding Machine looks like. You need to generate the C++ code, and compile and link the application. To generate the C++ code in the Composition Editor you can either select the **Save and generate** button or you select the **File** item on the menu, select **Save and generate...**, and then select **Part source**. Generating the **Part source** creates the following files:

DDERVIEW.CPP

DDERVIEW.HPP

DDERVIEW.RCI

You may wonder what happened to the names of the files. The part's name is **AdderView**, but the generated files are named DDERVIEW.XXX. Remember in Chapter 2 you set the Visual Builder option so the file names would conform to the FAT file system. FAT file names are restricted to eight characters for the file name and three characters for the file extension. If the name of a part exceeds eight characters, the Visual Builder needs to adjust the file names so they are only eight characters in length. The algorithm used to achieve this works as follows:

1. From left to right, start removing vowels until either the length of the name is eight characters or the end of the name is reached

2. If all the vowels have been removed and the name is still more than eight characters, the name is truncated to eight characters.

Remember that you need to generate the **main()** function so you can compile an executable file.

❑ Select File, Save and generate..., and main() for part

Generating the **main() for part** creates the following files:

DDERVIEW.APP

DDERVIEW.RCX

DDERVIEW.MAK

❑ Switch to a Command prompt session so you can compile the **AdderView** application.

❑ Ensure that you are in the **x:\VABOOK\ADDER** directory. Use the **nmake** facility just as you did in the Hello World application. At the Command prompt enter **nmake dderview.mak**

Running the Adding Machine

The **nmake** should complete without errors because the Visual Builder generated all the user interface code, and you only made one simple connection. You can now run and test **DDERVIEW.EXE**. Make sure the panel looks the way you designed it to look, see Figure 53.

You can enter numbers or even text in the entry fields. This is good enough for now, but soon you will change the entry field so it only accepts numbers. Check for the limitations you imposed on the entry fields. The entry fields should only accept five characters. If you select the **Add** push button, nothing happens because you did not connect it to anything. When you are sure everything is working properly, press the **Exit** button to close the program. If something is not working as it should, you can look in the **answers** subdirectory, which has a working version of the Adding Machine.

The Adding Machine application is a repositionable and sizable window just like the Hello World application. The user interface is mostly complete, and you did not need to write any code. The Adding Machine needs to be able to add the numbers in the entry fields. You will add this C++ logic in the application using nonvisual parts.

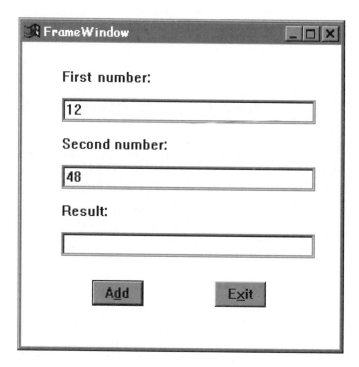

Figure 53: Running the AdderView application

Making a Nonvisual Part

There are many ways to get the Adding machine to add the two numbers. The best Object-Oriented method for providing the add function is to develop a nonvisual part which encapsulates the logic and data necessary to perform the addition of the two numbers. You can hand code the nonvisual part, or you can use the Visual Builder to define and generate the stub code for the nonvisual part. The better approach is to use the Visual Builder to define the public interface of the Calc nonvisual part. The Visual Builder will generate the C++ files for the Calc part as **stub code**. Stub code consists of the declaration of functions in the **.HPV** file and the skeleton definition of the function in the **.CPV** file (more about these file types later), providing the entry point to the function, the opening and closing braces, and the return statement.

Once the stub code is generated you add the C++ logic for the **add** function. Continue with the instructions and construct the nonvisual part, as shown in Figure 54, with the following steps:

❑ From the Visual Builder Parts Selector window, select **Part, New**. Enter **Calc** for the **Class name**.

❑ Enter the same **File name** you used for the Visual part; this way all the pieces that make up this application are in the same file. As you remember, you used **Adder**.

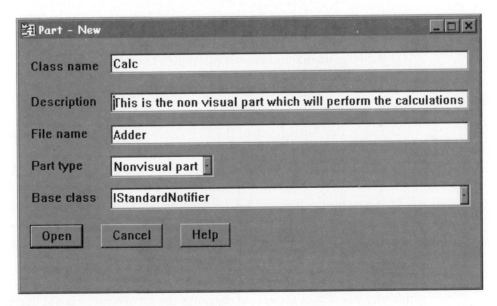

Figure 54: Creating the Calc nonvisual part

❑ Enter a suitable description such as **This is the nonvisual part which will perform the calculations** in the Description entry field.

❑ Select **Nonvisual** as the part type. The Base class for nonvisual parts is automatically IStandardNotifier. IStandardNotifier contains the necessary code to enable classes which derive from it to handle notifications.

❑ When all the fields have the been filled in, press the **Open** button to start defining the **Calc** part.

Using the Part Interface Editor

When you define a nonvisual part, the Visual Builder starts in the Parts Interface Editor, which can be referred to as the PIE for short. There are five pages in the PIE notebook; the first page is where you define the **attributes** of the class. Attribute is another word for public member data. This class has three attributes, all are type **int** for integer.

❑ In the **Attribute name** field enter **num1**.

❑ In the **Attribute type** list box enter **int**.

You can select primitive attribute types, like *int* or *long*, from the drop down list box. Nonprimitive types can be typed in. Press the **Add with defaults** push button. Notice how the get and set member functions for the attribute were created for you. You may now add a description like **Holds the first operand** and press the **Update** button, see Figure 55.

❑ Add the **num2** and **result** attributes the same way.

Now define the **add** action which is a public member function in the **Calc** class.

❑ Select the **Action** tab of the PIE notebook to switch to that page, see Figure 56.

❑ Type **add** in the **Action name** entry field and press the **Add with defaults** button at the bottom of the Action page.

❑ Now enter a description for this action such as **Performs the addition operation between num1 and num2**.

❑ Press the **Update** button to save this change to the part's action.

The default return type of the **add** action is *int*. This is fine; however, once you see how this part is used in the Visual Builder you will wonder why the return type is *int*, because the return value is not used by

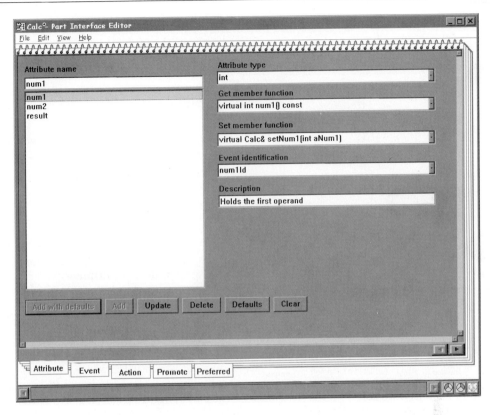

Figure 55: Parts Interface Editor for the Calc part

the application. In the C language, functions that produce unused return values should be coded as `void`; in C++ when you encounter this type of member function you usually return a reference to the object to which the member function belongs. This is done by returning *this* and typing the member function as *Calc& add()*. Returning a reference to the object also gives you the ability to chain calls to member functions of the same object. For example, you could write something like this:

```
main()
{
  Calc aCalculator;
  aCalculator.setNum1(2).setNum2(5);
  int result = aCalculator.add().result();
  // the int result would hold the number 7
}
```

Code segment 7: Chaining of functions

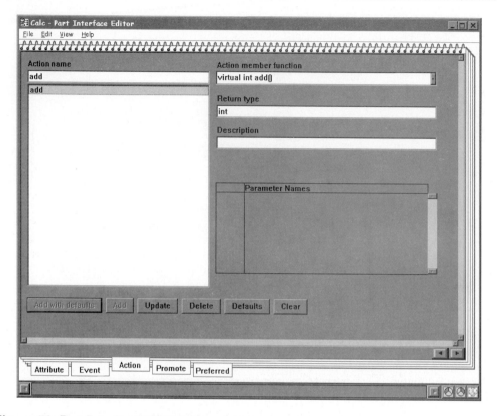

Figure 56: Part Interface Editor, Actions page

The code snippet in Code segment 7 does not perform a very complex operation, but in general a good Object-Oriented programming practice is to return a reference to the object if the return code is not used for anything else.

By default all actions generated by the Part Interface Editor are declared as virtual. Generally this is fine, but if the application depends on the highest performance you may want to take a closer look at each action and determine whether it really needs to be a virtual function. The overhead of a virtual function call is not great, especially with the caliber of common place machines today, but nevertheless it exists.

For the **Calc** part, modify the default action declaration by making the **add** action return a reference to the Calc object, and also make it a non virtual function:

❑ Change the **Action member function** to *Calc& add()*

❑ Change the **Return type** to *Calc&*

In the C or C++ language the add function would have been written like this:

```
int add( int num1, int num2);
```

for the Visual Builder you wrote:

```
Calc& add( );
```

You may wonder now, if the return type of the add action is not *int*, how is the result of the operation passed to the **result** entry field so it can be displayed? How are the values of **num1** and **num2** known to the Calc part if they are not passed? The answer is that the Calc part has its own copy of the **num1** and **num2** attributes, and these attributes are kept synchronized with the values of the entry fields by virtue of connections and the notification framework of the class library. The **add** action sets the **result** attribute in the Calc part, and this action generates the proper notification so that the **efResult** entry field is updated. You will see more details later.

There are no special events to be added to the **Event** page of the notebook, but notice that in the **attribute** page each attribute also has an **Event identification**. As attributes are changed by the program logic, events are generated to notify other parts of the event so that they can take appropriate action. This is one of the ways the notification framework sends messages to other parts.

The last page in the notebook is the **Preferred** page shown in Figure 57. In this page you define which features of the part are displayed in the pop-up menu to make quick connections.

- ❏ Go to the **Preferred Features** list box and select **remove all** from its pop-up menu; you can access the pop-up menu by pressing the right mouse button.
- ❏ Go to the **Actions** list box and select **add**, bring up the pop-up menu, and select **Add >>**. This adds the item to the **Preferred Features** list box and therefore to the pop-up menu.
- ❏ Do the same for the attributes **num1**, **num2**, and **result**.
- ❏ From the bottom right corner of the PIE, select the middle icon.

This switches you to the **Class Editor** for the **Calc** part as shown in Figure 58. This editor is used to define a variety of parameters for the part you are building. You are now going to use it to describe the names of the .HPV and .CPV files that will contain the stub code for the get and set functions for the attributes and also for the **add** action. The names of these files are entered under the **User files included in generation** section.

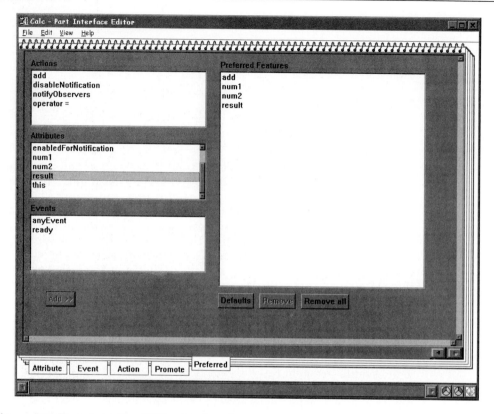

Figure 57: Parts Interface Editor, Preferred page

❑ In the **User .hpv** field enter **CALC.HPV** and in the **User .cpv** file enter **CALC.CPV**.

If you need additional include files to support the code you enter in this class, you can define the include files in the **Required include files** section. For example, if you use IColor parts in your code you would include **ICOLOR.HPP** here. However, you do not have any other classes within the **Calc** class, so leave this field blank.

You have now finished describing the part by defining its public interface. You can use the part in combination with other parts to make composite parts. You need to save this part definition and generate the C++ code for the part.

❑ Select **File**, **Save and Generate**, and **Part source** from the menu bar.

This saves the **Calc** nonvisual part in the ADDER.VBB file and then generates the following files:

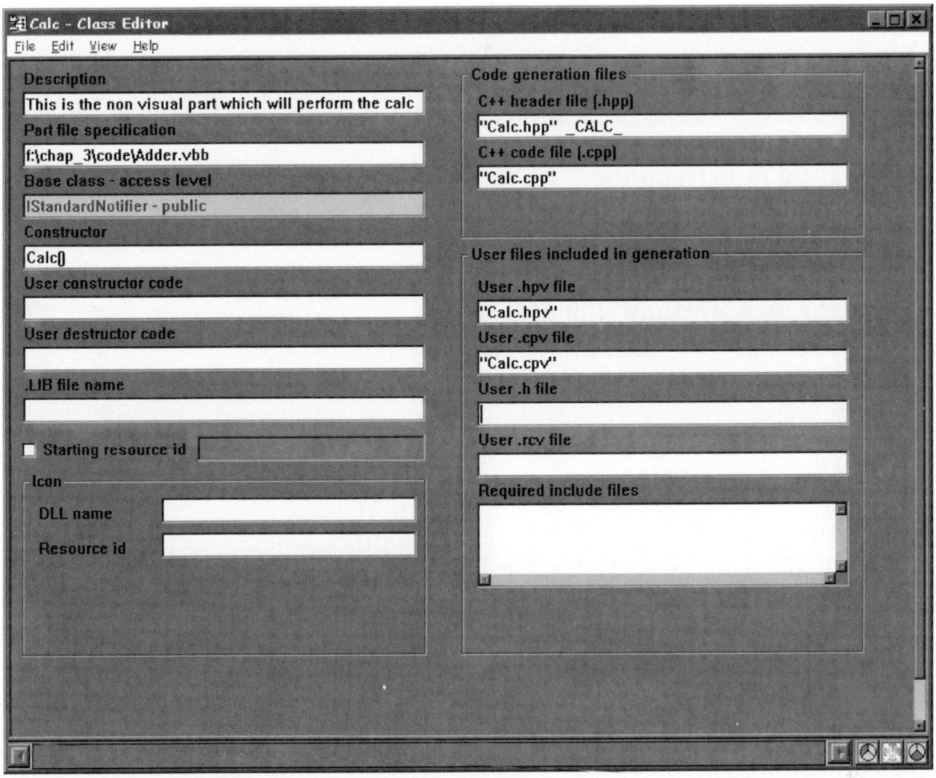

Figure 58: Class Editor for the Calc part

CALC.HPP

CALC.CPP

CALC.H

CALC.RCI

These files contain the skeleton for the part. Every time you select **Save and generate** and then **Part source** these files are regenerated, completely replacing previous versions without any warnings. Therefore, if you modify these files manually, your changes are lost the next time the C++ code is generated. User code should go in the **User files** with the .HPV and .CPV file extensions specified in the **Class editor** of the part.

❑ Now select **File**, **Save and Generate**, and **Feature source...** from the menu bar, see Figure 59. In this panel you can select the actions, attributes and events to be generated or generate all the part features.

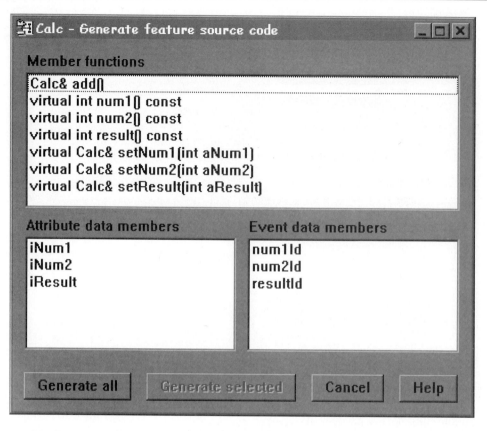

Figure 59: Generate feature source for the Calc part

❑ Select **Generate all** to create the stubs for the definitions by pushing the **Generate all** button.

This generates the following files:

CALC.CPV

CALC.HPV

The .HPV and .CPV files are included by the corresponding CALC.HPP and CALC.CPP, files which are generated C++ code for the part. If you add, delete, or modify the part attributes, actions, or events and regenerate the **Feature source**, the modified code is appended to the existing files. The code you have previously entered is not lost. You should only generate the code for features you have added or modified. Do not use the **Generate All** option after the first generation, or you will have duplicate declarations of the part features. The compiler does not accept the duplicate definitions; it will complain with

an error message, and you will need to remove the duplicate definitions before the application will compile.

❑ Exit the Class Editor and switch to your favorite text editor.

Now add the code to support the **add** action. VisualAge includes the
Program editor, which is a context sensitive editor and it is great for
writing C or C++ code. The Program editor works the same in both
the Windows and OS/2 versions of VisualAge for C++.

You need to add the logic to the **Calc** part to perform the addition of
num1 and **num2**. To do this you need to edit the CALC.CPV file. Locate the **add** member function and complete the code so it looks like
Code segment 8: add action for Calc part.

```
Calc& Calc::add()
{
  // user code for add function
  setResult( iNum1 + iNum2 );
  return *this;
}
```

Code segment 8: add action for Calc part

```
Calc& Calc::setResult(int aResult)
{
  if (!(iResult == aResult))
  {
    iResult = aResult;
    notifyObservers(INotificationEvent(Calc::resultId,
    *this));
  } // endif
  return *this;
}
```

Code segment 9: setResult member function for Calc part

In Code segment 9 you see the **setResult** member function, which in
addition to setting the value **iResult,** sends a notification to inform
observers that this value has changed.

The code generator has changed the name of the attributes by adding
the letter **i** at the beginning of the name and also by changing the
first letter of the original name to upper case. This is done to avoid
naming conflicts between the name of the attribute and its **get** member function. For the attribute **num1** the get function is also called
num1(), so the generator changed **num1** to **iNum1**.

❑ Save the **CALC.CPV** file and, if you need to conserve memory exit the editor.

You have completed creating the nonvisual part which performs the addition in the Adding Machine. In the next exercise you will improve this part to perform the subtraction, multiplication, and division operations.

Using Nonvisual Parts

Now you need to bring the nonvisual part into the **AdderView** Composition Editor and make the necessary connections.

❑ If not already open, select **AdderView** from the Parts Selector list box and open it.

❑ From the composition editor, select **Options**, **Add part...** .

❑ Type in the name of the adder part **Calc***. C++ is case sensitive, which means you must type **Calc*** exactly. Be extra careful and include the asterisk at the end of the class name.

❑ It is a good idea to name the part, so enter **calculator**. Press the **Add** push button to close the window.

The mouse pointer is now loaded with the **Calc** nonvisual part for you to drop on the free-form surface. Move the mouse pointer outside of the frame window, over the free-form surface, and press the left mouse button to drop the part. You should now have a part that looks like a puzzle piece available for connections. While the mouse pointer is loaded with a nonvisual part, the Composition Editor does not let you drop it on the visual part. You can only drop the part on the free-form surface, see Figure 60.

To use the **Calc** part in the application, you connect it to the visual part. The data from the **efNum1** entry field needs to be used by the **num1** attribute of the **Calc** nonvisual part. Make an attribute-to-attribute connection between the two parts as follows:

❑ To start a connection, place the tip of the mouse pointer on top of a part where you want to start a connection.

❑ Press the right mouse button to bring up the preferred connections pop-up menu. Remember that you defined the **num1** attribute to be of type **int**. Fortunately, the entry field has a data conversion function **valueAsInt**.

❑ Point to **valueAsInt** in the preferred list and press the left mouse button to start the connection.

The pop-up menu contains whatever actions and attributes were entered in the **Preferred list** when the entry field part was defined as

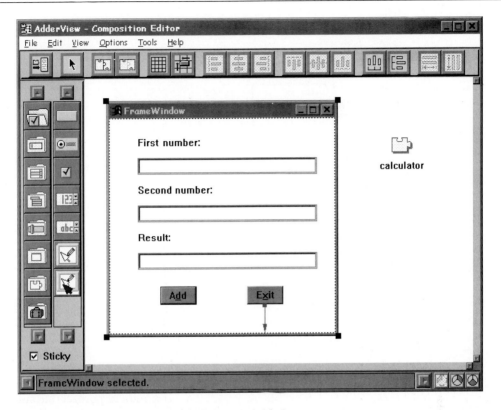

Figure 60: Composition Editor with Calc part added

shown in Figure 61. At the bottom of the **Preferred list** is the **More...** selection, which brings up a dialog box containing all possible Events, Attributes, and Actions for a part.

Now the mouse pointer has changed to a spider and there is a line which originates from the control you selected and follows your mouse movements.

❏ Move the spider to the **Calc** nonvisual part and press the left mouse button. This displays the preferred connections list for the **Calc** part.

❏ Select the **num1** item on the preferred list to complete the connection. This establishes a connection between the efNum1 **value-AsInt** attribute to the Calc **num1** attribute.

In a similar fashion, connect:

❏ efNum2 (valueAsInt) → calculator (num2)

❏ calculator (result) → efResult(valueAsInt)

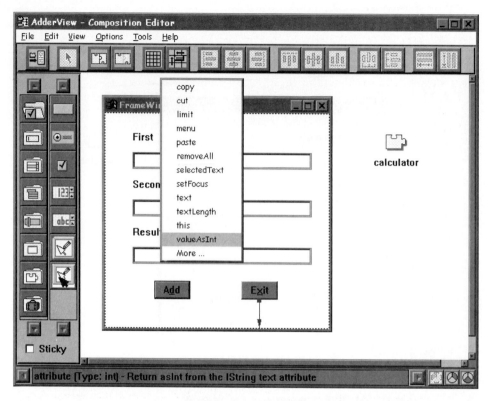

Figure 61: Preferred list for efNum1

❏ pbAdd (buttonClickEvent) → calculator(add)

Now that the connections are complete for this iteration of the Adding Machine, the title bar should have a meaningful name.

❏ Directly edit the title bar (Alt+left mouse button) and change the title to **Adding Machine**. The Composition Editor should now look like Figure 62.

When using lower resolution screens you will frequently you have to make connections to parts that are off the visible part of the free-form surface. This means that you have to scroll the free-form surface to reach the part to which you want to connect. If the spider connection pointer is on and you press the scroll bars, you lose the pointer and the connection. How can you scroll the free-form surface to reach the part without losing the starting point of the connection? The answer is: select the source of the connection, and while dragging the spider pointer, touch the edge of the free-form surface in the direction in which you want to shift it.

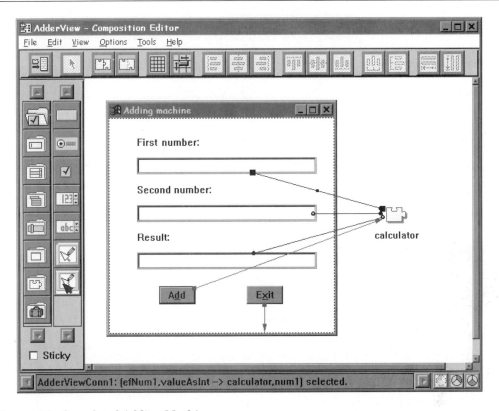

Figure 62: Completed Adding Machine

❑ Generate the **Part source** and the **main() for part**; both are found under the **File** action bar item.

❑ Switch over to a Command Prompt session to run **nmake,** which compiles and links the **Adding Machine**. At the Command prompt enter **nmake dderview.mak**.

Running the Finished Adding Machine

The processing of nmake should complete without errors, so run and test DDERVIEW.EXE. If the application does not compile or works incorrectly, remember to check completed Adding Machine supplied in the *answers* subdirectory.

When the application starts it should look like Figure 63. The user interface looks like it did the last time you ran the Adding Machine. Enter a number in the **Num1** entry field and another number in the **Num2** entry field. Remember that the numbers must be integers

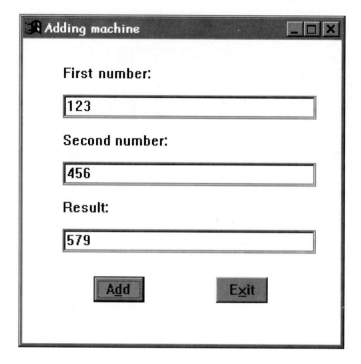

Figure 63: Running the Adding Machine

which are round numbers with no decimal point. You can use negative numbers because integers include negative numbers. If you try putting text in the fields it will be ignored.

Enter **123** for the first number and enter **456** for the second number; then select the **Add** push button and you see the number **579** in the Result field. You can try other integers, even negative integers, and you get the correct answer. Close the Adding Machine application by selecting the **Exit** button.

Chapter 3—Summary

This was a little tougher than the Hello World application, but it was still pretty easy. In this chapter you learned the following:

VisualAge Parts architecture including:

- ❏ Composite parts
- ❏ Visual parts
- ❏ Nonvisual parts

How to build the Adding Machine application user interface which included:

- ❏ Adding entry field, static text and push button controls
- ❏ Setting Tab order
- ❏ Creating nonvisual parts
- ❏ Making connections between visual and nonvisual parts

How to create a nonvisual part by:

- ❏ Defining attributes
- ❏ Defining actions
- ❏ Setting preferred features
- ❏ Working with the Class editor
- ❏ Adding user code to the generated files

These are the very basics elements to Visual Programming. In the following chapters you will build on these basic elements and learn how to build real applications.

What's in Chapter 4

You will build on what you learned making the Adding Machine and improve it in a number of ways. The new application will have a much more sophisticated user interface. In the next chapter you will add more math functions, and in this chapter you will add user interface controls which will support these new functions. To do this you will:

❑ Add a tool bar

❑ Add tool bar buttons

❑ Change connections

❑ Add fly over help

❑ Compile and run the new user interface

❑ Customize the entry fields to accept numbers only

❑ Add an icon to the system menu

❑ Compile and run the completed application

4

Making a
Calculator

Just as in the Adding Machine application, you will develop this application in stages. This chapter focuses on improving the user interface of the Adding Machine.

Copying Parts

The Calculator is based on the Adding Machine application, but you do not have to start by making new parts. You can copy the **Adder-View** visual part and reuse the **Calc** nonvisual part. Start the Visual Builder and load the ADDER.VBB file, which contains the parts from the Adding Machine application. As seen in Figure 64, copy the **AdderView** part by completing the following steps:

❑ Select **AdderView** in the Visual Builder Parts Selector.

❑ Select **Part**, **Copy** from the menu bar.

❑ The copy dialog appears because you need to pick a new name for this part. In the **Target part name** field enter **CalcView**.

❏ You will build the Calculator in the **x:\vabook\calcltor** directory. In the **Target file name** entry field enter **x:\vabook\ calcltor\calcltor.vbb**. Press the **Copy** button.

This creates the file CALCLTOR.VBB in the specified directory and place a copy of the **AdderView** part called **CalcView** in it.

When copying parts in the Visual Builder you must provide a unique name for the new part. Fortunately, this time there was no problem; but sometimes you may want to make a copy of a part and use the current part name without destroying the original part. This is useful when you want to use an existing part as a building block for a new part. The new part may have improvements or additions to the original part. Since the Visual Builder internal model maintains a registry of part names, the Visual Builder does not allow two parts with the same name to be loaded at the same time, even if the parts exist in different .VBB files. There are a few steps in copying a part to another file and keep the same file name. This requires a copy and rename operation using the following steps:

1. Copy the original part to the part file of your choice or to a new VBB file, using a different name:

   ❏ copy part **A** from *OLD.VBB* as part **B** to **NEW.VBB**.

2. Unload the part file which contained the original part.

3. Rename the new part to the original part name:

   ❏ Rename part **B** in *NEW.VBB* to part **A**.

In your case you need to copy the Calc part from the *ADDER.VBB* file to the x:\VABOOK\CALCLTOR\CALCLTOR.VBB file. Perform the following steps:

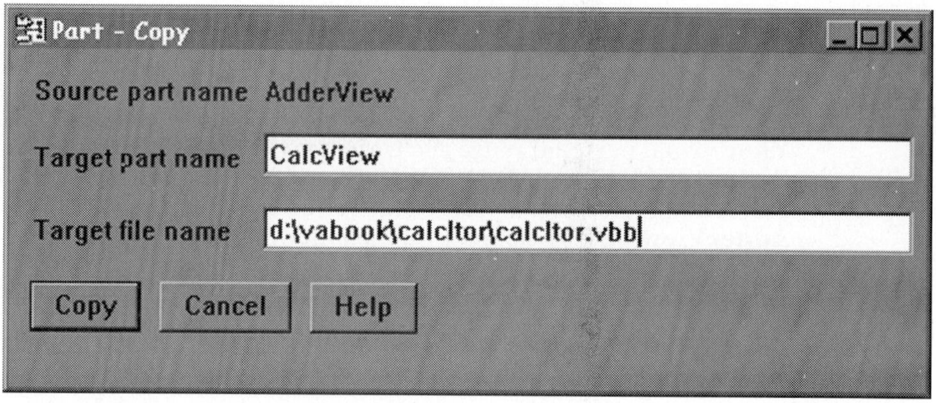

Figure 64: Copying AdderView into CalcView

❑ Select the **Calc** part, bring up its pop-up menu and select **Copy**.

❑ In the **Target part name** entry field type **NewCalc**.

❑ In the **Target file name** entry field type **x:\VABOOK\ CALCLTOR\CALCLTOR.VBB**. Press the **Copy** button.

❑ From the **Loaded Part Files** list box select the **ADDER.VBB** file. Bring up its pop-up menu and select **Unload...** .

❑ Select the **NewCalc** part, bring up its pop-up menu and select **Rename**. In the **New part name** entry field type **Calc**.

❑ Press the **Rename** button to complete the change.

Copying the Calc part allows you to use it whenever the CALCLTOR. VBB is loaded. You should be aware that all you have copied is the Visual Builder definition of the part. The actual source files did not get copied by this operation. You have two options to correct this problem:

1. Copy the Calc.* files from the x:\VABOOK\ADDER directory to the x:\VABOOK\CALCLTOR directory

2. Regenerate the Part Source and Feature source for the Calc part in the x:\VABOOK\CALCLTOR directory. You will have to add the code to perform the addition operation in the CALC.CPV file.

From now on you will not be required to do any copying and renaming as part of the instructions in this book, but as you work with the Visual Builder you may want to reorganize the parts. You need to manage where you save parts, for example, saving backup copies of files. Becoming familiar with the part management functions in the Visual Builder like copy, move, rename, and delete can help you be more productive.

Constructing the Calculator

Now let's get back to building the Calculator. From the Options menu bar change the working directory to **x:\VABOOK\CALCLTOR.** You should always make sure that the working directory is pointing to where you want your files saved.

❑ Select **CalcView** and double click the left mouse button to open the Composition Editor for the part.

❑ Directly edit the title of the frame window and change the title to **Calculator** as shown in Figure 65.

Adding an IToolBar control

New applications have tool bars which are easier to use than just menus and can be customized by the user. Tool bars also come with a

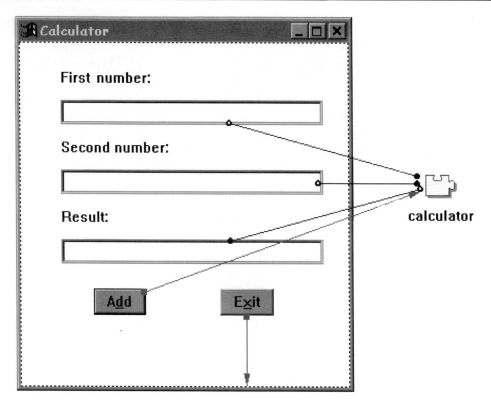

Figure 65: Calculator with buttons

special type of push button which can contain text, graphics, or both text and graphics. The **IToolBar** control works in Windows 95, Windows NT, Windows 3.1, and OS/2.

The tool bar is a very flexible control which can have tool bar buttons, regular push buttons, static text, animated buttons, or just about any other control. You can also have multiple tool bars on the application. The Calculator uses a single tool bar with multiple tool bar buttons.

The **IToolBar** control is located in the Frame Extensions category because tool bars are always associated with a specific frame window. Add a tool bar to the calculator:

❏ From the Frame Extensions category, select the **IToolBar*** control and add it to the frame window. In order to place the tool bar control on the frame window, the mouse pointer should be on the title bar of the frame window. The result is shown in Figure 66.

When you place a tool bar control on the frame window, the tool bar makes room for itself below the title bar and moves the canvas down.

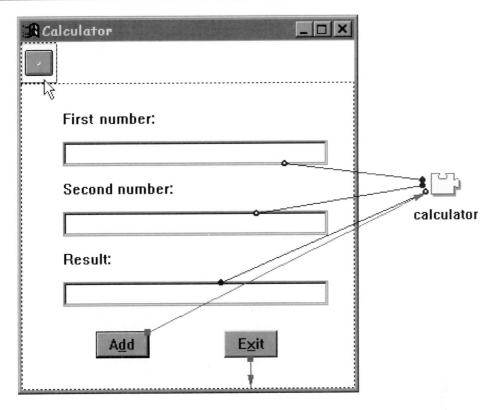

Figure 66: An IToolBar control added

The tool bar control also comes with one tool bar button. The **ITool-BarButton** is a very flexible control which shows a bitmap as a default view. Additionally, the tool bar button can have text and a bitmap, or only text as its view. IToolBarButton controls can actually be used on a canvas, just like the IPushButton control, and are not required to be on a tool bar. Each tool bar button has unique settings, so you can easily set the bitmap and text. You can even have different sized tool bar buttons on a tool bar. These features facilitate the construction of very slick and useful custom tool bars.

Tool Bar Options

The **IToolBar** control has many options and styles that can be changed in its settings notebook. It is a little tricky to open the tool bar settings notebook. Remember that the Visual Builder opens the settings for the part which is under the tip of the mouse pointer. To select the tool bar, the tip of the mouse pointer must be pointing to the area of the tool bar where there are no other controls, see the pointer position in Figure 66. This is a very small area on the screen and can be difficult to select. If the mouse pointer is on the title bar, you will accidentally select the settings notebook for the frame window, or if the mouse pointer is on the tool bar button, you will select the settings notebook for the tool bar button.

Let's make some changes to the tool bar settings:

❏ Place the tip of the mouse pointer on the tool bar and double-click the left mouse button to open the tool bar settings notebook.

❏ In the **Subpart name** field enter **tbCalc.**

❏ Enter **Calculator tool bar** in the **Floating title** field.

The **Floating title** appears when you detach the tool bar from the frame window. This is accomplished by dragging and dropping the tool bar from the frame window to the desktop when the application is running. If you have more than one tool bar in you application, you may want to select the **Group with preceding tool bar** check box. This allows multiple tool bars to be grouped next to each other in a row. The default behavior stacks the tool bars on top of each other. Since there is only one tool bar in the application, there is no need set this option.

Another feature of the tool bar is the default position. The default position is **aboveClient** which means just below the title bar of the frame window. You can select a different position, such as on the either side or at the bottom of the frame window. As mentioned earlier, the tool bar control can be detached from the frame window when the application is running. You can also reattach the tool bar to any of the four sides of the frame window. So, even though the default tool bar is at the top of the frame window, when the application is running the user can easily change the tool bar location. Change the location of the tool bar to **belowClient** as shown in Figure 67.

Tool Bar Views

Let's have this tool bar show both bitmaps and text.

❏ Turn to the **Styles** page of the settings notebook to change the default view for the tool bar control.

As mentioned earlier, there are three views for the tool bar **text**, **bitmap**, and **text and bitmap**. Since tool bar buttons are not required to be placed on a tool bar, they also have the same three views. The tool bar view setting overrides the tool bar button settings, so all the tool bar buttons used on a tool bar should have the default view set.

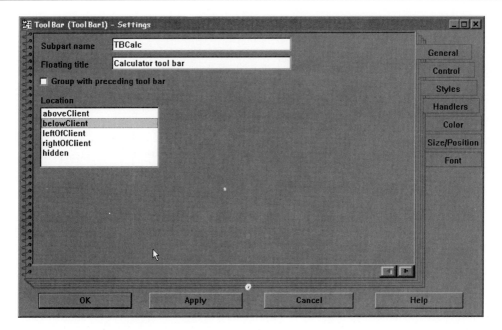

Figure 67: IToolBar General settings page

When you use tool bar buttons on a tool bar, the type of view must be set by the tool bar because you can not have tool bar buttons with different views on the same tool bar. If you make a mistake and set different styles on the tool bar and the tool bar button, the Visual Builder displays an error message in place of the button as shown in Figure 68. If you see this error message, check the styles for the tool bar buttons and ensure that their styles are set to the default; then set the desired style for the buttons on the tool bar settings.

Set the default view to show both text and a bitmap as shown in Figure 69.

❏ Select the **On** radio button for the **buttonBitmapAndText-Visible** style.

For some applications you may want the default view to be **button-TextVisible** where only text shows on the buttons. Since the three different view settings are mutually exclusive, you should only have one of the three styles selected as **On**, and the other two should be **Off**. Making these explicit settings in the **Styles** page ensures that the Visual Builder displays the buttons correctly.

There is a **noDragDrop** option on the styles page. If you do not want the users of the application dragging, dropping, and repositioning the

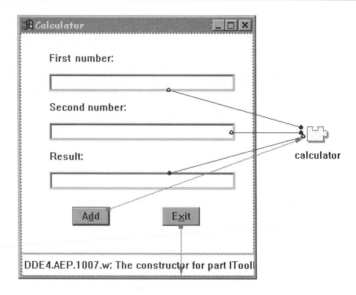

Figure 68: Error message shown instead of tool bar button

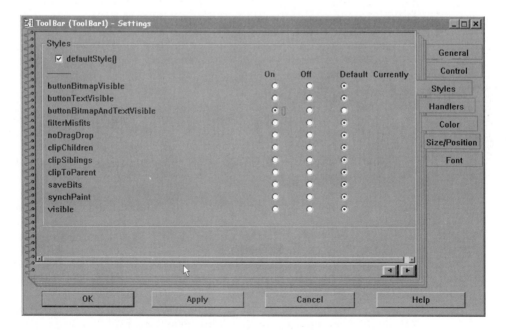

Figure 69: Select tool bar buttons style

tool bar; then select this option. Be careful to select the **On** button. You need to think about the settings because **Off** to **noDragDrop** is a double negative and means you want drag and drop.

❑ When you are finished changing the tool bar settings, select the **OK** button to close the notebook and save the changes.

Next, the tool bar needs four more tool bar button controls for the other math functions.

❑ Select the tool bar button control from the frame extensions category and add the buttons to the tool bar.

❑ The first button is the **add** button, so directly edit the button. Point to the button with the mouse, press Atl+left mouse button, and enter **Add**.

❑ Directly edit the other four buttons and add the text to read **Subtract**, **Multiply**, **Divide**, and **Clear**.

Connecting Tool Bar Buttons

Now that there is a new **Add** tool bar button, you do not need the old **Add** push button on the canvas. The new **Add** tool bar button should call the **add** action in the **Calc** nonvisual part when the tool bar button is pressed. You could delete the old push button and then redraw the connection from the new tool bar button. To save the time of redrawing and making the connection, you can move the starting point of the connection with the following steps:

❑ Select the pbAdd(buttonClickEvent) → Calc(add) connection by clicking on it.

❑ Place the tip of the mouse pointer at the square connection handle at the button end of the connection.

❑ To move the connection starting point, hold down the right mouse button and drag the starting point for the connection to the new **Add** tool bar button and release the mouse button to set the connection.

This is a very helpful feature and can save you a lot of time when you change the application.

Since both the push button and the tool bar button have a **buttonClickEvent**, the move is a perfect match. If you move a connection to a part that does not have the same event, action, or attribute, the Visual Builder displays the preferred connections list. You must then complete the connection by selecting the appropriate event, action, or attribute. If you accidentally select the wrong target, press the ESC (escape) key to stop the move and retry these steps.

Now that you have moved the **add** connection, you can delete the old **Add** push button very easily:

❏ Select the push button with the mouse pointer.

❏ Press the Delete key.

❏ Delete the **Exit** push button. When deleting a part which has connections, a warning dialog displays to inform you that, along with the part, all the connections to and from the part will also be deleted. Press **OK** on this dialog.

The Composition Editor should look like Figure 70.

Adding Bitmaps to a Tool Bar

Add a custom bitmap to make the tool bar buttons look more professional. Bitmaps can not be loaded directly into the Visual Builder; they must first be compiled into a resource Dynamic Link Library (DLL). This may seem a little restrictive, but you need this DLL to run the application. Also, other applications may use this bitmap, when it is used in a DLL it is only used once in memory and is easier to update. It is a good idea to group many bitmaps into one DLL to reduce the number of files associated with the application.

Here is an important reminder about using DLLs, they must be placed in a directory accessible to the program. In OS/2 this means placing the DLL in a directory which appears in the LIBPATH statement in the CONFIG.SYS file. In Windows the DLL must be placed in

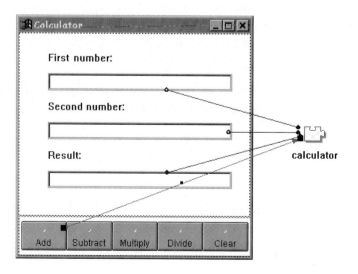

Figure 70: Four more tool bar buttons added

a directory which appears in the PATH statement in the AUTO-EXEC.BAT file. Of course, both operating systems will find the DLL if it is located in the current working directory.

❏ Open the settings notebook for the **Add** tool bar button by double-clicking the left mouse button while the pointer is over the control.

The Visual Builder includes some predefined bitmaps for tool bar buttons. Try using one of the predefined bitmaps as shown in Figure 71:

❏ Check the box for **Select from type list** and the list of bitmaps becomes enabled for selection.

❏ Select the IC_ID_OPEN item from the **Type list.**

❏ Then select the **Apply** push button. The **Apply** push button makes the changes to the part in the Composition Editor and leaves the Settings notebook open.

Let's see how that changed the tool bar button. Move the settings notebook so you can see the **CalcView** part. Do this by moving the mouse to the title bar of the settings notebook and holding down left mouse button. Now drag the settings notebook down to the bottom of the screen to make the actual tool bar on the Composition Editor visible. The tool bar button now has a nice folder icon as seen in Figure 72.

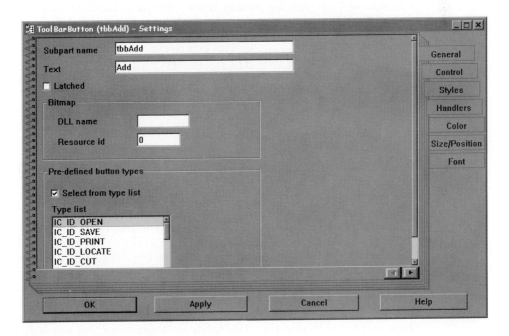

Figure 71: Selecting a predefined bitmap

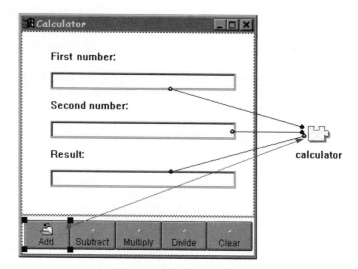

Figure 72: Open folder bitmap on the Add tool bar button

The folder bitmap is nice, but it really does not belong on the **Add** button. If you moved the settings notebook, bring it back to where you can change the settings. If you closed the settings notebook, then re-open it. Remove the folder bitmap.

❑ Deselect the box for **Select from type list** and scroll to the top of the General page.

The installation program on the CD-ROM included with this book copies the file **BITMAPS.DLL** to the x:\VABOOK\CALCLTOR directory. This file has bitmaps for all the functions in the Calculator. A later chapter covers the details of building a DLL for bitmap resources. Both icons and bitmaps can be included in the same DLL. With scanners and bitmap libraries it is easy to get high quality bitmaps for your applications.

The BITMAPS.DLL must be accessible to the Visual Builder while you are constructing the part and when you run the application. Remember to make sure the DLL is placed in the proper directory.

You can specify tool bar button bitmaps in the tool bar button setting notebook by supplying the .DLL file name and the resource number. You can enter a fully qualified file name for the .DLL file in this field, but this is hard coded into the application. When the application runs, this requires that the bitmap DLL be located in that exact path. It is not a good idea to hard code the path where the DLL can be found, because when you distribute the application to other systems there is no guarantee that the other systems have the same drives and paths as you have specified.

Each of the bitmaps has a defined resource number which is set in an .RC file and bound to the DLL when it is compiled. The **add** bitmap resource id is 1 in the DLL.

❏ On the General Page of the setting notebook as shown in Figure 73, scroll down to the **Bitmap** group box.

❏ Enter **bitmaps** in the **DLL name** entry field

❏ Enter **1** in the **Resource id** field

This provides the correct bitmap for the **Add** tool bar button. Press the **Apply** push button to check the new bitmap on the tool bar button.

If the Visual Builder could not access the BITMAPS.DLL file, or if you entered an invalid resource number, you see a question mark icon on the **Add** tool bar button. If this happens, go back to the settings notebook and correct the mistake.

In OS/2 you can enter the text for the tool bar button and include a mnemonic. However even though you enter a mnemonic for the Add button by typing the tilde character (~) in front of the letter **A** of the word Add, you will not see an underscore under the letter **A** in the **tool bar button.** The mnemonic is still active and you can access the **Add** action by pressing **Alt-A**.

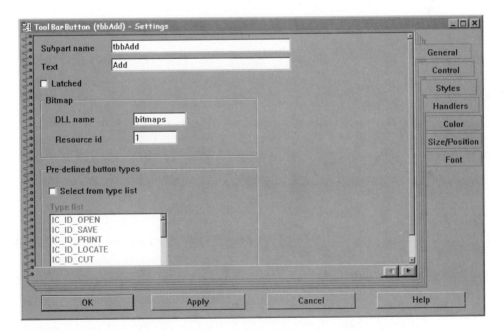

Figure 73: Selecting the bitmap for the tool bar button

In Windows you see an ampersand (&) where you typed the tilde. This appears to be a bug in the Windows version, and until it gets fixed you should not use mnemonics in the tool bar button.

Completing the Tool Bar

The other tool bar buttons need to get all the changes made to the **Add** tool bar button.

❑ Open the settings notebook for each of the tool bar buttons and make the necessary changes.

❑ On the General page, give each tool bar button an appropriate **subpart name.**

❑ Add the bitmap resources to the tool bar buttons using the same file BITMAPS.DLL. Use the resource numbers shown in Table 2.

Table 2: Mapping of resource numbers in BITMAPS.DLL

Bitmap	Resource number
add	1
subtract	2
multiply	3
divide	4
clear	5

Adding Fly Over Help

With the advent of tool bars the use of many little icons in applications has proliferated. There are so many icons it is difficult to remember what many of the tool bar buttons represent. An innovation for user interfaces is the use of a small tag of help which acts as a reminder. This help has many names, such as fly over help, bubble help, and hover help. Fly over help adds a small rectangle with short help text which shows next to a control and is commonly seen with tool bars. Fly over help can be associated with any control, not just tool bar buttons. It can be used on entry fields, push buttons, and any other control in the application. Add fly over help to the Calculator toolbar buttons as seen in Figure 74:

❑ Turn to the **Control** page of the settings notebook of the **Add** tool bar button.

❑ In the Fly over short text field enter Add 2 numbers.

❑ Select the OK push button to save these changes.

Repeat these steps and add **Fly over short text** to the remaining tool bar buttons. Use your creativity to define some short descriptive text. The completed tool bar control looks like Figure 75.

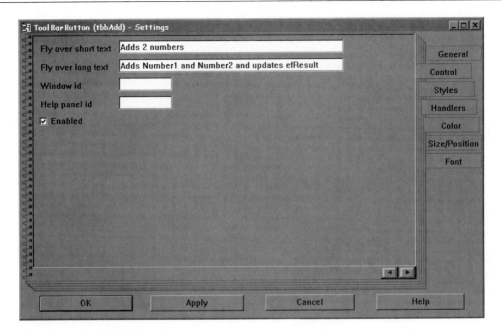

Figure 74: Entering fly over text

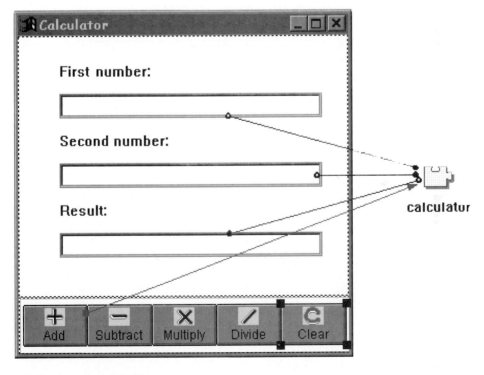

Figure 75: Completed tool bar

Using Fly Over Help

Although you specified fly over help in the tool bar buttons, you still have one more step for fly over help to work. The application needs an **IVBFlyText*** control added to the Composition Editor of the Calculator part to display the fly over help at runtime.

❏ From the **Other** category, select the **IVBFlyText*** control, and place it anywhere on the free-form surface, as shown in Figure 76.

This control is required if you want to see the fly over help when you run the Calculator application. This control is somewhat unique in that it needs no connections to perform its function. Dropping the control on the free-form surface instantiates the object and starts it handling fly over text messages for the frame window.

Testing the Calculator User Interface

Let's compile what you have built so far and see how the tool bar works at runtime.

❏ Save and Generate the part source files by selecting the generate button.

❏ Generate the .MAK file and the C++ code with the main() by selecting **File**, **Save and generate**, and **main() for part**.

❏ Switch over to a command prompt session and at the prompt enter **nmake calcview.mak**.

❏ After the compile and link is finished, start the application by entering **CALCVIEW** at the command prompt.

The Calculator is a bit fancier than the Adding Machine, but you have only improved the user interface. Test the Calculator by entering **123** in the **First number** entry field and **456** in the **Second number** field. The **Add** function still works correctly. See Figure 77.

The tool bar has a special feature. You can drag it from the frame window and have it float, separate from the frame window, on the desktop, as shown in Figure 78. This can be a little tricky to do. The following steps show you how to make the tool bar float:

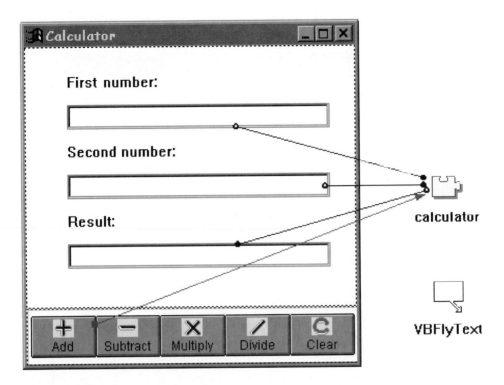

Figure 76: Added IVBFlyText control

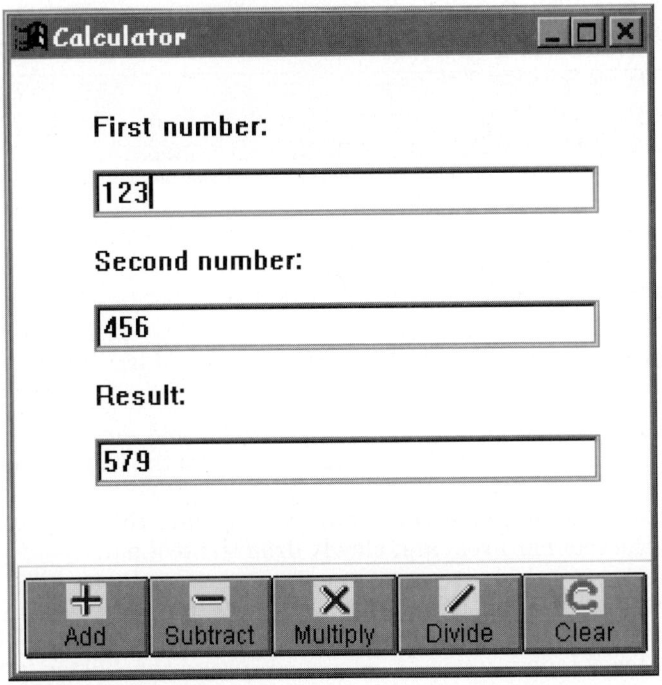

Figure 77: Running Calculator

Figure 78: Floating tool bar

❏ Point the tip of the mouse pointer on the tool bar. Remember and point at the area of the tool bar around the tool bar buttons, see Figure 66.

❏ Hold down the left mouse button (in OS/2, hold down the right mouse button) and drag the tool bar away from the frame window.

If the tool bar does not move, try again, making sure the mouse tip is pointing to the tool bar area, and slowly drag the tool bar.

Now move the Calculator window by dragging the title bar and the tool bar remains fixed on the screen. If you want the tool bar to follow the Calculator window when it is moved, press the button which looks like a push pin on the tool bar title bar. This is referred to as "pinning" the tool bar to its parent window. While pinned, the tool bar follows the application window and maintains its relative position to the application window. Sorry Windows users, you were looking for the pin. Pinning the tool bar is only available in OS/2.

The floating tool bar has a system menu. If you close the floating tool-bar while it is detached from its frame window, you will not be able to get the tool bar back.

The **Add** function still works fine by pressing the tool bar button. The fly over help appears when the mouse pointer remains on top of a tool bar button for a few seconds.

The tool bar can be reattached to any side of the frame window at runtime. Let's reattach it to the side of the Calculator window as shown in Figure 79.

❏ Point the mouse to the tool bar and drag it to the side of the frame window.

❏ To reattach the tool bar, the tip of the mouse needs to point to the window border. When the tool bar is positioned over the window border, drop the tool bar.

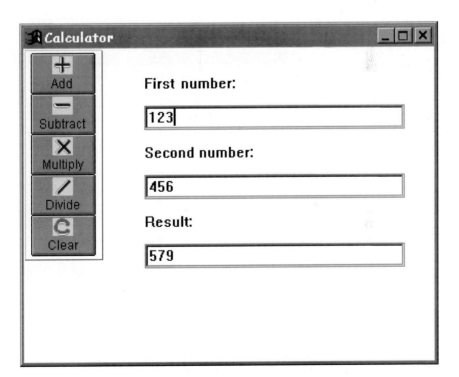

Figure 79: Tool bar reattached to the frame window

The mouse position is very critical in making the tool bar reattach. When the tip of the mouse is on the frame window border, a little icon appears that looks like a window with a tool bar. If you move the mouse too quickly you will not see the icon. When you reattach the tool bar to the top of the window, you can not merely point to the title bar; you must drag the tool bar and point to the top frame border. In Windows you must drag the tool bar with the mouse pointer on the actual tool bar, not the tool bar title bar, in order to be able to reattach it.

Nothing happens when you select the other tool bar buttons because there are no connections from these controls. Close the Calculator application so you can continue working on the user interface.

Adding Handlers

Handlers are very useful classes that can be added to controls to modify their behavior. The Open Class Library has an **IHandler** class which is the base class for all handlers as seen in Figure 80. There are many handlers which you can use. An important function needed in the Calculator is to restrict what type of characters can be entered in the entry fields. To do this, the program needs to be able to

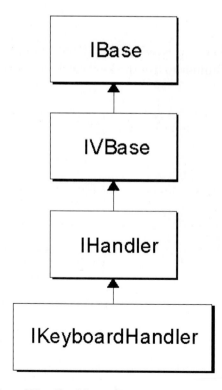

Figure 80: IKeyboardHandler hierarchy

see what key is pressed before the key character is displayed in the entry field. If the key pressed is not a number, then it is rejected; optionally a beep can be emitted to warn the user. The Open Class Library provides a class called **IKeyboardHandler** which contains the proper virtual functions to help you build specialized handlers using sub-classing. All of the keyboard handlers in Table 3 are subclassed from IKeyboardHandler.

The file **KBDHDR.VBB** is included with the files on the CD-ROM. This file contains several keyboard handlers which can be attached to entry fields or multiple line entry fields to restrict the type of characters that can be typed into these fields. Table 3 shows the handler names and their purposes:

More than one handler can be attached to a control. For example, if you need an entry field that should accept only upper case hex numbers, you would attach both a **HexOnlyKbdHandler** and an **UpperCaseKbdHandler** to that entry field.

The default entry field allows entering any text including special characters. This version of the Calculator will work with double precision numbers; thus, the entry fields should only accept the numbers 0 through 9, the decimal point, and a plus or minus sign in the first position of the number. Looking at Table 3, the **NumDecOnlyKbd-Handler** provides the function required.

The part files containing these classes must be loaded into the Visual Builder to use the keyboard handlers. Refer to Figure 81 as you follow this step:

❑ From the Visual Builder Parts Selector, load the KBDHDR.VBB file by selecting **File**, **Load**.

Table 3: Supplied keyboard handlers

Handler Name	Function
NumOnlyKbdHandler	Allows numbers 0–9, Also a minus (−) or plus (+) as the first character
NumDecOnlyKbdHandler	Allows numbers 0–9 and a period(.) Also a minus (−) or plus (+) as the first character
PosNumOnlyKbdHandler	Allows numbers 0–9
PosNumDecOnlyKbdHandler	Allows numbers 0–9 and a period(.)
UpperCaseKbdHandler	Allows any character and lower case characters are converted to upper case
LowerCaseKbdHandler	Allows any character, and lower case characters are converted to lower case
HexOnlyKbdHandler	Allows numbers 0–9 and characters a–f and A–F

Figure 81: KBDHDR.VBB loaded

To attach the handler to the **efNum1** and **efNum2** entry fields, follow these steps:

❏ Open their settings notebooks by double-clicking the left mouse button on each of them.

❏ Select the **Handler** page of the notebook and enter **NumDec-OnlyKbdHandler** in the handler field.

❏ Press the **Add after** push button. Depending on the resolution of your display, you might need to scroll to the bottom of this page to see this button.

While the settings notebook is open, there is one more thing to set on this entry field. A default entry field has a length of 32 characters.

This is a very large number, in the Adder you changed the limit to 5 characters, since the Calculator handles decimal numbers restrict the number of characters that can be typed into the entry fields to 10 characters with the following steps:

❏ Select the **General** page of the notebook.

❏ In the Limit field enter 10.

❏ Press the **OK** button to save the changes and close the notebook.

❏ Repeat these steps and change the efNum2 entry field.

When designing and building an application, changing the default values of many controls to the same values can get very tedious. There is an easier way: using the copy and paste functions of the clipboard, under the **Edit** menu, you can duplicate controls maintaining any changed settings, only the actual name of the control changes. A second way to duplicate a control is to select it by clicking on it, pressing and holding the Ctrl key, and dragging the control with the left mouse button to a new location. When you release the mouse button, a new control with the same attributes will be dropped.

Clearing the Entry Fields

The **Clear** tool bar button can clear the contents of the entry fields by simply drawing connections. This is possible because the **IEntry-Field** control has a **removeAll** action. This action, as its name implies, removes all the characters from the entry field. You can find the other actions implemented for the **IEntryField** control and its parent classes documented in the Open Class Library on-line reference book. This can be a time consuming exercise if you do not know what you are looking for, like looking for a needle in a haystack. There is a very useful feature in the Visual Builder that shows information about a specific part without leaving the Visual Builder.

Suppose you do not know that the **removeAll** action was part of the implementation for the IEntryField control, but your instinct tells you that it would make sense to have such an action for this part. Since you want to clear an entry field:

❏ Select the **efNum1** entry field and display its pop-up menu by pressing the right mouse button.

❏ Select the **Browse Part Features ...** menu item which displays a dialog window as shown in Figure 82. This shows all of the actions, attributes, and events for the **IEntryField** part.

❏ Move the mouse to the **Actions** column and select the **clear** item.

The **Description** field at the bottom of the window shows **Replaces the selected text in the entry field with blanks.** This action is not

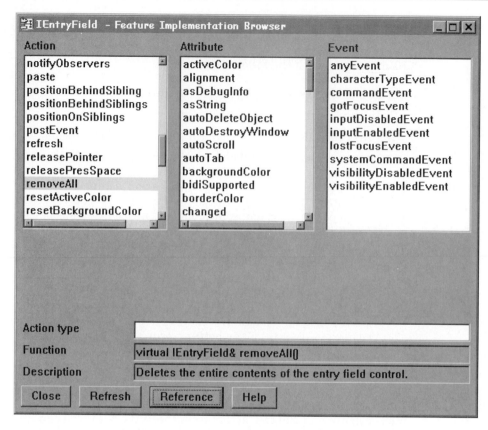

Figure 82: Browse Parts Features for the IEntryField part

the one you want. This action replaces the selected text, so it requires that the user first selects the text, then presses the **Clear** button. Scroll down the **Actions** list and look for one that looks appropriate. Select the **removeAll** action and look at its description which reads **Deletes the entire contents of the entry field control**.

It looks like the **removeAll** action has the function you need. You found the action you needed by inspecting the feature descriptions. This is a good reason to have concise and accurate descriptions for the features you create. As you make other connections with the Visual Builder, you should use the **Browse Part Features** function to inspect a part. This is very helpful in learning more information about features. Browsing a part also gives you insight to the number and types of parameters for the actions.

In the Windows version, notice the **Reference** push button in Figure 82. Pressing this button invokes the VisualAge for C++ help facility and opens a window showing the help for the type of control you are browsing.

❑ Select the **Clear** tool bar button and start a connection by pressing the right mouse button.

❑ Select the **buttonClickEvent** and move the mouse to the **efNum1** entry field.

❑ Press the left mouse button to make a connection.

❑ On the preferred list for the entry field, find the **removeAll** action. Select it to complete the connection.

❑ Repeat the above steps for **efNum2**. These connections a shown in Figure 83.

In the OS/2 version, the key combination Alt+right mouse button can be used as a shortcut to display the preferred list for a part to initiate a connection. In Windows this key combination does not work well with the current version and fix level of the product; therefore, you should not use it.

Setting the Result Field

You could have connected the **Clear** button to the **efResult** entry field **removeAll** action. It is better to set efResult to 0 than to clear

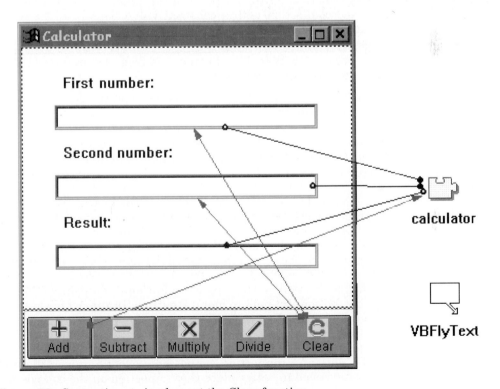

Figure 83: Connections to implement the Clear function

the contents and leave an empty entry field. There are a number of ways to set the efResult to 0.

1. Add a new **initResult** action to the **Calc** nonvisual part which would set the result attribute to 0. You would connect the tool bar button to the initResult action. This is not the best choice for a single connection because it adds additional code to the **Calc** part. It makes more sense to set all three attributes number1, number2, and result with an **initAttributes** action. If the init-Attributes action sets all three attributes, you would only need to make one connection to the Calc nonvisual part. The Visual Builder generates code for each connection, so you can have more efficient code with fewer connections by making efficient actions or member functions in your parts.

2. Connect the **Clear** tool bar button to the **add** action in the **Calc** nonvisual part. Since the **Clear** button already causes the values of the number1 and number2 attributes to be removed, when you add number1 and number2 the result is set to 0 (zero).

3. Connect the **Clear** tool bar button to the **result** entry field's **text** attribute.

The third option is a good option because it directly changes the **result** entry field and, for the purposes of this book, demonstrates a parameterized connection with a constant value. This is an **Event to Attribute** connection. Let's use option 3 in the following steps:

❑ Point to the **Clear** tool bar button, and from the preferred list select the **buttonClickEvent**.

❑ Drag the mouse pointer to the **efResult** entry field and select the text attribute.

The connection line is dashed as shown in Figure 84. This means the connection requires a parameter and there is no default parameter specified.

You can modify the connection and set the needed parameter. Connections can be selected and reshaped. To reshape a connection, point to the midpoint of the connection which is indicated by a black square. Then hold down the left mouse button and drag the connection midpoint to a place on the screen that makes the connection easier to view.

In the Windows version, this creates additional midpoints. There is an item on the connect pop-up menu **Restore Shape**, which removes the added midpoints. Sometimes you can make a real mess if you are not careful.

The end points of a connection cannot be moved; however, the midpoint can be moved to better place the connection on the composition

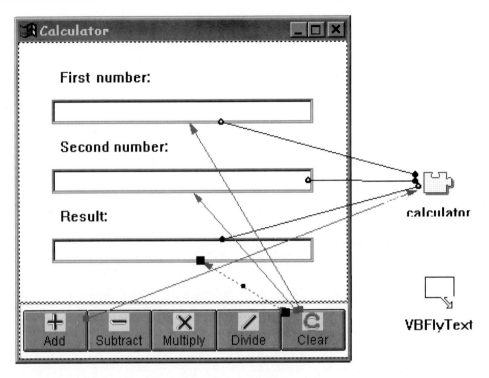

Figure 84: Incomplete pbClear to efResult connection

editor. A connection cannot be selected from the starting point, the end point, or any midpoint. When the mouse is over one of these points the Visual Builder interprets the mouse clicks as instructions for repositioning the connection point. Select the connection with these steps:

❑ Move the mouse pointer to the dashed line part of the connection.

❑ Press the right mouse button to see the pop-up menu for the connection.

You recognize a connection's pop-up menu because it is very small and contains only a few items.

❑ Select the **Open settings** item and a dialog box for modifying this connection opens.

The **Set parameters...** push button is at the bottom of the dialog. This button is only enabled when there are parameters for the connection.

❏ Press the **Set parameters...** button and the parameters dialog opens.

You have made an event-to-attribute connection which means the **Clear** button sets the text attribute of the **efResult** entry field. The Visual Builder needs to know what value to use for this connection.

❏ Enter a **0** (zero) in the **text** entry field and select the **OK** button at the bottom of the dialog as shown in Figure 85.

❏ Press **OK** again in the parameters dialog.

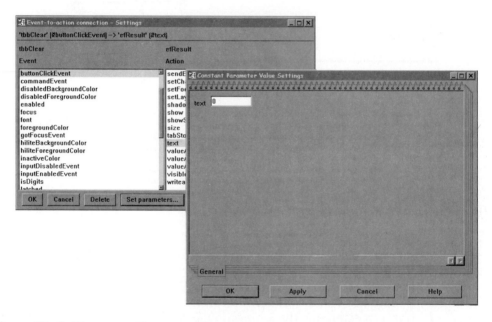

Figure 85: Setting connection parameter

Now that you have specified the parameter the dashed line becomes solid as shown in Figure 86. The Visual Builder needs specified or default parameters for all connections that have parameters before the Visual Builder can generate the C++ code for the part. As you develop your own nonvisual parts, remember to design the classes with as many default parameters as possible.

Adding an Application Icon

The upper left corner of a frame window has a small icon called the **System Icon**. By default the application window gets the system icon provided by the operating system. The system icon provides a menu of actions you can select for the frame window at runtime. The Visual

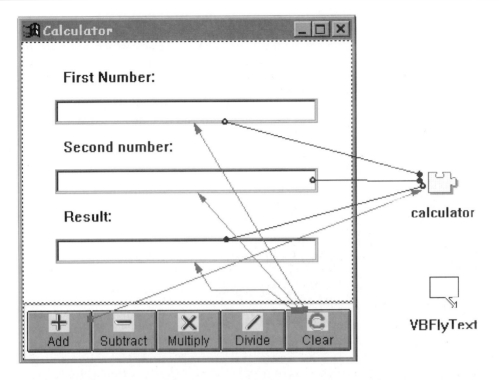

Figure 86: Completed connections for Clear button

Builder generates a default **system menu** for the frame window, and you can assign a custom icon for the frame window at runtime. This application icon is shown when the frame window is minimized.

To set the system icon you need to use an event which is generated after all the components for the part have been constructed and after the part has been properly initialized. This event is called the **ready** event. It occurs only once for each window, and it can be found for connections on the free-form surface.

Add an icon to the system menu using the following steps:

❏ Connect the **ready event** from the free-form surface to the **icon** attribute of the frame window.

❏ Open the settings notebook for the connection. Press the **Set parameters...** button.

❏ Enter **bitmaps** as the .DLL name for the icon, and the resource number of the icon which is 6. That is how easy it is.

Even though you have made all the proper connections to add an icon to the system menu you will not see it until you run the program.

Adding a Pop-up Menu to the Tool Bar

Pop-up menus are useful user interface items which are used to provide control dependent choice items to the user at runtime. They can be made to appear by placing the mouse pointer over the control and pressing the right mouse button. You will add a pop-up menu to the tool bar of the Calculator. From this menu you can change the view style of the tool bar buttons by setting the tool bar **buttonView** attribute. The views available are:

1. Bitmap
2. Text
3. Bitmap and text

  Pop-up menus are frame extensions and they are built from the **IMenu** and **IMenuItem** controls supplied with the product.

❏ To start building the pop-up menu, select the frame extensions parts folder.

❏ Select and drop an **IMenu** part on the free-form surface.

The Visual Builder names this object **Menu1**. Menu items need to be associated with a visual part on the Composition Editor. Virtually any visual part can have a pop-up menu associated with it. In the Calculator the **Menu1** object is associated with the tool bar control. Make the following connection:

❏ Menu1(this) → tbCalc(menu)

 The **IMenu** part is a container for **IMenuItem** parts. On its own it does not do anything.

❏ Drop three **IMenuItem** parts on top of the Menu1 part.

The only place you can drop these parts is on top of an **IMenu** part.

❏ Directly edit the text of the three IMenuItem parts to read:
1. bitmap
2. text
3. bitmap and text

The IMenuItem does not have a buttonClickEvent, instead it has a commandEvent. This terminology is from the underlying message in the operating system. IMenuItems can emit other events when selected, but for now you will use the **commandEvent**.

❏ Make the following connections:

❏ IMenuItem **bitmap commandEvent** to tool bar **buttonView**. In order to reach this attribute you need to select the **More...** option of the pop-up menu.

❏ IMenuItem **text commandEvent** to tool bar **buttonView**.

❏ IMenuItem **bitmap and text commandEvent** to tool bar **buttonView**.

There are three dashed lines indicating the connections. As you remember, a dashed line means that the connection is incomplete. These connections need to know the attribute for the buttonView. To set this value, double-click on each of the connections and press the **Set parameters** button on the settings dialog for the connection. This opens yet another dialog which has the options available for this connection:

1. bitmapView

2. textView

3. bitmapAndTextView

Set each **buttonView** style respectively for each of the connections. All of the connections should now be solid lines as shown in Figure 87.

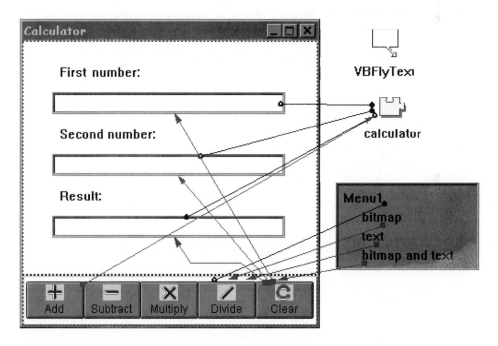

Figure 87: Connections to the Pop-up Menu

Press the Generate button to save and generate the code for the application; then run the make file to compile and run the application.

When the application runs, test the pop-up menu by clicking the right mouse button while its pointer is over the tool bar or one of its buttons. The menu should display and you can select a different view for the tool bar buttons as shown in Figure 88.

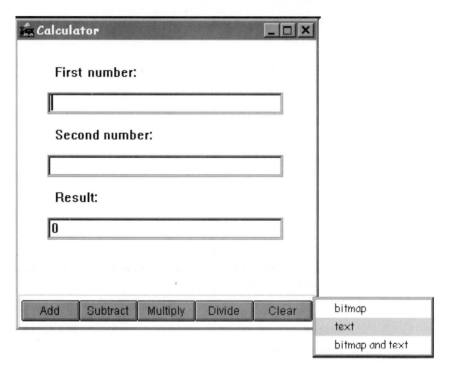

Figure 88: User interface completed

Preventing the Frame Window from Sizing

There is no reason for the Calculator to be built in a frame window with a variable size. You can prevent the user from changing frame window size by setting the **dialogBorder** style to **on** and the **sizing-Border** style to **off**. Both these styles can be found on the **Styles** page of the settings notebook for the frame window.

Making the Completed Calculator User Interface

Now you have a fairly complete user interface. There is a lot of detail and special features incorporated into this user interface. To see it work, select **Save and Generate** the **Part source**. Then generate the **main()** for the CalcView. This is required because when you generate the **main()**, the Visual Builder also generates the .MAK file. You need a new make file because of the added entry field handler. The Visual Builder generates all the C++ code for the user interface changes you made, including the C++ code for the connections. Now, from a command prompt, compile the code by entering **nmake calcview.mak**

After the compile and link is complete, run the application by typing **CalcView** at the command prompt.

Testing the Completed Calculator User Interface

Try typing in the **First Number** entry field. If the keyboard handler is working you should only be able to enter numbers. Also, you can only enter ten numbers. Enter another number in the **Second Number** entry field. Select the **Add** tool bar button. The **Result** is still correct. The custom icon appears in the upper left corner of the Calculator window.

The amazing thing is that you were able to build the entire user interface for the Calculator using the Visual Builder. The Visual Builder generated the C++ code for the entire application. The generated code is efficient; the compiled user interface with the **add** and the **clear** functions is about 40 Kb in size. This does not include the Open Class Library runtime DLLs, but it is still a pretty impressive feat. In the next chapter, continue to improve the Calculator by enhancing the **Calc** nonvisual part and completing the Calculator application.

Chapter 4—Summary

You improved the Adding Machine in a number of ways and made it a Calculator. To do this you:

❑ Used a tool bar control which has the add, subtract, multiply, divide, and clear functions

❑ Added bubble help to tool bar buttons

❑ Used handlers to limit input to decimal numeric characters only

❑ Used the removeAll function to clear the entry fields

❑ Worked with connections that use parameters

❑ Added an Icon to the system menu

❑ Added a pop-up menu to customize the view of the tool bar at runtime

❑ Changed the frame window settings

What's in Chapter 5

In this chapter you build on what you learned with the Adding Machine about developing and using nonvisual parts. You improve the Calculator with more math functions. Then you integrate these new functions into the Calculator user interface you built in the previous chapter. To do this you:

❏ Provide the additional operations of subtract, multiply, divide, and clear in the Calc nonvisual part

❏ Make the necessary connections to support the new operations.

❏ Add items to the connections preferred list pop-up menu of the Calc part

❏ Use Custom logic to signal a divide by zero exception

❏ Use exception handling to catch a divide by zero exception

❏ Use the IMessageBox control to display an error

5

Completing the Calculator

In the first few chapters of this book you learned some basics about VisualAge for C++ parts and their components. Using this information you developed the Adding Machine. Now that you have completed the Calculator visual part, you can focus on improving the **Calc** nonvisual part. In this chapter you will complete the Calculator application by:

❑ Improving the Calc nonvisual part with additional actions

❑ Editing and completing the generated code

❑ Completing the connections in the Composition Editor

❑ Emitting a beep when an error occurs

❑ Adding a message box to display errors

❑ Compiling and running the application

Understanding VisualAge Parts

The Visual Builder is a powerful application development tool. The Visual Builder has the necessary function for developing the graphical user interface for an application. The Visual Builder also supports the unique method of construction from parts. This method provides a visual metaphor to connect visual and nonvisual parts using the Attribute/Action/Event paradigm. You still need to do Object-Oriented Analysis and Design for applications because the Visual Builder does not prevent you from making implementation errors. The Visual Builder makes it a lot easier and faster to create C++ based Object-Oriented applications and allows the developer to focus on the domain specific coding required for the application.

The Parts Architecture is covered in great detail in the document *Building VisualAge for C++ Parts for Fun and Profit* which comes with the product as an on-line book. Assuming you installed the documentation, you can find it in the **VisualAge for C++ On-line Information** folder. It makes no sense to duplicate the *Building VisualAge for C++ Parts for Fun and Profit* document in this book. Instead, you will learn the bare essentials to get you started. You can refer to the on-line book for more details on specific topics.

Actions, Attributes, and Events

The Open Class Library has a notification framework which provides C++ classes with a special messaging system. The behavior for the notification framework is provided by the base classes **INotifier** and **IObserver**. The notification framework is new in version 3.0 of VisualAge for C++. For this reason the classes using the notification framework only work on the OS/2 and Windows versions of VisualAge for C++. The next AIX version should include the notification framework in the Open Class Library.

C++ Parts are specialized C++ classes which derive from the **INotifier** base class. Parts whose features are defined in terms of, actions, attributes, and events. These items define a part's public interface and can be used in the Visual Builder to construct applications with connections. The following paragraphs describe these terms.

Actions are member functions in a class which can be called by other classes. Actions are implemented as public member functions within the class. The classes in the Open Class Library are rich in functions. An example of an action in the Hello World sample is the **close** action of the **IFrameWindow** control.

Attributes are data members in the class. The data items are implemented as private data within the class and can only be accessed through a **get** function and changed through a **set** function. An example from the Hello World sample is the **text** attribute of the **IStatic Text** control.

Events signal occurrences within a part to notify that a specific change has occurred in the part. An example from the Hello World sample is the IPushButton **buttonClickEvent,** which sends a message indicating that the button was pressed. Another example you will see later is the signal that a file has reached its end. This event can be used, for example, to close the file.

The connections in the Composition Editor are observers for the notification of events. In the generated code from the Visual Builder, the connections are subclasses of the **IObserver** class which has the base methods to handle the connections.

Adding Actions to the Calculator

Now continue to work on the **CalcView** visual part and the **Calc** nonvisual part which you developed in the last chapter. If you are just starting the Visual Builder, make sure your working directory is set to x:\VABOOK\CALCLTOR, and from the Visual Builder Parts Selector load the ADDER.VBB file which contains the Calculator parts and the KBDHDR.VBB file which contains the keyboard handlers.

❑ From the Visual Builder Parts Selector, open the **Calc** part. This opens the Part Interface Editor (PIE) which is the default view for nonvisual parts.

❑ In the **Actions** page of the PIE as shown in Figure 89, add the actions listed in Table 4. Entering the information from the table and press the **Add** push button for each action.

You pressed the **Add** push button because the return type of these actions is a reference to the object **Calc**, **Calc&**. If you had pressed **Add with defaults**, the return code would have been **int** which is inadequate for these actions.

The **add** action is still in the part from the Adding Machine application.

Adding Preferred Features

Now that you have defined these new actions for the part, it is helpful to add these actions to the **Preferred** list. As a parts builder, which is what you do most of the time while using the Visual Builder, it is a good idea to put the commonly used part features on the **Preferred** list. This makes it easier for users of your parts, including yourself, to make connections to other parts.

By no means is it a requirement for all features to be on the Preferred list, in fact putting too many entries in the list can cause a situation where there is not enough room on the screen to display all the choices. You are more likely to run into this problem when using lower resolution displays.

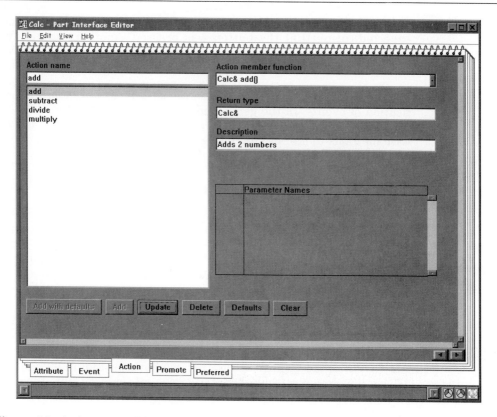

Figure 89: Action page of the Calc part PIE

Any features not on the Preferred list can still be connected by accessing them through the **More...** item on the Preferred list.

❑ Select the **Preferred** tab in the PIE. Once on the preferred page, you find all the actions in the **Actions** list box listed in alphabetic order as shown in Figure 90.

❑ Select one of the new actions by pressing the right mouse button to bring up the pop-up menu for the Actions list.

❑ Select **Add>>** to copy the selected action to the **Preferred Features** list. Repeat this for the other actions.

Table 4: New actions for the Calc part

Action Name	Action Member Function	Return Type	Description
subtract	Calc& subtract()	Calc&	Subtracts two values
multiply	Calc& multiply()	Calc&	Multiplies two values
divide	Calc& divide()	Calc&	Divides two values

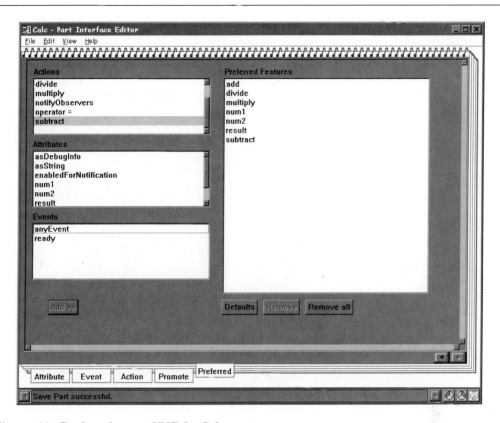

Figure 90: Preferred page of PIE for Calc part

Changing Attribute Types

The Adding Machine can only add two integer numbers. The Calculator application can be made to do double precision operations. To make this possible you need to change the type of the attributes **num1**, **num2**, and **result** from **int** to **double**.

❑ Select the **Attribute** page of the PIE.

❑ Select each of the attributes and change the word **int** to **double** in the **Attribute type**, **Get member function** and **Set member function** entry fields as seen in Figure 91.

❑ Press the **Update** button after making the three changes for each attribute.

Generating the Calc Code

❑ Save the **Calc** part by selecting **File**, **Save and generate**, and **Part source**. This saves the modified part definition in the .VBB

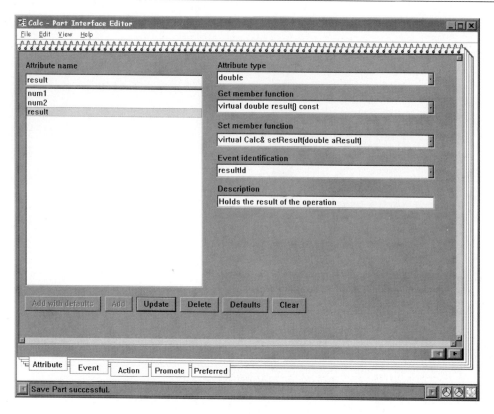

Figure 91: Attributes type changed from int to double

file and regenerates the CALC.HPP and the CALC.CPP file. Now that you have defined the new actions in the Calc part, you need to generate the C++ code for the Calc features.

❏ From the menu bar select **File**, **Save and Generate**, and **Feature source code...** to display the Generate feature source code window.

When the Visual Builder generates C++ code into the .CPV and .HPV files, the generated code is appended to these files if they already exist. This is a good feature because it preserves the code you have already written while appending new function to the same files. However, there is a small danger. If you always select the **Generate all** option, then you end up with duplicate definitions in the files and the compiler complains. Typically, you only need to generate the code for all features the first time you generate code for a part, thereafter you select the new features added to the part and press the **Generate selected** push button. If you accidentally generate code for features which were already generated, you have to manually edit the CPV and HPV files and remove the duplicate definitions. Code generation is enclosed by a begin line and an end line in the code as shown in Code segment 10. This makes it is easy to identify what code was generated by each press of the generate button.

```
// Feature source code generation begins here...
public:
virtual int num1() const;
virtual int setNum1() const;
virtual int num2() const;
virtual int setNum2() const;
virtual int result() const;
virtual int setResult() const;

Calc& add();

private:
int iNum1;
int iNum2;
int iResult;

// Feature source code generation ends here.

// Feature source code generation begins here...
public:
  virtual double num1() const;
  virtual Calc& setNum1(double aNum1);
  virtual double num2() const;
  virtual Calc& setNum2(double aNum2);
  virtual double result() const;
  virtual Calc& setResult(double aResult);
  Calc& add();
  Calc& subtract();
  Calc& multiply();
  Calc& divide();

  static const INotificationId IVB_IMPORT num1Id;
  static const INotificationId IVB_IMPORT num2Id;
  static const INotificationId IVB_IMPORT resultId;
private:
  double iNum1;
  double iNum2;
  double iResult;
// Feature source code generation ends here.
```

Code segment 10: CALC.HPV Duplicate definitions

The Generate Features window shown in Figure 92 has three lists:

1. Member functions

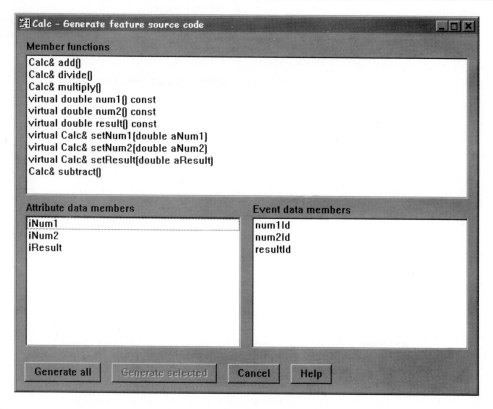

Figure 92: Generate feature source code dialog box

2. Attribute data members

3. Event data members

The existing CALC.HPV and CALC.CPV files already contain the **add** function with your modifications and the code for handling the attributes **num1**, **num2** and **result** as integers. As mentioned before, generating the **Feature code** will append to the existing files, this will create different problems depending on what you do next. You basically have three choices:

1. Delete the existing CALC.HPV and CALC.CPV files. Press the **Generate all** push button and reenter the code for the add function in the new CALC.CPV file.

2. Select the new items from the **Member functions** list box. They are the lines for **subtract**, **multiply** and **divide** member functions. Press the **Generate selected** push button. Edit the generated files and globally change **int** to **double**.

3. Select **Generate all**. Edit the files and remove the old definitions and declarations for the **int** attributes and the **new** add member function.

The first choice looks like the best. The feature generation appends the required C++ code stubs to CALC.HPV and CALC.CPV. After you have completed this step you should close the PIE. This closes the editing session for the **Calc** nonvisual part.

Remember, when you make a new nonvisual part you must specify the .HPV and .CPV files in the Class Editor. If these files are not specified you get an error message when you select one of the **Generate** buttons. The error message indicates you must set the USER.HPV and USER.CPV file fields in the Class Editor. To do this open the Class Editor by pressing the middle button at the bottom right corner of the PIE. This switches the Visual Builder to its Class Editor view, where you can enter the appropriate file names.

There is another default behavior you should know. When you copy a nonvisual part, you copy all the attributes of the part. This is generally what you want to happen, but the new part maintains the .HPV and .CPV file names of the original part. If you generate feature code in this new part, the Visual Builder generates the feature code in the old .HPV and .CPV files. This becomes a mess because, after you modify them the old feature source files only work with the new part. You should switch to the Class Editor and enter new file names for the .CPV and .HPV files to correspond to the new part name. It is impractical to remember all the tool behavior. When copying a part and you run into this problem, you will remember that you read about it in this book.

Adding C++ Code to the Calc Part

When you generated the feature source code into the CALC.CPV file, the Visual Builder generated the stub code for the new actions. Edit these files to add the C++ code for the new actions. Use any text editor you wish because the generated files are plain ASCII text. The example in this book uses the **Program Editor** that comes with VisualAge for C++.

❑ Start the editor and load the **CALC.CPV** file using the **File**, and **Open** menu item selections in the Program editor.

The Editor starts and displays the CALC.CPV file as seen in Figure 93. First look for the **add** function you originally added to the generated code as shown in Code segment 11.

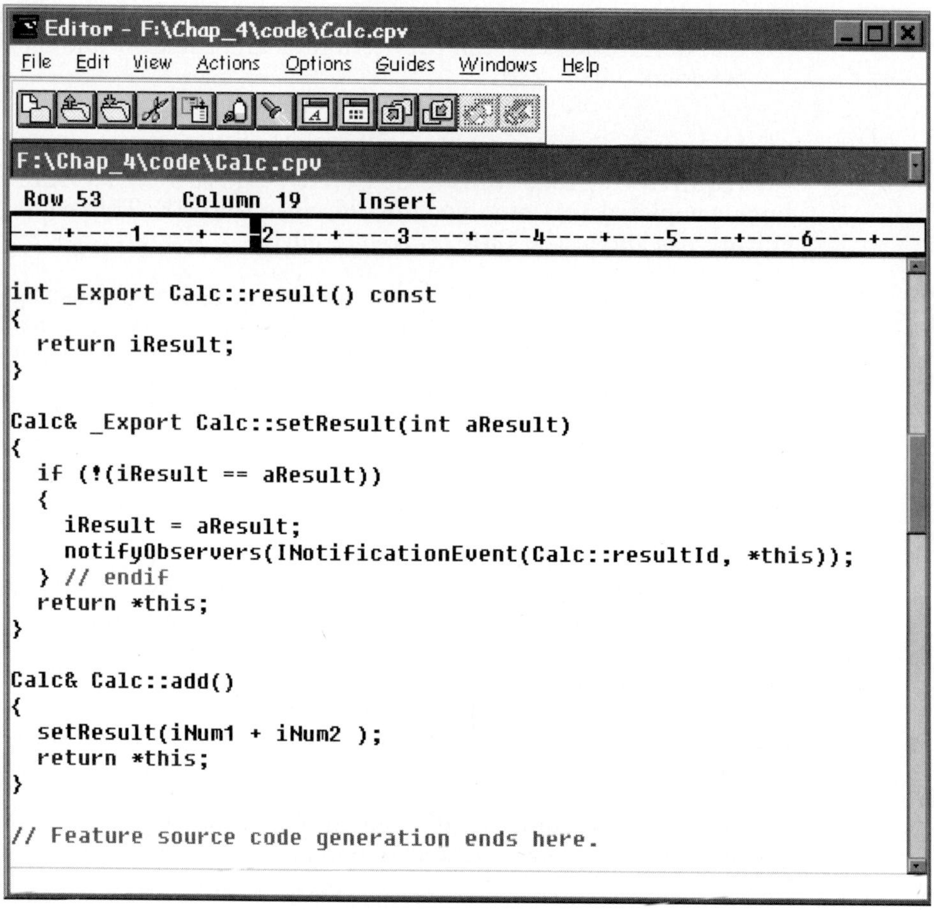

```
Editor - F:\Chap_4\code\Calc.cpv                    _ □ x
 File   Edit   View   Actions   Options   Guides   Windows   Help

F:\Chap_4\code\Calc.cpv
 Row 53          Column 19       Insert
----+----1----+---2----+----3----+----4----+----5----+----6----+---

int _Export Calc::result() const
{
  return iResult;
}

Calc& _Export Calc::setResult(int aResult)
{
  if (!(iResult == aResult))
  {
    iResult = aResult;
    notifyObservers(INotificationEvent(Calc::resultId, *this));
  } // endif
  return *this;
}

Calc& Calc::add()
{
  setResult(iNum1 + iNum2 );
  return *this;
}

// Feature source code generation ends here.
```

Figure 93: Programmers Editor—CALC.CPV

```
Calc& Calc::add()
{
  setResult(iNum1 + iNum2 );
  return *this;
}
```

Code segment 11: Calc add function

❑ Using the same approach as the **add** function, add the necessary code to the **subtract**, **multiply** and **divide** actions to perform these operations.

Throwing Exceptions

Some additional code is needed for the divide function. The computer can not divide numbers by zero. Exception handling is the proper method for handling this condition. The divide function can test for the 0 and throw an exception. The completed **divide** member function looks like Code segment 12.

❑ Add code to the **divide** member function. It should throw an **IInvalidParameter** exception when a divide by zero operation is attempted.

```
Calc& Calc::divide()
{
  // check if the second number is zero
  if( iNum2 == 0 )
  {
    IInvalidParameter exception =
      IInvalidParameter("Divide by zero not allowed");
    ITHROW(exception);
  }
  setResult(iNum1 / iNum2 );
  return *this;
}
```

Code segment 12: Exception handling in divide member function

For more information on the different **IException** derived classes available as parameters to the **ITHROW** macro, consult the on-line Open Class Library Reference manual.

❑ Save CALC.CPV and, if you need to conserve memory, close the editor.

Using the Improved Calc Nonvisual Part

Ensure that the Composition Editor for the CalcView part is open. If you still have the **CalcView** part Composition Editor open, there is no need to close it. The new actions that were added to the Calc nonvisual part are accessible through the **calculator** part on the free-form surface. To activate the new actions you need to connect them to the tool bar buttons, just like you did in the previous chapter for the **add** function.

❑ Connect the **buttonClickEvent** of each tool bar button to the appropriate action on the **calculator** part. The CalcView part should look like Figure 94.

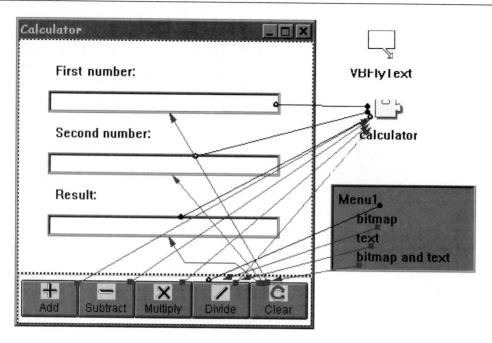

Figure 94: New actions connected to the calculator part

Initializing an Entry Field

When you write a program in C++ there are usually a number of ways to implement your ideas. There are different benefits to each implementation. One implementation may have a better design, another implementation may perform better, and yet another implementation may be the easiest to implement. When you have schedules to meet it usually boils down to just getting the application working. Then, if the application is not fast enough and you still have time to make changes, you look at performance issues.

The recommended way to initialize instance or member variables in C++ programming is through the use of an **initialization list**. This is the method that compiles the most efficient code, see Code segment 13. However, code generated by the Visual Builder does not directly support initialization lists. You can alter the generated .CPP file, but your changes will be lost the next time you generate the **Part source**.

There are at least three other ways to achieve the same result by initializing the instance variables for our Calc part.

1. Open the settings notebook for the Calc part. On the **General** page, enter the values which you want to initialize the instance variables. Any attributes that were identified when the part was defined are automatically placed on this page.

```
Calc:Calc()
      : iNum1(0)
      , iNum2(0)
      , iResult(0)
{// initialization list, before opening brace
      ...
}
```

Code segment 13: Calc constructor with initialization list

2. In the Class Editor for the **Calc** part, you can enter both custom constructor and destructor code. There is only 1 line to write your code, so you can either type a long line, separating your statements with semicolons, for example, iNum1 = 0; iNum2 = 0; iResult = 0; If your constructor code is more complex, you can enter a single call to a private member function in your .CPV file to perform the initialization, for example, **callInitialization-Function();**

3. Connect the **ready** event of the free-form surface to the attribute you want to initialize and pass the initial value as a parameter to the connection.

Of the three methods, 1 and 2 are more desirable. Method 3 works, but could get complicated if many attributes are initialized. In the Calculator application use method 1 to initialize the attributes on the **calculator** object.

Changing the Attribute-to-Attribute Connections

Because you changed the type of the num1, num2, and result attributes from **int** to **double**, you must also change the attribute-to-attribute connection between the CalcView and the calculator parts. To do this, follow these steps:

❑ Double-click on the connection to open the Settings dialog for the connection.

❑ The **efNum1** list box shows possible choices, you see **valueAsInt** selected. Select **valueAsDouble** as the new attribute for the connection and press the **OK** button.

❑ Repeat these steps for the other two attributes.

❑ Set the default values by using method one as described above.

Ensure that the source of the connection, the left side list box, is the **calculator** part and the target, the right side list box, is the **entry field**, see Figure 95. If your connection is backwards, press the **Reverse** push button.

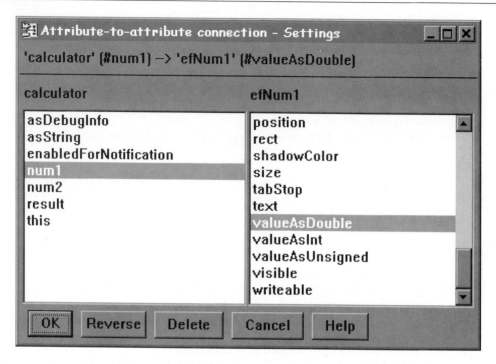

Figure 95: Changing Attribute-to-Attribute Connection

Attribute-to-attribute connections are bi-directional, which means that the values are kept the same no matter which side of the connection changes. The source and target are important at the time the connection is initialized, because the value at the source will be set for the target. In a previous step you initialized the attributes in the calculator part to zeros; if your source and target are set correctly, they will initialize the contents of the entry fields to zero.

Incorporating Exception Handling

In C programming, functions are passed parameters and upon completion they return an error code or value. Usually a return code of zero (0) means successful completion and any other return code indicates some type of failure. In C++ the recommended mechanism for handling errors is through exception handling. You can read about exception handling in any current C++ textbook, including the C/C++ Language Reference on-line book included with the product.

Basically, a C++ program can *try* to execute a C++ statement and if that statement *throws* an exception the program can *catch* the exception and do something about it. This mechanism is called the *try/catch* block as shown in Code segment 14.

```
do
{
  try
  {
    iPart = new CalcView();
    iPart->initializePart();
  }
  catch (IException& exc)
  {
    resp =IMessageBox(IWindow::desktopWindow())
            .show(exc.text()
            , IMessageBox::retryCancelButton);
  }

}while (resp == IMessageBox::retry);
```

Code segment 14: Try / catch block in main ()

If you examine the code generated by the Visual Builder you see that it uses this technique extensively. All connections are executed within a try statement.

You will take advantage of this feature while checking for an attempt to divide a number by zero. The computer cannot handle division by zero. If you actually try a division by zero the processor detects this condition and terminates your program with an unfriendly message.

You have already added the code to test if num2 is equal to zero and to throw an exception in that case in Code segment 12.

Custom Logic

You are going to catch the exception and emit a beep on the speaker to indicate that an invalid operation has occurred. Since the Open Class Library does not provide a class that can be used to beep, you will implement this function using a feature of the Visual Builder called **custom logic**.

Custom logic allows you to write C++ code by hand, which will be inserted at the appropriate spot in the code for the part that uses it. The custom logic code is executed as a result of a connection. In this case, when the exception is thrown by the divide operation the speaker will beep.

You have already made the connection:
    pbDivide(buttonClickEvent) → calculator(divide)

You need to catch the exception thrown by this connection if the operation it executes fails. You can connect to the connection by selecting it and bringing up its pop-up menu. On the **Connect** menu select **exceptionOccurred**, move the spider pointer to the free-form surface and click. From the free-form surface's pop-up menu select **Custom logic...** . The dialog box shown in Figure 96 appears.

In this dialog you can enter any valid C++ statements you need. Notice that you have access to the source and the target of the connection. You can use these buttons as shortcuts to get to the supported functions of the parts you are connecting. All you need to enter is the following:

❏ Beep(1000, 500); // In Windows

❏ DosBeep(1000, 500); // In OS/2

The first parameter is the frequency of the sound, the second parameter is the duration. In Windows 95 these values are ignored and substituted by whatever system sound you have set up for the **Default sound**.

You should also enter a description for the custom logic as it will appear on the information area of the Composition Editor when you select the connection, enter **Beeps on Exception**.

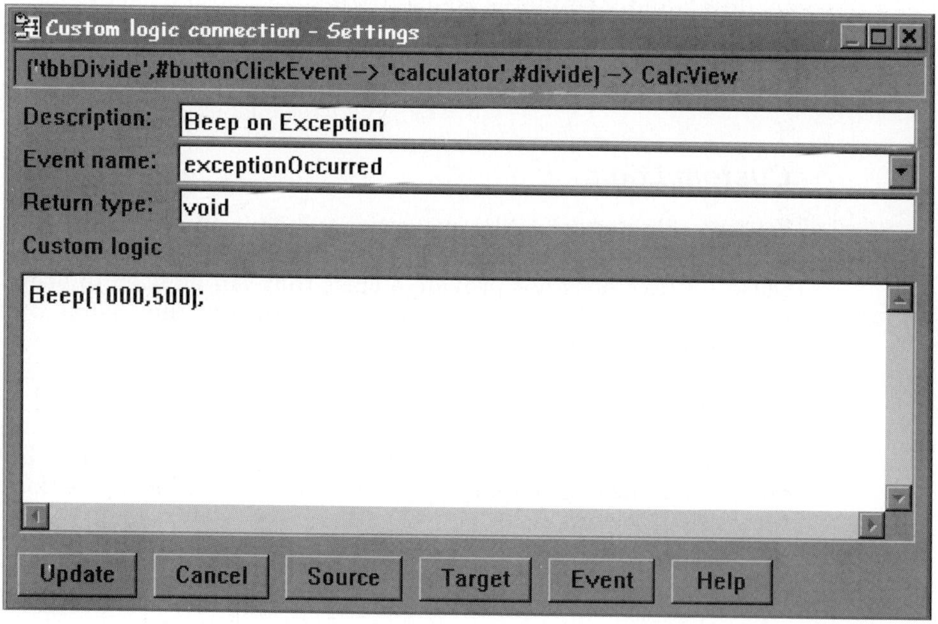

Figure 96: Custom logic dialog

The segment of the code generated by the custom logic can be seen in Code segment 15. Custom logic can also be referred to as a *code snippet*.

```
. . .
void perform(const INotificationEvent & anEvent)
{
  IFUNCTRACE_DEVELOP();
  ITRACE_DEVELOP(" firing connection :
      Conn24(exceptionOccurred) to (customLogic,
      \"Beep on Exception\"))");
  codeSnippet(&anEvent);
};
private:
//---------------------------
// private member functions
//---------------------------
void codeSnippet(const INotificationEvent* event)
{
  Beep(1000,500);
};
. . .
```

Code segment 15: Custom logic snippet

In the current version of the Visual Builder custom logic connections appear as blue lines. Selecting the custom logic connections inserts the description you entered in the info area of the Composition Editor, see Figure 97.

In order for the compiler to find the definitions of the Beep or Dos-Beep functions, you must turn to the Class Editor of the CalcView part and enter the following in the **Required include files** section:

❏ windows.h in Windows

❏ os2.h in OS/2

You can generate the Part source, compile, and test the CalcView application to make sure you get the beep when a divide by zero exception occurs.

You should be aware that custom logic should not be abused. You should only use it when doing a one-of-a-kind connection. Each custom logic connection is a self contained piece of code and adds code to your application, making it larger and more difficult to maintain. For

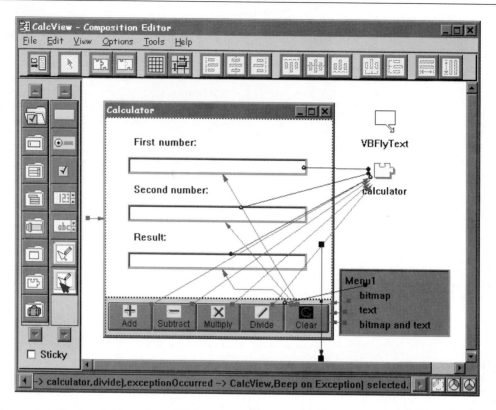

Figure 97: Custom logic connection

example, if you have more than one connection which causes a beep, probably for different reasons or conditions encountered by the program, and the user of your application wanted a different sounding beep; you would have to edit each and every one of the custom logic connections to make the changes. It is almost always better to construct a simple nonvisual part, which can be reused, than to write custom logic code.

This example provides a very rudimentary mechanism to inform the user that an error has occurred, and was presented mainly as an introduction to using custom logic. A more effective and user friendly way to handle errors is through the use of message boxes. The instructions below will guide you through the necessary steps to handle the exception in this way.

Message Boxes

After you have tested the custom logic connection and understand how it works, delete the connection. Follow these steps to catch the exception and display a friendly message:

❑ From the **Other** category, add an **IMessageBox** part to the free-form surface and name it **errorMessageBox**.

❑ Connect the **exceptionOcurred** event of the divide connection to the **errorMessageBox(showException)** action. In order to be able to connect to a connection, you select the connection by clicking on it, then bring up its pop-up menu by clicking the selected connection with the right mouse button. This connection should like Figure 98.

Compile and Test the Calculator

Generate the Part source one last time, switch to a command prompt session and enter **nmake calcview.mak**.

After the compile and link is finished, start the application. The Calculator application looks the same as the last time you ran it. Test the math functions and see how they work.

❑ Enter **123.45** in the **First number** entry field and enter **678.91** in the **Second number** entry field.

❑ Select the **Add** button and check that the Result is **802.36**.

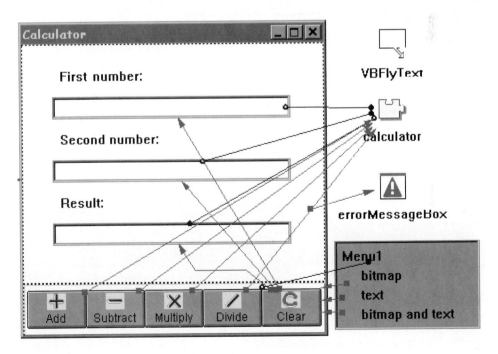

Figure 98: Connecting exceptionOccurred to the message box

❑ Now select the **Subtract** button and you see the Result is -**555.46**.

❑ Select the **Multiply** button and the Result is **83811.4395**.

❑ Finally select the **Divide** button and the Result is **0.181835589400657**.

The last test is to try to divide by zero.

❑ Change the entry for **Second number** to **0** and select the **Divide** button.

The exception thrown by the connection is caught and the appropriate message box displayed as seen in Figure 99.

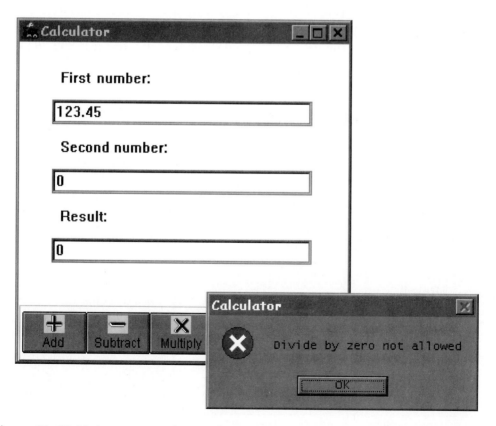

Figure 99: Divide by zero exception caught

Chapter 5—Summary

You completed the Calculator application and improved it in a number of ways. In this chapter you:

❏ Included additional operations of subtract, multiply, and divide in the Calc nonvisual part

❏ Made the necessary connections to support the new operations

❏ Added items to the connections preferred list pop-up menu

❏ Used exception handling to catch divide by zero exceptions

❏ Used the IMessageBox control to display an error

This is the last you will add to the Calculator application. It is a good example of many of the key elements that go into a good Object-Oriented C++ application. In the next chapter you will use the Calculator application to learn tracing and debugging.

What's in Chapter 6

This chapter provides you with an introduction to using the debugging aids available with VisualAge for C++. You will be exposed to:

❑ The Open Class Library trace facility as an aid to debugging programs

❑ The source level debugger to step through a program and find execution errors

These are very helpful tools for debugging applications. In Visual Programming the tools generate a lot of the code for you. This gives you a false sense of security as though the software knows what you want it to do. These debugging tools are only covered in this chapter, but you should use them in the other chapters if you have problems with your applications.

6

Debugging Applications

In the first few chapters of this book you learned the basics about VisualAge C++ Parts and their components. You built and tested the Adding Machine and Calculator applications. These applications are fairly simple and not very error prone. They were meant to introduce you to the basic user interface controls and the mechanics involved in composing, building, and running an application using the Building from Parts paradigm. You were also introduced to the world of connections and how they are used to "make things happen" in an application.

Introduction to the Trace Facility

By now you are beginning to understand that programs generated using the VisualAge for C++ Visual Builder are event driven and rely on the underlying notification framework provided by the Open Class Library.

In traditional programming when you receive unexpected results while executing the program, you resort to examining the code, analyzing the logic flow and operations, and often find yourself using the debugger to step through the program execution step-by-step.

Visual programming introduces a new type of complexity through debugging connections. There are at least three things that can go wrong with connections:

1. The connection does not fire.
2. The connection fires at the wrong time (out of sequence).
3. The wrong connection fires.

You need to have the ability to "see" the connections firing in order to help you determine what the problem is. Luckily, the code generated by the Visual Builder incorporates tracing information for each of the visual connections. You can also add trace information within the classes you create.

Using Trace to Understand a Program

In this chapter a bug will be introduced in the Calculator program. You need to erase all the .OBJ and .EXE files from the directory containing the files for the Calculator. This ensures that new files are compiled with the proper information for debugging and tracing.

Tracing information is not compiled into the program by default. To include it you need to define the pre-compiler macro **IC_TRACE_DEVELOP**.

To include trace and debugging information in the Windows version of the product, start the **nmake** program defining the VBDEBUG macro. This can be easily done by invoking **nmake** as shown below:

    nmake VBDEBUG=ON calcview.mak

The VBDEBUG macro is interpreted in the file IVBDEFS.MAK, which is included at the beginning of every make file generated by the Windows version of the Visual Builder. This file is in the **x:\IBMCPPW\BIN** directory.

In the OS/2 version, you must type the **IC_TRACE_DEVELOP** macro definition in the make file. Edit the CALCVIEW.MAK file and add **/DIC_TRACE_DEVELOP** to the end of the **PARTCPPFLAGS** and **APPCPPFLAGS** lines. To include debugging information in an OS/2 program, you also need to include the **-Ti** compiler flag. Modify the same lines as above to include debug information. These lines are at the top of the make file, as shown in Code segment 16.

Trace and debugging information are two different and independent components of the compiled code. Trace information is added by the Visual Builder or the programmer at strategic points in the execution path of the program. Debugging information is added by the compiler to the executable file and this information enables the application to be viewed and executed step-by-step in the Source Level Debugger.

You can compile the code with any combination of trace and debug information:

1. One or the other
2. Both
3. None

```
#*******************************************************************
#FILE NAME: CalcView.mak                                          *
#                                                                 *
# DESCRIPTION:                                                    *
#   Make file for class:                                          *
#     CalcView- View for the adder application                    *
# -------------------------                                       *
# Warning: This file was generated by thc VisualAge C++           *
#  Visual Builder.                                                *
# Modifications to this source file will be lost when             *
# the part is regenerated.                                        *
#******************************************************************/
PARTCPPFLAGS=-FtCalcView -Gm+ -Tdp -Gd+ -I. -DIC_TRACE_
DEVELOP -Ti
APPCPPFLAGS=-FtCalcView -Gm+ -Tdp -Gd+ -I.  -DIC_TRACE_
DEVELOP -Ti

all:   CalcView

CalcView:   CalcView.exe

CalcView.exe:   CalcView.o CalcView.obj Calc.obj \
       CalcView.res
         icc $(PARTCPPFLAGS) /B"CalcView.o /pmtype:pm" \
           CalcView.obj Calc.obj \
           /FeCalcView.exe /FmCalcView.map \
           os2386.lib
         rc CalcView.res CalcView.exe
. . .
```

Code segment 16: OS/2 make file with trace macro defined

Now recompile the **CalcView** application with the new make file. After the make process finishes building the code, both trace and debug information is included in the executable file. The final version of the program should be recompiled without the trace macro defined and without debugging information to minimize the size of the executable file. This also eliminates the overhead that results from tracing the connections.

Inserting Trace Points in a Program

As mentioned previously, the Visual Builder adds trace points for every connection. This is very useful because it enables you to see what connections are firing as the results of actions or events in the program. You can also add your own trace information to find out what is happening while the program is executing. This is done by inserting trace macros at the appropriate points in the program.

The Open Class Library provides several trace macros, two of the most useful are:

1. IFUNCTRACE_DEVELOP
2. ITRACE_DEVELOP

Use the IFUNCTRACE_DEVELOP macro to trace the entry and exit points of a member function. IFUNCTRACE_DEVELOP can only be used once in each function. It is usually the first line after the opening brace. Enter this macro in the **Calc add** member function, as shown in Code segment 17.

```
Calc& Calc::add()
{
  IFUNCTRACE_DEVELOP();
  setResult(iNum1 + iNum2);
  return *this;
}
```

Code segment 17: Trace macro in the add member function

Use the ITRACE_DEVELOP macro as you used the **printf** function in your C language programs. The **printf** function is used to send messages to yourself from within a program. This is a useful technique to indicate progress or to display the value of variables at execution time.

The ITRACE_DEVELOP macro takes an **IString** object as a parameter. This string object can contain virtually anything since the **IString** class provides conversions from many other types. For example, to trace the result of the operation just performed by the Calculator, enter a line of code in the **setResult** member function shown in Code segment 18.

```
Calc& Calc::setResult(double aResult)
{
  IFUNCTRACE_DEVELOP();
  if (!(iResult == aResult))
  {
    iResult = aResult;
    ITRACE_DEVELOP("The result is:" + IString(iResult));
    notifyObservers(INotificationEvent(Calc::resultId,
        *this));
  } // endif
  return *this;
}
```

Code segment 18: ITRACE_DEVELOP macro in setResult

System settings for Running Trace

The **ITRACE** statement uses the built-in **IString** conversion function and converts the double **iResult** to an **IString** object. In addition to including trace macros in the program, the operating system needs an environment variable set to enable displaying the trace information. To enable tracing the CONFIG.SYS file of your computer must have the following line:

```
SET ICLUI_TRACE=ON
```

This line must appear exactly as shown. There are spaces between the first two words and no spaces on either side of the equal sign. Without this environment variable properly set, you can not get the trace information from the program. If your CONFIG.SYS file does not set this environment variable, you can temporarily set it from a command prompt session and then start your program from the same session.

By default, the trace information in OS/2 is sent to queue called **\\QUEUES\PRINTF32**. You do not need to understand how OS/2 queues work because there is a program supplied in the CD-ROM included with this book called **pmprintf**. This utility program displays the trace information sent to this queue by the program. The trace information is conveniently displayed in a window. Read the documentation and licensing information supplied with **pmprintf**.

An alternative for viewing the trace information is to send the trace output to a file. While you run your application, the trace information is written to a file as the tracing occurs. You must then edit the trace file to view the trace information. Another operating system environment variable needs to be changed to capture the trace information in a file. Set the ICLUI_TRACETO environment variable as follows:

```
SET ICLUI_TRACETO=STDOUT
```

Again, this line must appear exactly as shown. There are spaces between the first two words and no spaces on either side of the equal sign. Without this environment variable properly set, the trace information is not redirected to **stdout**. If you choose to send the trace output **stdout**, pass the name of the file for the trace information when you start the application. Start the program from a command prompt window and redirect the output of the program to a file, for example:

calcview >trace.out

It is possible to write a utility like **pmprintf** for the Windows version, but by the time of printing this book none could be found. Until one is developed, you need to send the trace output to a file when using the Windows version.

When the **calculator** program exits, you can edit the file **TRACE. OUT** and analyze the trace information.

Understanding Trace Output

The output generated by the trace macros is displayed in Code segment 19. The trace output looks the same whether the trace was sent to a file or to the output screen of the **pmprintf** tool.

```
00000034 726263:54 +CalcViewConn4::perform(const INotification Event&)(242)
00000035 726263:54   > firing connection : tbbAdd
  (buttonClickEvent)to                          calculator(add))
00000036 726263:54  +Calc::add()(55)
00000037 726263:54   +Calc::setResult(double)(43)
00000038 726263:54    >The result is:36
00000039 726263:54    +CalcViewConn3::performSetTarget()(196)
00000040 726263:54     > firing connection : calculator(result)
to                      efResult(valueAsDouble))
00000041 726263:54     > setting target from source
00000042 726263:54    -CalcViewConn3::performSetTarget()
00000043 726263:54   -Calc::setResult(double)
00000044 726263:54  -Calc::add()
00000045 726263:54 -CalcViewConn4::perform(const
INotificationEvent&)
```

Code segment 19: Trace output for the Add operation

The numbers in the columns of the trace output provide you with the information as shown in Table 5: Trace information description.

Table 5: Trace information description

Column	Description
ICLUI	Trace generated by ICLUI (old name for the IBM Open Class Library) This column does not appear in the Windows trace
00000034–45	Sequence number within the trace file
000153:01	Process number:thread number
Trace information	+CalcViewConn1::dispatchNotificationEvent(const INotificationEvent&)(129)

The plus (+) sign indicates entering a member function and the minus (−) sign indicates leaving a member function. The greater than (>) sign indicates a trace produced by the ITRACE_DEVELOP macro. For a complete description of all the tracing functions available and trace formatting macros, please see the Open Class Library Reference Guide, under the ITrace class.

The trace output is slightly different between Windows and OS/2, but basically it contains all the same information.

Introduction to the Source Level Debugger

Sometimes studying the output of trace information does not provide enough insight to determine what is causing the program to go haywire. At other times, the logic of a particular function or algorithm may be very complex and you want to better understand how it works. Sometimes programs get a general protection fault (GPF) in Windows or a Trap D in OS/2. These are storage protection violations, meaning that the program has attempted to access an area of memory it has no access to. For all these cases you need to examine the code more closely, perhaps by setting a breakpoint at a particular instruction and monitoring state variables. The source level debugger which is part of the VisualAge for C++ product is an excellent tool to use in the above cases.

Debugging the Calculator Application

Since you are familiar with the Calculator application, you will now introduce a coding error and use the debugger to track the offending source instruction.

❏ Open the CALC.CPV file, locate the divide member function and change it to look like Code segment 20.

```
Calc& Calc::divide()
{
  IFUNCTRACE_DEVELOP();
  // check if the second number is zero
  if( iNum2 = 0) // Error should be ==
  {
    IInvalidParameter exception
= IInvalidParameter("Divide by zero not
allowed");
    IInvalidParameter("Divide by zero");
    ITHROW(exception);
  }

  setResult(iNum1 / iNum2);
  return *this;
}
```

Code segment 20: divide function with an error

Save and recompile; do not forget to tell the compiler to add debug information to the executable. The compiler may at this point give an informational error, saying that you are using an assignment in a conditional statement. Of course, good programmers ignore warning and information messages (just joking of course), so let the compile continue and test the application.

When you run the changed program in Windows, everything appears to work fine with the exception of the division operation. The operating system is giving you a nasty error and terminating the program.

In OS/2, the Result entry field may display the word **infinity** or **nan** (not a number) instead of the more nasty effect of terminating your program.

You suspect something is wrong with the operating system, the compiler, the computer, or possibly the division code.

Starting the Debugger

Use the debugger to step through the code that performs the division. A good way to start the debugger is from a command line session in the directory that has the source files. This way, everything the debugger needs can be found. You can also start the Debugger from the icon in the VisualAge for C++ folder. Start the debugger in the directory with the Calculator files, at a command prompt enter:

- idebug calcview.exe, in Windows
- icsdebug calcview.exe, in OS/2

The **Debug session control** dialog appears (refer to Figure 100) and the debugger starts loading the executable program. This step may take a while depending on your computer configuration.

After the file has been loaded, the **Source** window opens and displays the file containing the **main()** function as shown in Figure 101.

Viewing Source Code in the Debugger

The source window is implemented as a notebook and you can open any files included by the displayed file. Most of the time the code you are looking for is not part of the **main()** function. You can easily pinpoint the function you need by expanding the contents of the modules shown in the **Debug Session Control** panel as shown in Figure 102. Press the plus button to the left of the CALCVIEW.EXE entry. This exposes the files that comprise the application. They can be further expanded to show the member functions in each file. You know the divide member function is part of the **Calc** class. Press the plus button on the left of **Calc** to see its member functions.

Double-click on the Calc::divide entry to open its source file. Once it opens, the cursor is placed at the entry point of the selected member function as shown in Figure 103.

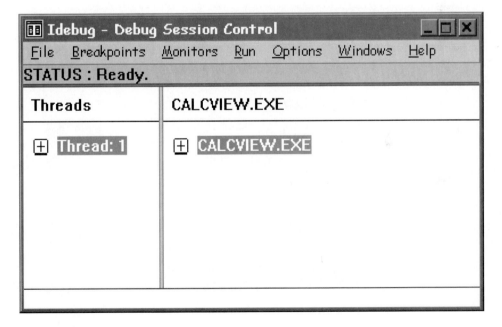

Figure 100: Debugger session control dialog

```
Source: CalcView - Thread :1                                          _ □ ×
File  View  Breakpoints  Monitors  Run  Options  Windows  Help

18  //-----------------------------------------------------------------
19  int main(int argc, char ** argv)
20  {
21       IApplication::current().setArgs(argc, argv);
22
23       CalcView *iPart;
24       IMessageBox::Response resp = IMessageBox::unknown;
25
26       do {
27          try {
28              iPart = new CalcView();
29              iPart->initializePart();
30          }
31          catch (IException& exc) {
32              resp = IMessageBox(IWindow::desktopWindow()).show(
33                      exc.text(),
34                      IMessageBox::retryCancelButton);
35          }
36       }
37       while (resp == IMessageBox::retry);

CALCVIEW.APP   ISTRING.INL
```

Figure 101: Source notebook for calcview.app

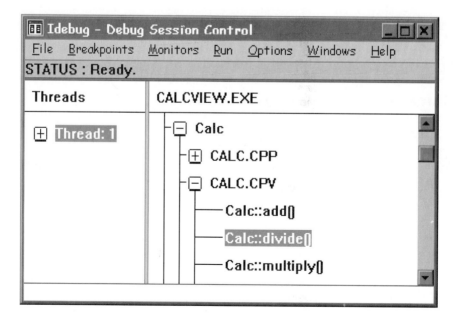

Figure 102: Selecting the divide member function of Calc

```
Source: Calc - Thread :1                                    _ □ X
File  View  Breakpoints  Monitors  Run  Options  Windows  Help

[toolbar icons]

70    setResult(iNum1 * iNum2);
71    return *this;
72  }
73
74  Calc& Calc::divide()
75  {
76    IFUNCTRACE_DEVELOP();
77    // check if the second number is zero
78    if( iNum2 = 0)
79    {
80      IInvalidParameter exception = IInvalidParameter("Divide by
81      ITHROW(exception);
82    }
83
84    setResult(iNum1 / iNum2);
85    return *this;
86  }
87
88  // Feature source code generation ends here.

                        CALC.CPV
      CALC.CPP    IEVTDATA.INL
```

Figure 103: Source for the divide member function

Setting Breakpoints in the Debugger

The next step is to set a breakpoint on line 74 of the source file. This is easily done by double-clicking on the line number. The number is now red. When you have many breakpoints selected it can be difficult to remember where they are. You can manage all the breakpoints for a debugging session by opening the **Breakpoints List** dialog as shown in Figure 104. Open this dialog by selecting **Breakpoints**, then **List** from the menu bar or by pressing Ctrl+X.

From this dialog you can enable, disable, modify, or jump to the location of the breakpoint. These functions are available from the pop-up menu of each breakpoint. Close this dialog.

Now that the breakpoint is set, you can start running the program by pressing the run button on the debugger tool bar or selecting **Run**, **Run** from the menu bar.

The program runs normally. Enter **12** in the **First number** and **3** in the **Second number** fields as shown in Figure 105. You know the application should perform this division and that the answer is 4. Press the Divide button on the calculator tool bar.

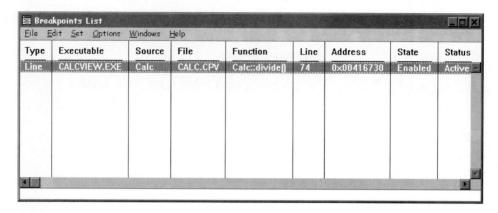

Figure 104: Breakpoints List dialog

Stepping through Source Code

As you press the **Divide** button, the application stops at the break-point and the source window appears with the line containing the breakpoint highlighted. You can step through the code line by line by pressing the first toolbar button called the **Step over** button. This

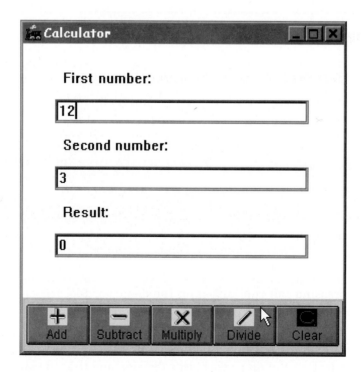

Figure 105: About to press the divide button

button is used if the line to be executed calls another function. That function is executed without taking the debugger into the call. You can experiment with the other **Step** buttons and read about their function in the on-line book "Debugger Reference". For this problem stepping over is fine.

Step the program execution until the selected statement is at the point where the comparison is made **if(iNum2 = 0)**. At this point it is a good idea to examine the current value of the **iNum2** variable. Click on the word **iNum2** to select it and then double-click it to open a Program Monitor dialog. In this dialog you see the value of **iNum2** as shown in Figure 106.

Note: there appears to be a problem in the OS/2 version of the class libraries which prevents the debugger from displaying the error message box in Figure 107. In order for you to see the box, when a floating point divide by zero exception is detected by the CPU, do the following before executing the next instruction:

❑ display the CPU registers

❑ locate the FPCW register and change its current value of 037F to 0362 by typing over the numbers displayed. Press enter for the new value to take effect.

The above change restores the FPCW floating point register to the proper value allowing the error to be detected by the debugger.

In the monitor window you see that the value for **iNum2** is indeed 3, which is what you entered in the **Second number** entry field. Certainly 3 is not 0, and the exception should not be occurring. You are getting an operation system error, not your own message box catching the exception. Execute the next statement by pressing the **Step over** button again. Execution jumped to the **setResult(iNum1 / iNum2);** line. This should set the result after the computer divides the two

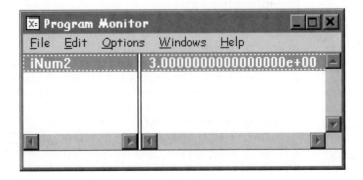

Figure 106: Program Monitor for iNum2

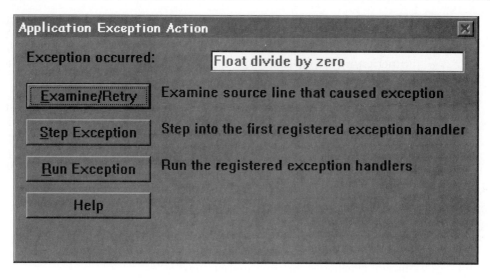

Figure 107: Exception Action dialog

numbers. Press **Step** again and the program stops with an error. This time the error presented by the debugger is a lot more exact as shown in Figure 107.

The problem appears to be that the application attempted a divide by zero operation. Computers, and people, cannot divide by zero. So the CPU signaled the operating system that the error had occurred, and the operating system terminated the program.

What really happened? You inspected the **iNum2** variable and its value was 3. Why did the CPU think it was 0? Press the **Examine/ Retry** button; the debugger handles the clean up required and resets the debugger so you can restart the application by selecting **Run, Restart**. When the debugger is ready, press the **Run** button to start the application again.

When the Calculator displays, enter the same numbers again and press the **Divide** button. The debugger stops at the breakpoint again. This time proceed more slowly. Step until the **if** statement. The Program Monitor still indicates that **iNum2**'s value is 3. Step once more and check the monitor. The value of **iNum2** is now 0 as shown in Figure 108. Now you understand why the computer complained, but how did the value get changed?

The error happened somewhere between the **if** and the **setResult** statements. A close examination of the *if(iNum2 = 0)* statement reveals that instead of comparing iNum2 to 0, you were assigning 0 to iNum2.

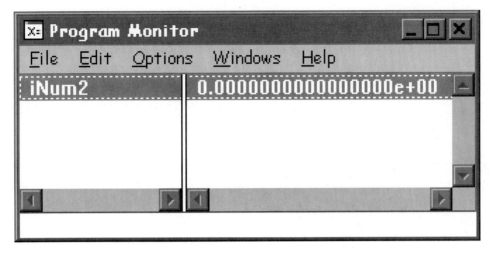

Figure 108: iNum2 value is now 0

Close the debugger, add another equal sign to the offending line, re-compile, test and everything is fine again. When you close the debugger it saves information about the last debug session for each program you debug. This feature restores the debugging environment across invocations of the debugger for a particular program.

This was a very simple introduction to a very powerful tool in your arsenal against bugs. As your applications become more complex and the logic in your nonvisual parts contain more algorithms and involved calculations, you will find yourself using the debugger more and more and you will become familiar with its advanced functions. The on-line help for the debugger is excellent and contains many details and techniques to help you debug programs.

Chapter 6—Summary

In this chapter you were introduced to the trace and debugging facilities of VisualAge for C++. This chapter included the following activities:

- ❑ Adding trace information to a program by entering your own trace statements in the code.
- ❑ Setting the correct environment for tracing
- ❑ Recompiling the Calculator application to include both tracing and debugging information.
- ❑ Debugging the Calculator application to fix a logic error

What's in Chapter 7

In this chapter you will learn about several new controls available in the Open Class Library and you cover techniques for using these controls in the Visual Builder. You will build a reminder application that uses the following controls:

❑ Menus

❑ Submenus

❑ Pop-up menus

❑ Subparts

❑ Multicell Canvas

❑ Set Canvas

❑ Radio buttons

❑ Multiple line edit fields

❑ Information Area

❑ Long fly over text

This chapter also covers adding Help to an application. You will enable an application to provide help for:

❑ Help Index

❑ General Help

❑ Using Help

❑ Keys Help

❑ Product Information

7

Making a Reminder List

In this chapter you start a totally new application. Since you are building on the material already covered in this book, the very basic steps are described in less detail. For example, instead of giving you step-by-step details on how to add a part to the Composition Editor, the instructions just direct you to add or drop a certain part. By now you should be able to locate a part in the parts palette, select it, and drag it to the correct Composition Editor area. You should also be getting used to making connections. The convention used to describe connections consists of the source part name, the source feature in parenthesis, an arrow, the target part name, and the target feature in parenthesis. The following connection is an example of this convention:

pbOk (buttonClickEvent) → myWindow (close) action

This connection translates to mean "connect the **OK** push button's **buttonClickEvent** to the frame window's, called myWindow, **close** action". When the feature of the part needed for the connection could be ambiguous, it is clearly specified whether it is an action, attribute, or event. In the example above you could have confused the **close** action with the **closeEvent** of the IFrameWindow part.

Using Subparts

This chapter introduces a key concept in VisualAge for C++ called subparts. This technique utilizes the power of Object-Oriented technology to build custom visual and nonvisual components which can be used and reused in many applications.

Requirements for the Reminder List

This application saves and retrieves information related to six categories, and provides the functions of a Reminder or Todo list as shown in Figure 109.

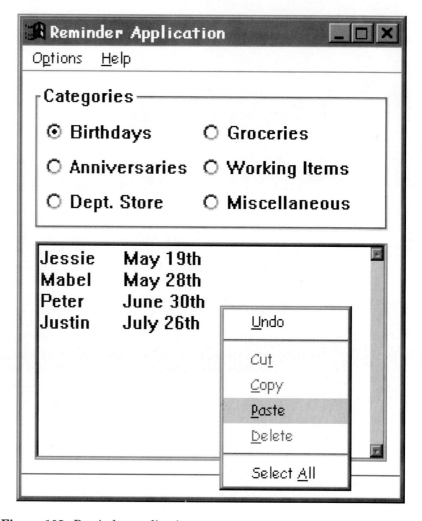

Figure 109: Reminder application.

As the user selects a radio button, the information related to that selection is displayed in the input/output area. The user can edit the text displayed. The input/output area is implemented using an **IMultiLineEdit** part (MLE).

The first radio button is preselected when the application starts, and the MLE displays the information associated with the first radio button. When a different radio button is selected the current text in the MLE is saved, and the text associated with the newly selected radio button is displayed in the MLE. When the user exits the program the current text in the MLE is saved.

Data persistence is provided by the **IProfile** nonvisual part in the Open Class Library. The internal implementation of this part is quite different between OS/2 and Windows. In fact, this is an excellent example of Object-Oriented technology. This application can be developed on Windows or OS/2 the same way, however the underlying implementation details are different. When using the **IProfile** class the Open Class Library internally compensates for different operating systems. With a well defined part interface, the user of this part can use the part's public interface and does not have to worry about the implementation. In Windows the data is saved in the **registry,** and in OS/2 the data is saved in an .INI file

The application has a menu bar with the structure pictured in Figure 110.

The **Clear** function removes the contents of the MLE and can also be accessed using the Alt+C key combination.

The program can be ended by selecting the **Exit** menu item or pressing the Alt+X key combination. At exit any information displayed on the MLE is associated with the currently selected radio button and saved.

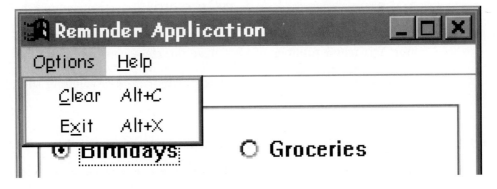

Figure 110: Menu bar for Reminder application

Help is context sensitive, which means specific help appears for the individual items in the Reminder List depending on which control has the focus. Help text is contained in a separate file which can eventually be translated to other languages, and its contents can generally be changed without affecting the application code.

Each menu item has a line of help displayed on the information area at the bottom of the screen.

When the mouse pointer is over the MLE or the area containing the radio buttons, appropriate bubble help describes their function. Long fly over help displays in the information area at the bottom of the frame window.

There is a pop-up menu associated with the MLE to perform **Cut**, **Copy** and **Paste** functions upon the contents of the MLE. This function is part of the built-in behavior of the IMultiLineEdit part in Windows. In OS/2 you must build this pop-up menu.

A couple of nonvisual parts are used to provide the business logic to the Reminder application. In addition to the **IProfile** part, used to provide data persistence, the INIMgr nonvisual part acts as a controller between the radio buttons and the **IProfile** part. These nonvisual parts are incorporated into the Reminder application in the next chapter.

Constructing the Reminder Application

Once again, you start by building the visual component of the project first; then you add the nonvisual parts, connect the components, and finish the application.

The application is built on a frame window, just like the Calculator. However, instead of adding the other visual parts to the standard **ICanvas** part, which comes as a default with the frame window, you use the much more versatile **IMultiCellCanvas** part.

The Reminder application is a bit more complicated than the Calculator. You use a number of new user interface controls including the multicell canvas. Because of the many new parts introduced in this application, this chapter is devoted primarily to developing the user interface.

Reminder Application Visual Components

From the Visual Builder Parts Selector set your working directory to **x:\VABOOK\REMINDER** and create a new visual part as shown in Figure 111.

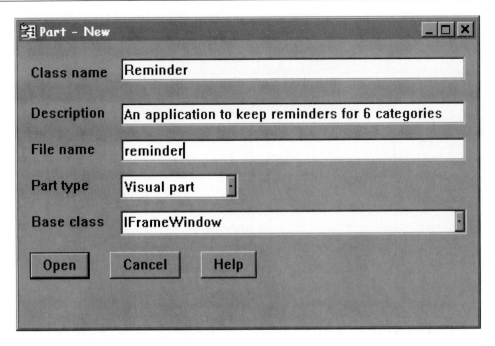

Figure 111: New visual part Reminder

❑ Enter **Reminder** in the **Class** name field.

❑ Enter **An application to keep reminders for 6 categories** in the Description field.

❑ Enter **reminder** in the File name field.

❑ The Part type is **Visual part**.

❑ The Base class for this part is **IFrameWindow**.

❑ Select the **Open** button to create the Reminder part and display the Visual Builder Composition Editor.

The first step is to remove the **ICanvas** control which is automatically inserted as the client of the frame window. Click on the client area inside the frame window to select the **ICanvas** control, click the right mouse button, and select **Delete** from the pop-up menu as shown in Figure 112. This technique can be used to delete any part on the composition area.

Next, select an **IMultiCellCanvas** part from the Composers folder and drop it in the frame window client area.

The multicell canvas expanded to occupy all of the client area as shown in Figure 113. No matter what the size of the frame window,

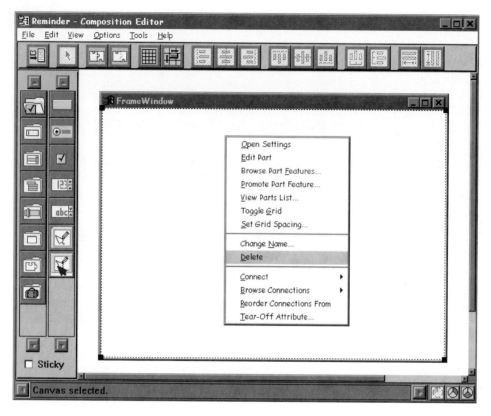

Figure 112: Deleting the ICanvas inside the frame window

the part occupying the client area of the frame window expands to fit the size of the window.

IMultiCellCanvas Settings

The **IMultiCellCanvas** control is a very powerful control that automatically resizes controls which are placed on top of it at runtime. This is very useful for controls like list boxes and containers. When a frame window with a multicell canvas is stretched at runtime, these controls can expand, allowing more information to be displayed. This helps users see more information in parts like entry fields, list boxes, and containers. The ability to automatically size controls also benefits translating applications to other languages. This is because words in different language can be different lengths than those of the original languages for which the application was first designed. Controls on a multicell canvas adjust to accommodate these longer or shorter words.

Figure 113: IMultiCellCanvas in a frame window

This added function is not free. Design considerations must be taken when implementing a multicell canvas since additional code is generated when using a **IMultiCellCanvas** part instead of an **ICanvas** part. Some of the additional generated code is required to position each control within its cell in the **IMultiCellCanvas** and to resize the control dynamically as the cell grows and shrinks. This added code makes the C++ files and the compiled executable bigger, but the additional function is well worth it.

Each control is assigned to a cell, this is the cell where you placed the control. Only one control can be placed in a particular cell. Any attempt to drop a control on a cell already occupied generates an error message.

The **IMultiCellCanvas** control, along with the **ISetCanvas** control, are also known as *minimum size canvases*. This means that the minimum size of a column or row is controlled by the size of the controls placed on that column or row. For example, if you place a static text, an entry field and a push button in the same column of the **IMulti-CellCanvas**, the width of that column is as wide as the widest control in the column.

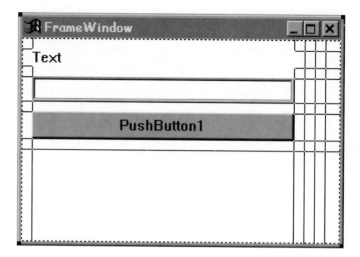

Figure 114: IMultiCellCanvas with controls

In Figure 114, you see a somewhat disproportional push button. Since it has been placed on the same column as the other controls, its width is determined by the width of the other controls. In this case the entry field, with a default width of 32 characters, is forcing the push button to be too wide.

If you want the entry field to hold 32 characters and also want the push button to keep its smaller size, you need to do two things. First make the entry field span more than one column, then set the column not occupied by the button as expandable as shown in Figure 115.

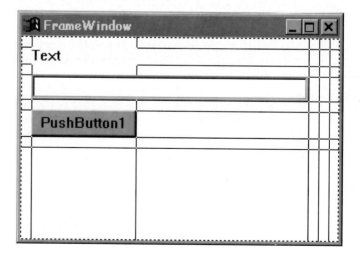

Figure 115: Entry field in cols 2 and 3, col 3 expandable

Each row and column of the **IMultiCellCanvas** can be set to expand, by default nothing is expandable. When you set a row or column as expandable, all controls in that row or column expand at runtime.

To get an individual control to expand, as in the case of the entry field above, without affecting other controls in the same column, you need to add additional rows and columns to the canvas. For canvases with a lot of controls, it is helpful to do a little paper planning of the canvas layout.

As you see in the crude paper design in Figure 116 row 4 and column 2 are designated as expandable. This provides a design that allows the MLE to expand and contract, in both height and width, as the frame window is sized. This is a good design because it allows users with higher resolution displays to make the frame window larger and see more of the information in the MLE. Because of this setting, all controls in row 4 and column 2 expand. This causes a side effect; the area containing the radio buttons also becomes wider as the MLE becomes wider. This may or may not be acceptable for your taste or your customer's requirements.

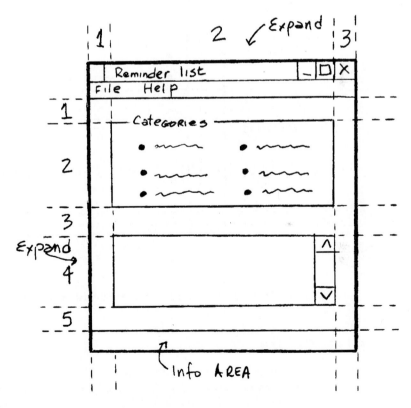

Figure 116: Paper design of the Reminder visual part

Figure 117 has a revised design for the multicell canvas that keeps the area containing the radio buttons a constant size and centered in relation to the MLE. This is achieved by adding two columns to the **IMultiCellCanvas** and making the MLE span columns 2 through 4. Also, making these two columns expand still allows the MLE to change size without affecting the **ISetCanvas** which contains the radio button cluster.

Implement the simpler design of Figure 116. Instructions for the design of Figure 117 are not included in this book, but you can implement it on your own initiative.

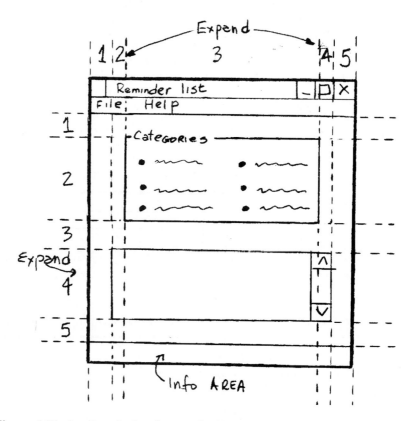

Figure 117: Another design, keep radio buttons centered

Using an ISetCanvas

There is another canvas that is very helpful when using radio buttons, or other controls which need to be automatically aligned and distributed on the area defined by the canvas. The **ISetCanvas** performs this automatic alignment function. There are many features available to customize the set canvas, and you will use them later in this chapter when you start building the application.

The Visual Builder allows you to combine many Open Class controls into composite parts, which would be very difficult to do if you had to hand code in C++. Some users learn how to use certain controls and then rely on them for implementations in very creative, but not necessarily correct, ways. Programmers have put a set canvas inside a group box to get the benefits of an outline, text, and distribution of controls. This is unnecessary because the set canvas already has an outline and text capabilities. Other users have put radio buttons in an **IMultiCellCanvas** to get the automatic alignment, then put the **IMultiCellCanvas** inside a group box to get an outline, this is even more wasteful. Usually when you think radio buttons, you should think about using a set canvas.

Using IRadioButton Controls

Radio buttons are used when you need to select one and only one option from a group of choices. Radio buttons are always used as a group of two or more choices; although each radio button is a separate control, clusters of radio buttons behave as a single control. For example, when any button is selected from a cluster a single **selected** event is generated. You can then look at the **selectedIndex** attribute on any radio button in the cluster to find out which button was just selected.

You should never use a single radio button to give the user a binary choice. The **ICheckBox** control should be used for that purpose. If multiple selections are allowed in a group of choices, you should also use ICheckBox controls.

Adding Visual Components to the Canvas

So far, you have created the new Reminder visual part which is a frame window. You have removed the canvas which was inside the window and replaced it with an **IMultiCellCanvas**. The part looks like Figure 113.

❑ Click the right mouse button on the frame window within the Composition Editor to display the pop-up menu.

❑ Select **Change name...** and enter **frmMainWindow** in the entry field to name the part.

❑ Select and drop an **ISetCanvas** part on row 2 column 2 of the **IMultiCellCanvas**.

As you can see, once the mouse pointer is loaded with the part and positioned over the **IMultiCellCanvas** it changes to a cross (+). The hot spot or drop point for this pointer is in the middle of the cross. A hot spot is a one pixel location in an icon which determines the pointer location. The rows and columns are a bit narrow, so you need to be careful when dropping controls into cells. If the control ends up in the wrong cell, you can select it and drag it to the right cell. You can also change the location of each control in the settings notebook for the multicell canvas.

At this time all you see is the dashed outline of the set canvas as shown in Figure 118. This control will hold the radio buttons. In order to make room for the six radio buttons, select and stretch the set canvas.

Adding Radio Buttons

From the **Button** category add six radio buttons to the set canvas. To make things go faster use the **sticky** feature to drop many controls at a time.

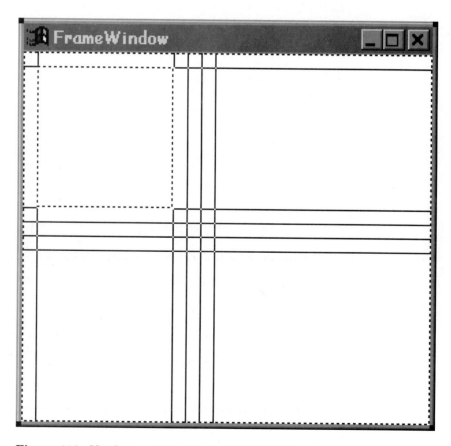

Figure 118: ISetCanvas Added to the IMultiCellCanvas

Figure 119 shows the radio buttons added to the set canvas. The reason the radio buttons are not showing properly is that the default settings for the set canvas control are just not right for this application. Open the settings notebook for the set canvas by double-clicking on it (remember to avoid double-clicking on the radio buttons). The settings notebook is shown in Figure 120.

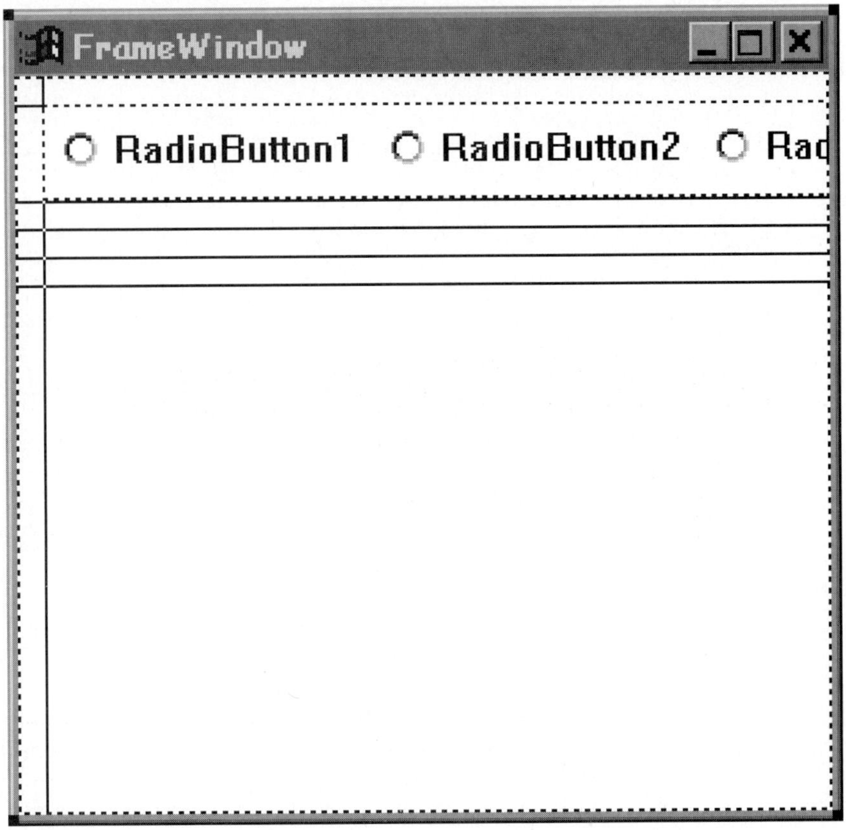

Figure 119: Radio buttons added to set canvas

By default the set canvas aligns the controls horizontally in one deck. For the Reminder application the radio buttons need to appear in two columns. It is very easy to change the way the set canvas aligns the controls with the following steps:

❑ In the **Deck Orientation** group select the **Vertical** radio button.

❑ In the **Text** entry field enter **Categories**.

❑ In the **Deck Count** entry field enter **2**.

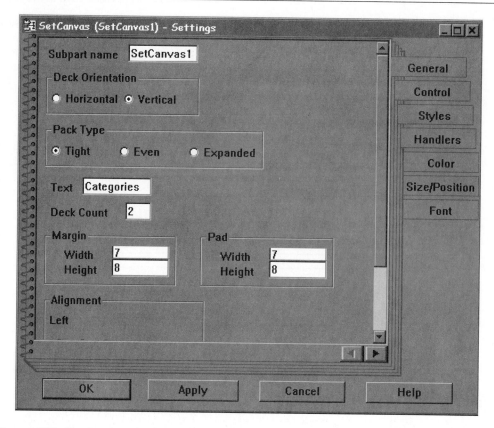

Figure 120: Settings notebook for the set canvas

❑ Switch to the **Control** page of the settings notebook. Add **Fly over short text** for the set canvas. The text should be short, enter **Pick a category**.

❑ Press the **OK** button.

There are two additional attributes that can be changed for the set canvas. The **Margin** and **Pad** settings manage the spacing of controls within the set canvas. The default values for **Margin** and **Pad** are fine for the Reminder application. Reduce the values if you want the controls to be more closely positioned within the set canvas; and conversely, **Margin** and **Pad** can be increased if the canvas design requires that the controls have greater spacing.

You can experiment with the other settings available on the **General** page of the notebook and press the **Apply** button to see the changes on the set canvas without closing the notebook.

Be careful when closing a settings notebook. Closing the notebook by double-clicking its system icon is not the same as pressing **OK**, in fact, it is the same as pressing **Cancel**. Pressing **Apply** and then **Cancel** does not cancel the changes just applied. To revert to a previous setting use the **Undo** function under the **Edit** pull down menu, or press Alt+Backspace after closing the notebook. This behavior applies to all the settings notebooks in the Visual Builder.

❑ Resize the set canvas so that all six radio buttons can be seen as shown in Figure 121.

Now you need to change the settings for each radio button, so open the settings notebook for the first radio button. Use the following steps and refer to Figure 122.

❑ On the **General** page enter **rbBirthdays** for the **Subpart name**.

❑ Enter **Birthdays** in the **Text** entry field.

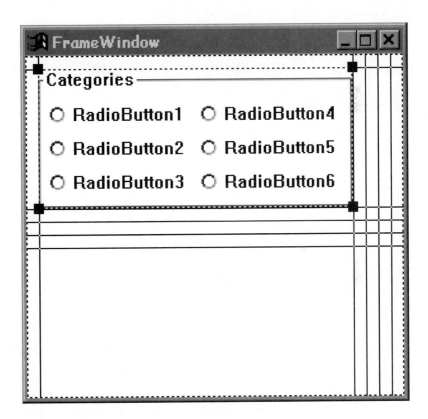

Figure 121: Set canvas after applying the correct settings

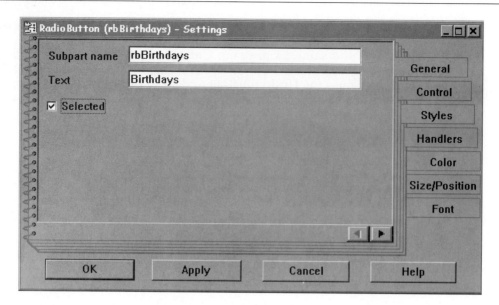

Figure 122: Settings notebook for a radio button

- ❏ Only the first radio button needs the **Selected** check box marked. This selects the first radio button at runtime when the application first starts.

In order for a radio button cluster to behave as one control you need to designate the first radio button as the beginning of the group. This can be done in a couple of ways:

1. In the settings notebook of the first radio button, turn to the **Styles** page and select the **group** style radio button.
2. In the Windows version: click the right mouse on the first radio button, select **Set tabbing**, select **Group**
3. In the OS/2 version: bring up the pop-up menu of the setCanvas and select **Set tabbing and depth order**. Select the group check box for the first radio button.

Now finish the settings for the first radio button:

- ❏ On the **Control** page of the settings notebook, enter **205** as the **Help panel id**. This id number matches the id in the Help file and provides context sensitive help.
- ❏ Save the settings and close the notebook by selecting **OK**.

Repeat as appropriate for the other radio buttons by individually opening the settings notebooks for each control. Set the Help panel id in all of the radio buttons to **205**.

Use the following list of categories for the Reminder application so that it looks like Figure 123.

- ❏ Birthdays
- ❏ Groceries
- ❏ Anniversaries
- ❏ Work Items
- ❏ Shopping List
- ❏ Other

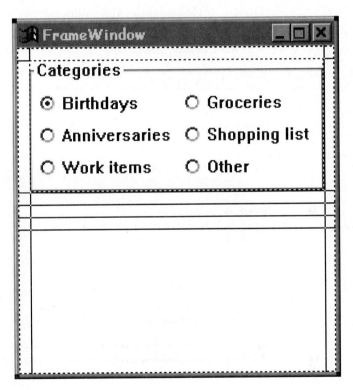

Figure 123: All radio button settings complete

Adding an IMultiLineEdit Control

You need an area to show the items for each of the different categories. There is a powerful control that expands the functions of a simple entry field. The **IMultiLineEdit** control, or MLE for short, provides the function of a simple editor and is a good control for displaying and editing text which can occupy more than one line on the screen. It can be sized vertically and horizontally at runtime and it supports word-wrap.

❑ From the **Data entry** category, select and drop an **IMultiLine-Edit** part.

❑ Place the **IMultiLineEdit** on row 4, column 2 of the **IMultiCell-Canvas** as shown in Figure 124.

This leaves an empty row in the multicell canvas between the set canvas and the MLE. Since the MLE is in the same column as the set canvas in the multicell canvas, the MLE expands to the size of the set canvas.

❑ Open the settings notebook for the MLE, and on the **General** page enter **mleReminder** for the subpart name.

❑ On the **Styles** page set the following radio buttons to on:

❑ **wordWrap** to allow text to wrap to the next line of the MLE when the line is full

❑ **ignoreTab** to allow the tab key to move from group to group in the OS/2 version

❑ **group**

❑ **tabStop**

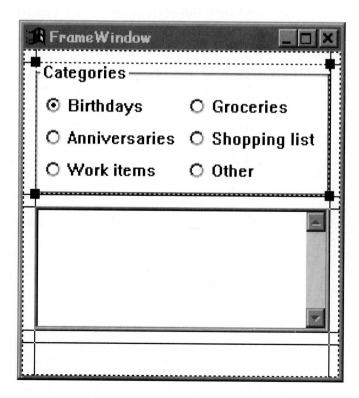

Figure 124: IMultiLineEdit added to an IMultiCellCanvas

- ❏ Turn to the **Control** page and enter:
  - ❏ Fly over short text enter Current list
  - ❏ Fly over long text enter The reminder items for the selected category
  - ❏ Help panel id enter 204
- ❏ Save these settings by selecting the **OK** button.

Adding an IVBFlyText Control

 From the parts palette select an **IVBFlyText** control and drop it on the free-form surface. Name it **flyOverHelp.** No connections are necessary at this time.

Running the Reminder List User Interface

Before you compile and run your application, open the frame window's settings notebook:

- ❏ Enter **Reminder Application** in the Title text field.
- ❏ Switch to the **Control** page and enter **200** in the **Help panel id** field.

You have made quite a bit of progress on this application and you are ready to compile and run it for the first time. If everything is working correctly, you are ready to move to the next step.

- ❏ Select **Save and Generate**, **Part source** and **Save and Generate**, **main() for part** for the Reminder part.
- ❏ Either minimize the Composition Editor for the Reminder part or, if you need to save memory, close the Composition Editor.
- ❏ Switch over to a Command prompt session and type **nmake reminder.mak**.

When the application is finished compiling, run the Reminder application as shown in Figure 125. You can select the radio buttons, only one at a time can be selected, but nothing really happens. This is because you have not implemented any logic with nonvisual parts. The fly over help appears when the mouse pointer is over the set canvas or the MLE. You can enter text in the MLE and, as you reach the end of the line, the text wraps to the next line. You can size the frame window, but the controls inside remain the same size and in the same position. This is because by default the multicell canvas does not size any of its controls. You need to set the options in the **IMultiCellCanvas** settings notebook. Later in this chapter you will set it up properly to achieve the desired action for this application.

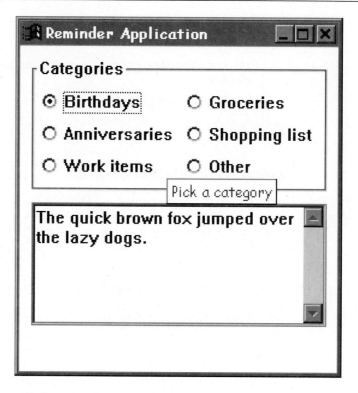

Figure 125: Running Reminder application

Building the Menu Bar for the Reminder Window

Menu bars and pop-up menus are built from the same components and are similar in structure. Menu bars, also known as Action bars, are connected to the **menu** attribute the frame window of the application. Pop-up menus can be attached to the **menu** attribute of most controls.

When building Menu bars for your applications, keep in mind this simple guidelines:

1. The **IMenu** part is associated with the **IFrameWindow** part.

2. There can only be one menu bar in a frame window.

3. If the menu item on the menu bar has a pull down menu to expose more choices, you use an **IMenuCascade** part instead of an **IMenuItem** part.

Drop down menus are built by adding an **IMenuCascade** part to an existing **IMenu** object, then adding a new **IMenu** part to the free-form surface and connecting them together. There is a shortcut for building pull down menu items. You can drop an **IMenu** part on top of another **IMenu** part, this creates an **IMenuCascade** object and places the **IMenu** object you dropped beside it. It also connects the two parts created, all in one action.

To build the menu structure for your application follow these steps:

- ❏ Drop an **IMenu** part on to the free-form surface, this part represents the actual menu bar with no items.

- ❏ Drop another **IMenu** part on top of the first part.

This creates an **IMenuCascade** object and another IMenu object. A connection associating the two is also created. Directly edit the text on the menu cascade part and call it **~Options**. Refer to Figure 126.

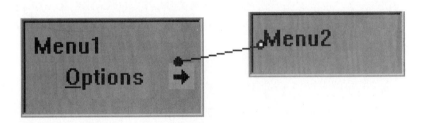

Figure 126: Initial menu bar components

At runtime, when you click on Options a drop down menu appears, and the actions **Clear** and **Exit** appear below it. To code this:

- ❏ From the **Frame extensions** category, drop two **IMenuItem** parts on top of **Menu2**.

- ❏ Change their text to **~Clear** and **E~xit**.

- ❏ Drop an **IMenuSeparator** part between the **Clear** and **Exit** items.

Typing the tilde (**~**) character in front of a letter of text, as in **E~xit**, provides a mnemonic at runtime. The **x** in **Exit** becomes underscored, and when the **Options** menu is pulled down you can either click on the word **Exit** or press the letter **x** to terminate the program.

If you drop menu parts in the wrong sequence, you can reposition them by dragging and dropping them to the right position. There are no special commands or dialog for this function. You can directly drag and drop the menu items within the menu on the Composition Editor free-form surface.

- ❏ Add accelerator keys to the **Clear** and **Exit** menu items by opening their settings notebooks as shown in Figure 127. Use Alt+C and F3 respectively.

- ❏ Name the parts **miClear** and **miExit** respectively.

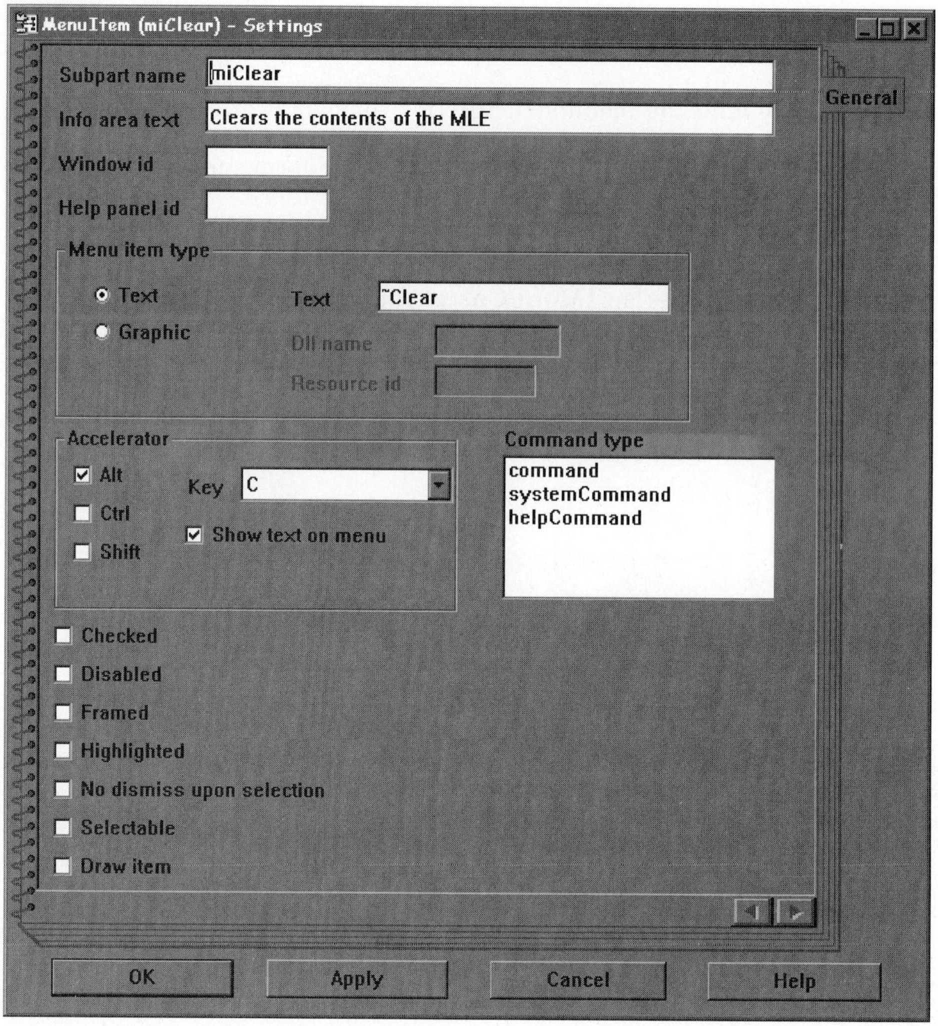

Figure 127: Settings notebook for IMenuItem

Accelerator keys can be pressed at any time, whether the menu item is pulled down or not, to execute their actions.

Even though the **Show text on menu** check box is checked, the accelerator keys do not show on the menu item in the Composition Editor. The accelerator key text shows on menu items when the application runs. Add an accelerator key to the Options menu item. When using top level menu bar items, do not check the **Show text on menu** check box. If you check this option the menu bars do not look right at runtime.

Finally you need to connect the menu items to the appropriate actions:

- ❑ Menu1 (this) → frameWindow (menu)
- ❑ miClear (commandEvent → mleReminder (removeAll)
- ❑ miExit (commandEvent → frameWindow (close)

Building the Help menu structure

Drop an **IMenu** part on Menu1 and label it **~Help**, name this menu **miHelp**. This is the first level of the **Help** menu item. Notice that, just like in the case of the **Options** menu item, what really happens is that **IMenuCascade** and **IMenu** objects were created and connected to each other. If you click on this connection and look at the information area of the composition editor, you see that this connection is:

Menu3(this) → miHelp(menu)

- ❑ Now drop five **IMenuItem** parts on **Menu3**. Label and name these objects as shown in Table 6: Help system menu.

Table 6: Help system menu

Label	Name
~Help Index	miHelpIndex
~General Help	miHelpGeneral
~Using Help	miUsingHelp
~Keys Help	miKeysHelp
~Product Information	miProductInfo

 In order for **Help** to work you need to drop an **IHelpWindow** part on the free-form surface. There are no connections required to make the help object work, but some values need to be set in the **General** page of its settings notebook using the following steps:

- ❑ set Title to **Reminder Application**.
- ❑ set Help Libraries to **REMINDER.HLP**.
- ❑ If you are working in Windows, switch to the Styles page and set the **ipfCompatible** radio button to on.

Make the connections shown in Table 7: Help menu connections.

- ❑ Drop an **IMenuSeparator** part between the miKeysHelp and miProductInfo.

All of the connections for the menus are shown in Figure 128.

Table 7: Help menu connections

Source	Target
miHelpIndex(commandEvent)	helpWindow(showIndexHelp)
miHelpGeneral(commandEvent)	helpWindow(showGeneralHelp)
miUsingHelp(commandEvent)	helpWindow(showUsingHelp)
miKeysHelp(commandEvent)	helpWindow(showKeysHelp)

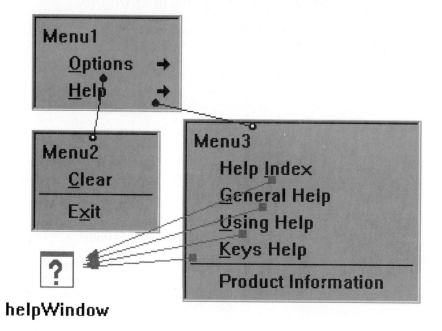

Figure 128: All menu connections

Product information window

In commercial applications it is customary to include a Product Information window, also known as the "About box". In this window the name and version of the application are shown. This is very useful information when updating or reporting a bug on the product. You will now build this window.

The Product Information window is called a **secondary window** as shown in Figure 129. Secondary windows may or may not be show during any one session while running the program. It is therefore good practice to dynamically create these windows as a result of some user initiated action like pressing a button or double-clicking on a list item. When secondary windows are used in this fashion, they are built as a separate reusable part and created on demand at runtime. Since this book has not yet covered how to dynamically create and al-

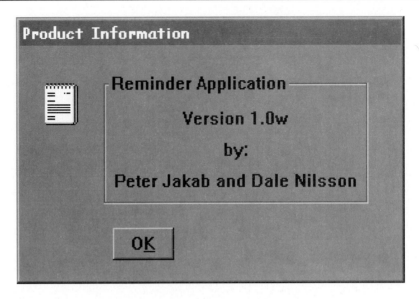

Figure 129: Product Information dialog

locate objects, you create the Product Information window using an alternate method. Implementing secondary windows with this alternate method imposes additional overhead on the application initialization. All the C++ classes, including the user interface parts, are instantiated when the application is started. Therefore, the secondary window is created and initialized before the main window is displayed.

Add the following user interface controls and name them appropriately:

- ❑ **IFrameWindow** part on the free-form surface near the main window. The position of the window in the Composition Editor is exactly where it appears at runtime. Make the subpart name for the part **frmProductInfo**. Directly edit the title bar to read **Product Information**.

- ❑ **IMultiCellCanvas** control inside the frame window.

- ❑ **ISetCanvas** control on cell 3,2 (row, column); subpart name is **scvIcon**.

- ❑ **ISetCanvas** control on cell 3,4; subpart name is **scvInfo**.

- ❑ **ISetCanvas** control on cell 5,4; subpart name is **scvButton**.

- ❑ **IIconControl** on scvIcon.

- ❑ Three **IStaticText** controls on scvInfo.

- ❑ **IPushButton** Control on **scvButton**. Name it **pbOK**.

The set canvas containing the three static text controls, **svcInfo**, needs to be set so that the text is distributed vertically and centered on the canvas.

❑ Open the settings notebook for the set canvas.

❑ Enter the settings in Table 8.

Table 8: scvInfo set canvas settings

Attribute	Setting
Deck Orientation	Horizontal
Pack Type	Pack Type
Text	Reminder Application
Deck Count	3
Alignment	center

In the Windows version, there is an easy way to name all the controls in one dialog box with the following steps:

❑ Select the **IMultiCellCanvas**, press the right mouse button and select **View Parts List**.

❑ Press the buttons with the + sign to expose the controls inside the set canvases.

❑ Now you can see all the parts and subparts on the multicell canvas.

You can now directly edit each of the labels, all in one place. On this screen you can also change the order of the controls within a part and open the settings notebook of any control. Use the names from Figure 130 as a guideline to naming your parts.

In OS/2, similar function is provided in the **Tabbing and depth order** dialog for the multicell canvas as shown in Figure 131. Unfortunately, direct editing of the subpart names is not supported in the current version, but should be available in the next version. Subpart names can be changed by selecting the part, bringing up the pop-up menu and selecting **Change Name...**.

❑ Double-click on the **IIconControl** to open its settings notebook.

❑ In the Bitmap group box enter **bitmaps** in the **DLL name** entry field and **7** in the **Resource id** entry field. This identifies the icon shown in Figure 129. This icon is also used as the icon on the system menu.

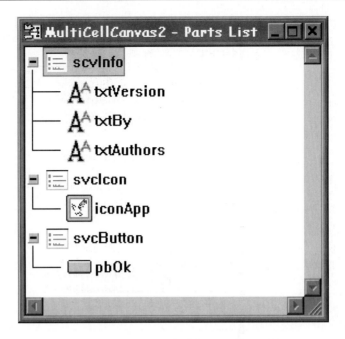

Figure 130: Windows version IMultiCellCanvas Parts List

❏ Connect:

free-form surface (ready) event → frmMainWindow (icon).

❏ Double-click the connection.

❏ Press the **Set parameters...** push button and enter the **DLL name** and **Resource id** information as you did previously.

The Product Information window needs to know who its owner is, because it needs to close when the main window closes. Connect:

❏ free-form surface(ready) → frmProductInfo(owner)

The above connection needs a parameter, connect:

❏ frmMainWindow(this) → connection (owner)

Directly edit the static text controls and the push button text to look like Figure 129.

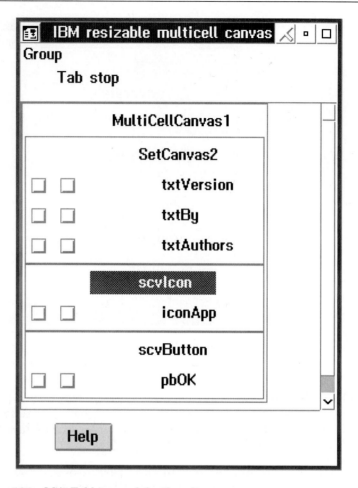

Figure 131: OS/2 Tabbing and depth order

To show the Product Information window when the **miProductInfo** menu item is selected, connect:

❑ miProductInfo (commandEvent) → frmProductInfo (visible)

❑ miProductInfo (commandEvent) → frmProductInfo (setFocus)

To cause the Product Information window to disappear when the **OK** button is pressed, connect:

❑ pbOk(buttonClickEvent) → frmProductInfo(hide)

❑ pbOk(buttonClickEvent) → frmMainWindow(setFocus)

Since you have created the Product Information window as part of the program main view, it is only created once when the program starts. The user must be prevented from closing this window, instead the user must hide the window. Closing the window destroys it and after that it can not be displayed anymore. To prevent the user from closing the window you must set the proper styles for this window and eliminate the system menu, the minimize, and maximize buttons on the frame window.

Open the settings notebook for the **frmProductInfo** window, select the Styles page. To make the window look like Figure 129 choose the Style settings in Table 9.

Table 9: Styles for Product Information window

Style	Setting
dialogBackground	On
dialogBorder	On
maximizeButton	Off
minimizeButton	Off
sizingBorder	Off
systemMenu	Off
visible	Off

Feel free to generate the code and compile the program at any time to ensure that you are getting the expected results or to try something different. Doing so often will expose any errors early enough to make it easier for you to find them.

When adding parts to the Composition Editor it is a good practice to also generate the **main() for part**, as doing so will include any dependencies on any new parts not previously accounted for.

Implementing a Pop-up Menu

The requirements statement indicates that a pop-up menu is needed to perform basic editing functions for the MLE. The Windows implementation of VisualAge for C++ includes this function as default behavior of the IMultiLineEdit part. In the OS/2 implementation, pop-up menus for MLEs have to be built manually. Therefore, if you are running on Windows you may skip this section.

In the pop-up menu you will implement the functions Cut, Copy, and Paste. Begin by dropping an **IMenu** part onto the free-form surface. Then, to build the pop-up menu, drop three **IMenuItem** parts onto the **IMenu** object you just added. From top to bottom name the menu item parts:

❑ Cut

❑ Copy

❑ Paste

You can either directly edit the text of the menu items or you can open their settings notebook and do it in the **General** page. You should also change the name of each menu item to something meaningful for example:

❑ miCut

❑ miCopy

❑ miPaste

Connecting the Reminder Pop-up Menu

It is very easy to implement the Cut, Copy, and Paste features because the **IMultiLineEdit** control comes with these actions predefined. All you need to do is connect the menu item's **commandEvent** to the appropriate MLE features:

❑ miCut (commandEvent) → mleReminder(cut)

❑ miCopy (commandEvent) → mleReminder(copy)

❑ miPaste (commandEvent) → mleReminder (paste)

The last connection associates the pop-up menu with the MLE:

❑ Menu4 (this) attribute → mleReminder(menu)

The completed pop-up menu is shown in Figure 132.

Using an IVBInfoArea

The **IVBInfoArea** control provides a display field to show help and information. The IVBInfoArea frame extension, which provides a dedicated area at the bottom of a frame window, looks like an entry field but occupies the whole width of the frame window. Drop an **IVBInfoArea** part on the frame window. Notice that you are only allowed to drop the part on the actual frame window, if you are having trouble finding a place to drop this part, drop it on the title bar.

The **IVBInfoArea** displays any **Fly over long text** that you have entered for any control on this frame window. In order to get this working you need to connect:

❑ flyOverHelp (longTextControl) → infoArea (this)

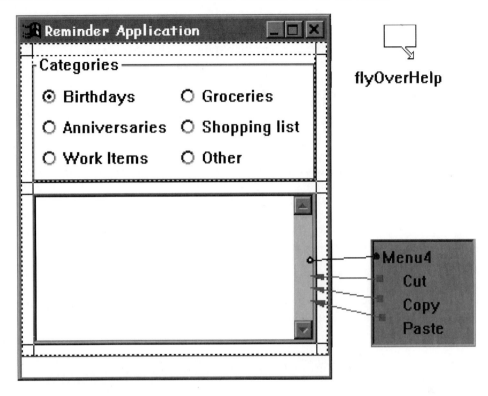

Figure 132: Pop-up menu for OS/2

You can display text in the **IInfoArea**, at runtime for each menu item. This text displays when the mouse pointer is over menu items and the right mouse button is pressed. Enter **Info area text** for any menu item on the **General** page of its settings notebook. Enter the **Info area text** as listed in Table 10.

Table 10: Menu item and info area text

Menu item	Info area text
Options	Clear the MLE and Exit the program
Clear	Clears the contents of the MLE
Exit	Terminates the program
Help	Invokes the Help system
Help Index	Show the index of the help file contents
General Help	Shows helps describing the program
Using Help	Shows information on how to use the Help facility
Keys Help	Shows how to use the keyboard in this program
Product Information	Show the Information or About box

Save and generate the source code for your application, compile and run the application. Figure 133 shows the application with the menu bar and long fly over text displaying in the **info area**.

Customizing the IMultiCellCanvas

You still need to set the **IMultiCellCanvas** options so that it expands and contracts at runtime as the frame window is sized. To get this behavior you need to set individual rows and/or columns in the **IMultiCellCanvas** as expandable. Open the settings notebook. Remember to do this you have to place the mouse pointer on a part of the **IMultiCellCanvas** which has no controls. If the mouse pointer is over any of the controls on the **IMultiCellCanvas**, you open the settings notebook for that control and not the **IMultiCellCanvas** as shown in Figure 134.

The settings notebook for the IMultiCellCanvas is very useful in changing how the canvas behaves. It is very productive to change the settings and press the Apply button, to see how the current settings affect the IMultiCellCanvas at runtime. On the notebook you can

Figure 133: Completed Reminder application user interface

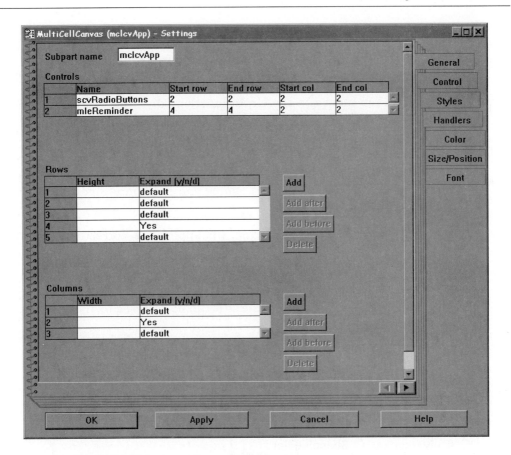

Figure 134: IMultiCellCanvas settings notebook

change the position of the controls and the amount of cells a control spans. You can also set which rows and/or columns expand.

If you are running on a low resolution screen, please note that this is a very large notebook and you need to use its scrollbars in order to reach all of its area.

If needed, refer to our paper design in Figure 116. On the General page in the **Row** table set the row that contains the MLE as expandable. This should be row number 4. In the **Column** table set the column that contains the MLE column to **Y**. This should be column 2.

It is always a good idea to leave an empty row at the top and bottom of the canvas and an empty column at the right and left of the canvas. If you place controls on the outer most rows or columns, these controls appear to touch the frame window at runtime.

Any excess rows or columns should be removed while the settings notebook is open. Do this by selecting them and pressing the delete button beside the Row and Column tables. Remember that if you accidentally delete too many rows or columns, you can use the **Edit**, **Undo** menu item in the Composition Editor to back out of your actions. You must run the **Undo** function only after you close the settings notebook. Remember that you can only change the multicell canvas in one place. You can change it in the settings notebook or the Composition Editor, but not in both at the same time.

Now the user interface is complete for the Reminder application. Save and generate the part source and run **nmake reminder.mak** to build the program.

As you can see in Figure 135, the application correctly resized the MLE when the frame window was stretched.

The user interface is finally finished. In the next section you will learn the Help file format and how to make changes to the file. You will also compile the Help file so it can be accessed by the application.

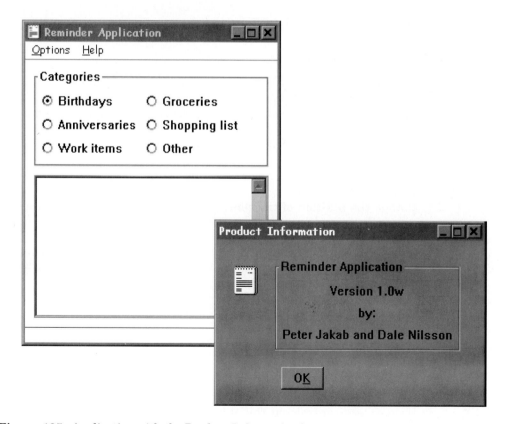

Figure 135: Application with the Product Information box

What Are Help files?

When you use VisualAge for C++ for Windows you have two choices for the format of your help file **IPF** (Information Processing Facility) and **RTF** (Rich Text Format). For OS/2 the choice is easy, it only supports **IPF**. If you are writing applications which need to run in both OS/2 and Windows you should use **IPF** for your help files, since this format is highly compatible between platforms. For this reason the application uses **IPF** as the help format.

The file REMINDER.IPF contains rudimentary help text and it gives you a good idea of the basics of developing Help for your applications.

```
:userdoc.
.*------------------------
:h1 res=200.REMINDER Application - Main Window Help
:i1.Main Window Help
:p.This is the help panel for the main window.
The main window contains the following areas:
:ul.
:li.The title bar icon, which provides access to the
system menu.
:li.The window title, which displays the title of the
window.
:li.The menu bar, which allows the user to select
specific actions.
:eul.
:p.Help is available for the following:
:ul.
:li.Items under :link reftype=hd
res=206.Options:elink. menu
:li.Reminder :link reftype=hd res=200.dialog box:elink
items .
:eul.
.*------------------------
:h1 res=204.MultiLineEdit field
:i1.Multi Line Edit field
:p.In this area you enter the reminder items
associated with the
currently selected radio button.
.*------------------------
:h1 res=205.Radio button help
:i1.Category Radio Buttons
:p.Use the Radio Buttons to select the Reminder
category you wish to see
reminder items for.
. . .
:euserdoc.
```

Code Segment 21: Excerpt of the REMINDER.IPF file

The content of the **.IPF** file is written using a tagged scripting language which is fully described in the on-line guide *IPF User's Guide*. For more information about how to enable your application for Help, consult the *IPF Programmer's Guide* also available on-line.

Feel free to modify the REMINDER.IPF file supplied on the CD-ROM to your liking. As you can see, the basics are very simple. The document starts with a **:userdoc.** tag and ends with an **:euserdoc.** tag. Sections begin with the **:h1.** or heading 1 tag. These sections correspond to areas in your program for which you are supplying Help. The headings are tied to the program by the **:res=xxxx.** tag where **xxxx** is the number you entered in the Control page of the settings notebook for that particular part, thus the line:

```
:h1 res=200.REMINDER Application - Main Window Help
```

This line means "start a new heading, associate it with the part or control which has **200** as the Help id and label this entry **REMINDER Application - Main Window Help.**"

Unnumbered lists start and end with **:ul.** and **:eul.** respectively. Numbered (or ordered) lists start and end with **:ol.** and **:eol.** respectively. List items are tagged with **:li.**.

Hot links to other parts of the IPF document can appear pretty well anywhere in the text and are tagged with **:link reftype=hd res=xxxx**. Where **xxxx** is the resource id of a heading in the document. Text can follow the **res=xxxx** tag. The **:link.** tag needs a corresponding **:elink.** tag.

Compiling a Help File

Help files need to be compiled by the Help compiler **IPFC**. The compiler can be executed from a command prompt or from within a make file. In the Windows version, **IPFC** is a Windows application and when it is called from a make file, **IPFC** starts the compiler and messages are shown inside the compiler's window. This window remains open until you select **File**, **Exit** or press F3 to close it. This is not the behavior you want from a make file, because execution of the make file is suspended until the **IPFC** window is closed. To prevent this behavior when running a make file in Windows, always run **IPFC** with the **/Q** (for quiet) flag. Edit the REMINDER.MAK file to include the compilation of the help file.

❑ Open the make file in a text editor.

❑ Change the following line in the make file:

```
Reminder: $(VBEXE)Reminder.exe
```

to

```
Reminder: $(VBEXE)Reminder.exe $(VBEXE)Reminder.hlp
```

❑ Then add Code Segment 22 at the end of the file.

```
$(VBEXE)Reminder.hlp: $(VBEXE)Reminder.ipf
        ipfc /q $(VBEXE)Reminder.ipf
```

Code Segment 22: Changes to Windows make file

In OS/2 the changes are similar:

❑ Change the following line in the make file:

```
all:   Reminder
```

to

```
all:   Reminder Reminder.hlp
```

❑ Then add Code segment 23 at the end of the file.

```
reminder.hlp: reminder.ipf
        ipfc reminder.ipf /x
```

Code segment 23: Changes to OS/2 make file

In the next chapter you will add some nonvisual parts to this application. This requires you to regenerate the **main**() for the program.
Whenever you select Generate **main**() the Visual Builder also generates a new make file if it is needed. Adding nonvisual parts to an application almost always causes the make file to be regenerated. When
the make file is regenerated the old make file is gone, and you have to
enter the changes to compile the Help file again.

Testing Application Help

Compile the Reminder application by running **nmake reminder.mak**
from a command prompt. As the make file messages display, see how
the REMINDER.IPF file gets compiled into REMINDER.HLP.

When running the application, it looks like Figure 136. From the
menu bar, select **Help**, **General Help**. The window showing the contents of res=200 displays. **General Help** is the **Help** associated with

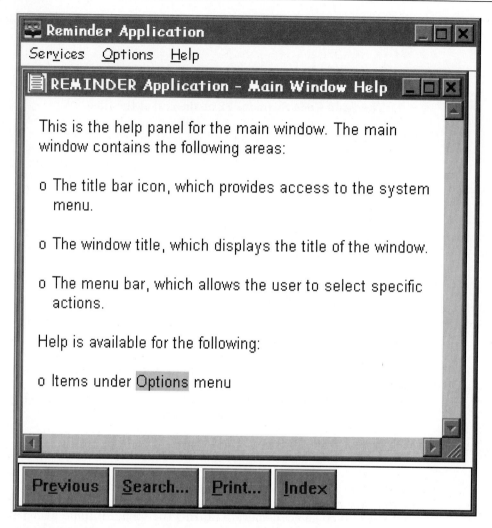

Figure 136: General Help for the Reminder application

the frame window. As you remember, Help id 200 is entered on the Control page of the settings notebook for **frmMainWindow**.

Try the other help items and compare the **Help** window contents with what is in the **IPF** file. When you are done viewing the help system, close the application.

Adding Keys Help

There is only one Help function left that needs to be completed for the Help System, the **Keys Help**. In order for **Keys Help** to work you need two elements:

1. Text for **Keys Help** must be included in the IPF file, with an id assigned.

2. The frame window needs a **Help handler**.

The implementation of **Keys Help** is a bit different than that of the other help items, such as the **General Help**. For the other items you just make the appropriate connection and the help works. The text for Keys Help is in your IPF file. You could have given it any id you wanted. This raises a question: How does the help system know the resource id of the item in the IPF file which describes the Keys Help item? The answer lies in the mechanism invoked by the help system when a request for **Keys Help** is received. When the user selects **Keys Help** an appropriate message is sent from the help window to the help system. The help system responds by sending a message back to the frame window which initiated the request. This message requests the **resource id** in the **.IPF** file for the Keys Help item.

Defining a Help Handler

If you do nothing to intercept this message, no help is displayed when you select this item from the help menu. To be able to act on this request from the help system you must attach a **HelpHandler** to the main frame window. This handler intercepts the request for the resource id and supplies the id number in the **.IPF** file corresponding to the Keys Help item. The complete code for the **Help-Handler** as it exists in the HELPHDR.HPP file is listed in the code in Code segment 24.

The help handler derives from the **IHelpHandler** class supplied as part of the Open Class Library. The member function keysHelpId (IEvent& event) is a protected member of IHelpHandler and is overridden in the derived class HelpHandler. The resource id for the section which contains the Keys Help in the .IPF file is used to set the result of the event, which is passed to the member function. This value comes from the integer constant helpForKeysId. Returning true from the function indicates that the event was handled by this handler and requires no further processing.

Importing a Handler

Before this handler can be used in the Visual Builder it needs to be made known to the Visual Builder's model. This is accomplished by creating a Visual Builder export file which describes the class. These files are known as .VBE files.

The format of .VBE files is fully described in the on-line document called *Building VisualAge C++ Parts for Fun and Profit*. The VBE file for the HelpHandler class is shown in Code Segment 25.

```
//*************************************************
*
// FILE NAME: HELPHDR.HPP
// Copyright (C) 1996, Peter M. Jakab
// All Rights Reserved.
//*************************************************
*
#ifndef _HELPHANDLER_
#define _HELPHANDLER_

#include "IHelphdr.hpp"
const int helpForKeysId = 9999; // IPF file ID
class HelpHandler : public IHelpHandler
{
protected:
   virtual Boolean keysHelpId ( IEvent& event )
   {
      event.setResult( helpForKeysId );// IPF file ID
      return true;
   }
};
#endif
```

Code segment 24: Help handler code in HLPHDR.HPP

```
//VBBeginPartInfo: HelpHandler
//VBParent: IHelpHandler
//VBIncludes: helphdr.hpp _HELPHANDLER_
//VBPartDataFile: 'helphdr.vbb'
//VBComposerInfo: class,204,dde4vr30
//VBEndPartInfo: HelpHandler
```

Code Segment 25: HELHHDR.VBE file

Once you have the .VBE file you need to import it into the Visual Builder. To import a part into the Visual Builder:

❑ Switch to the main Visual Builder window.

❑ Select **File, Import part information**.

❑ Select HELPHDR.VBE from the file selection dialog and press **OK**.

The Visual Builder reads and interprets the .VBE file and creates the binary file HELPHDR.VBB. The VBE is only used one time, and you should use the VBB part file whenever you need this of handler in the future.

❑ If the Composition Editor for the Reminder visual part is not open, open it now.

❑ Double-click on the **frmMainWindow** object to open its settings notebook.

❑ Turn to the **Handlers** page, enter **HelpHandler** and press **Add after**.

❑ Press **OK** to save.

These steps outlined above are used to bring classes into the Visual Builder which were created outside of the Visual Builder environment. These classes could be existing classes that you previously wrote and want to use in your application. Once these classes are imported they are available just like any other part. They can be dropped on the free-form surface and used in making connections to other parts.

Generate the **Part source**, compile, and test the program to make sure that **Keys Help** works.

Automatic Loading of VBB Files

Whenever you start the Visual Builder the VBBASE.VBB file is loaded. This file contains the base parts supporting the Open Class Library.

As you start building more complex applications you will need to load your own VBB files, which will contain the parts needed for the application you are building. For example, the file HELPHDR.VBB must be loaded every time you work with the Reminder application.

Of course, you can load the required VBB files by hand every time you start the Visual Builder. However, as you work with parts which require four, five or more VBB files to be loaded, doing it by hand can be time consuming and error prone.

When the Visual Builder starts it looks for a file named VBLOAD. DAT in the directory from which the Visual Builder was started. If it is not found there, it looks in the directories listed in Table 11.

Table 11: Default directory for VBLOAD.DAT

Operating System	Directory
Windows	x:\ibmcppw\ivb
OS/2	x:\ibmcpp\dde4vb

This file is created by you and contains the fully qualified path of the VBB files you want loaded when the Visual Builder starts. See Code segment 26 for an example which could be used in this chapter.

```
X:\VABOOK\reminder\reminder.vbb
X:\VABOOK\reminder\helphdr.vbb
```

Code segment 26: Contents of the VBLOAD.DAT file

Of course, your file will have the correct path to point to the files in your system.

If you are working with multiple projects, you might want to have a VBLOAD.DAT file in each of the directories containing the files for the project. In the Windows version you would then start the Visual Builder from that directory by typing IVB from a command session in that directory. In OS/2 you can start the Visual Builder by entering ICSVB.

If you are only working on one project at a time you can place the VBLOAD.DAT file in the directory mentioned in Table 11.

Chapter 7—Summary

In this chapter you have learned to use a number of new user interface components. You started to build the Reminder List application and learned how to:

❑ Make menu bars

❑ Create submenus

❑ Create Pop-Up menus

❑ Use the IMultiCellCanvas and the SetCanvas

❑ Use radio button clusters

❑ Use the IMultiLineEdit control

❑ Add Help to an application

❑ Add a handler to handle Keys Help

❑ Use an Information Area

❑ Use Long Fly Over text

❑ Use the VBLOAD.DAT file to preload the Visual Builder with the required .VBB files.

What's in Chapter 8

In this chapter you will complete the Reminder application by adding the logic to make the application work as specified. The logic is provided through the use of nonvisual parts. The major activities in this chapter are:

❏ Creating a part which manages a group of radio buttons called RBMgr

❏ Using an instance of IProfile which is part A in the Open Class Library.

8

Completing the Reminder List

In this chapter you complete the Reminder List application by adding the logic to the application using nonvisual parts.

The Reminder Application Reviewed

Let us review what you have built in the previous chapter and consider what still needs to be done to complete the application. You have constructed the visual component of the Reminder application. It is a very complete and fairly complex user interface. It includes a multicell canvas which will allow the multiple line entry field contained in the canvas to expand and contract as the main frame window is resized by the user. There is a set, or cluster, of radio buttons contained in a set canvas. You learned how the set canvas distributes and aligns the controls it holds.

There is a menu bar on the main window that holds drop down menus which allow the user to perform several functions including:

- Clearing the MLE

- Terminating the program
- Invoking the Help subsystem

You implemented a complete and fully functional Help submenu system which interfaces with the REMINDER.HLP file. Finally, you implemented an info area at the bottom of the main window to display menu help and long fly over text. If you are building on OS/2, you added a pop-up menu to the MLE.

This is quite an accomplishment, but the application still does not perform as specified in the requirements. To compete this application you need to provide the logic which acts upon user requests and the logic which saves the reminder information entered by the user.

Understanding the Requirements

The following is a list of expected actions for the Reminder List application which you need to understand before developing the rest of the application.

1. When the user selects a radio button the information related to that selection is displayed on the MLE.
2. The user can change this information and it is automatically saved by the program .
3. When the program starts, the first reminder category is selected, and the text associated with that category is displayed in the MLE.
4. As new categories are selected, their text is displayed in the MLE.
5. When the program ends, the information in the MLE at the time is associated with the currently selected category and saved.

At first glance it sounds pretty difficult, but by breaking down the development into individual steps it is simple to implement. For example:

1. Detect that a radio button was selected.
2. Get the text associated with that button.
3. Display it on the MLE.

That is simple enough, you should be able to do it without any custom nonvisual parts. You can, but what about the text displayed before the radio button was selected which belongs to another category? It needs to be saved under that category before the text for the newly selected radio button is retrieved and placed in the MLE. The application needs a nonvisual part that knows which radio button is currently pressed and which radio button was previously pressed.

As you start building nonvisual parts you should think of yourself as a parts builder, not an application developer. The problem this application solves is not unique. Therefore, the solution should be general enough so that you can use the components to solve a similar problem in a different application. If you do this, you are on your way to producing parts that are not only reusable, but parts that are actually reused in other applications.

Building the Radio Button Manager Nonvisual Part

The nonvisual part that knows the radio button states should:

1. Know how to deal with radio button clusters in general.

2. Know the index of the current button.

3. Remember the index of the previous button.

4. Generate events to let the users of the part know that the selection has changed.

The user can decide the action to perform when the radio button selection changes.

This part should not know that the text in the MLE is associated with the **previousButton**, or that this text needs to be stored before the text associated with the **currentButton** is retrieved and displayed in the MLE. It certainly should not know where the data is kept and how to store and retrieve the data; that is the responsibility of another part.

Now you are ready to design and build the **RBMgr** part which manages a cluster of radio buttons. First let's look at the features of the part listed in Table 12 through Table 15. Next, define the part using the Visual Builder and code the necessary logic by editing the stub files produced by the Visual Builder.

Table 12: Attributes of the RBMgr part

Attribute	Explanation
long currentButton	The zero based index of the button that is currently pressed.
long previousButton	The zero based index of the button that was pressed before the current button.
IString currentButtonAsString	An IString representation of the current-Button attribute to be used as a **key** with the **IProfile** part.
IString previousButtonAsString	An IString representation of the previous-Button attribute to be used as a **key** with the **IProfile** part.

Table 13: Actions of the RBMgr part

Actions	Explanation
RBMgr& startHandlingEvents()	Must be invoked before the part starts functioning. Wait until the view is constructed before issuing to avoid extraneous events.

Table 14: Events generated by the RBMgr part

Events	Occurs
currentButton	When the currentButton attribute changes.
previousButton	When the previousButton attribute changes.

Table 15: Implementation details for the Reminder Application

Implementation	Details
rbmgr.hpp and .cpp	Contain the skeleton for the part as generated by the PIE.
rbmgr.hpv and .cpv Usage notes for the Reminder application	Contain the actual part/class implementation. ❑ The startHandlingEvents action is needed to activate the part after the Reminder Canvas has been constructed. ❑ When the previousButton event occurs, it is time to store the MLE contents. ❑ When the currentButton event occurs, it is time to retrieve the data and place it in the MLE.

As you can see, this part is defined in terms of its attributes, actions and events. These represent the public interface of a part and are defined on the pages on the Part Interface Editor (PIE). By looking at the part description you see that two attributes are required, **previousButton** and **currentButton** . These attributes are available in numeric (long) and string (IString) representations. They generate events as their values change. Start building the **RBMgr** nonvisual part.

❑ If the Visual Builder is not already running, start the Visual Builder.

❑ Ensure the working directory is set to **x:\VABOOK\RE-MINDER**.

❑ From the Parts Selector, click the right mouse button on the Nonvisual Parts list box and select **New**. This is equivalent to selecting **Part**, **New** from the main menu, except this action assumes you want to create a new nonvisual part.

❑ Create a new nonvisual part called **RBMgr** as shown in Figure 137.

❑ Enter a description so people using this part have an idea of what this part does. For example **Radio button manager**.

❑ Enter **Reminder** as the **File name** to keep all parts for this application in the same file.

❑ The **Base class** is **IStandardNotifier** which is the base class for all nonvisual parts.

❑ Press the **Open** button to create the **RBMgr** part.

The Part Interface Editor opens and you can start defining the public interface of the part. Use Table 12 and Table 13 for the information needed to enter the attributes and the actions for this part. The only events required for this part are automatically generated when you define the long previousButton and currentButton attributes. Figure 138 shows these attributes listed in the PIE.

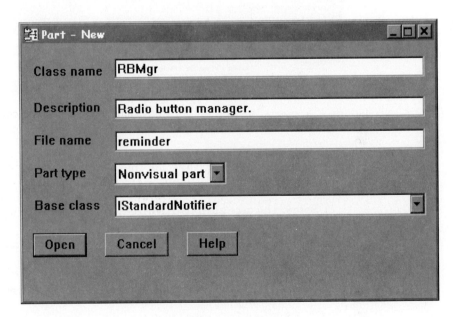

Figure 137: Creating the RBMgr nonvisual part

Defining the Attributes

The attributes **previousButtonAsString** and **currentButtonAs String** are read only, which means they cannot be set externally. It makes perfect sense to delete the **Set member function** from the PIE for these two attributes. By deleting these functions you reduce the amount of C++ code generated for the part and thus the size of

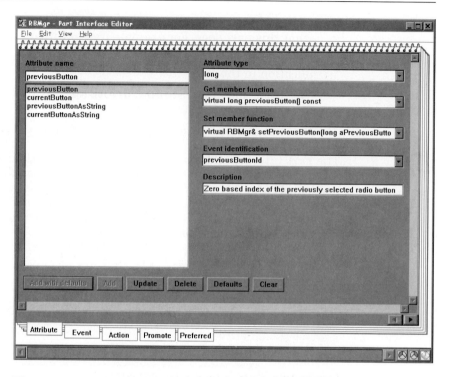

Figure 138: Attributes for the RBMgr part

the application. The strings for these attributes are constructed at runtime from the long attributes of the same name.

❏ Select the **previousButtonAsString** attribute which displays its **get** and **set** functions.

❏ Clear the contents of the **Set member function** field.

❏ Select the **Update** push button to change the part definition.

❏ Repeat these steps with the **currentButtonAsString** attribute.

Defining the Actions

Now you are ready to enter the actions for the part:

❏ Select the **Action** page of the PIE.

❏ Enter the definitions of the **startHandlingEvents** action as shown in Figure 139. The return type is **RBMgr&** and the function takes no parameters.

❏ Enter a description for this action which users of this part should understand.

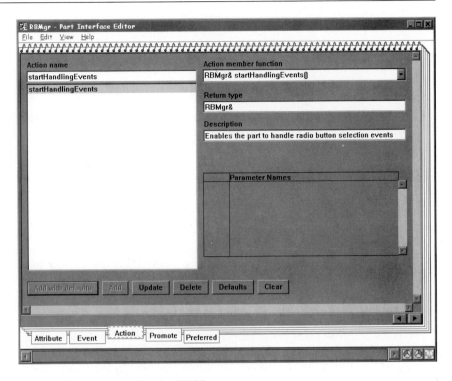

Figure 139: Actions for the RBMgr part

❑ Turn to the **Preferred** page of the PIE, and add the attributes and action you have just defined to the Preferred list. These appear on the pop-up menu which makes it easier to make connections.

❑ Save and generate the **Part Source**.

❑ Switch to the **Class editor** by pressing the middle button at the bottom right of the PIE, or by selecting **View**, **Class Editor** from the menu bar.

❑ Enter the name of the **User .hpv** and **User .cpv** files. Use the names **RBMGR.HPV** and **RBMGR.CPV** respectively.

❑ Generate the **Feature source** code for the part by selecting **File**, **Save and Generate**, **Feature source...**. Since this is the first time you generate the Feature source, select the **Generate all** button.

You just created six files in your working directory and they are:

1. RBMGR.CPP

2. RBMGR.HPP

3. RBMGR.H

4. RBMGR.RCI

5. RBMGR.CPV

6. RBMGR.HPV

The first four files were created as a result of the **File, Save and Generate**, **Part source** action and they are completely replaced, without warning, any time you generate the **Part source**. The last two files were created as a result of the **File, Save and Generate, Feature source...** action. Any subsequent time you generate the Feature source the Visual Builder appends the generated code to the existing .HPV and .CPV files. This can be good and bad news. The good news is that you can add C++ code to these generated files and re-generating does not destroy your work. The bad news is that if you regenerate code already in these files you end up with duplicate code and the compiler complains. This can be fixed by editing the generated files and removing any duplication. The way to prevent this from happening is to only select **Generate all** the first time you generate feature code. From then on, when you generate **Feature source**, you should not press the **Generate all** button, but instead carefully select any new feature(s) and then press the **Generate selected** button instead.

Adding User Code

Now comes the fun part, editing the feature source files to add the part logic. Start with the **RBMGR.HPV** file. You need a private data member to keep a state which remembers whether the part has been initialized by the **startHandlingEvents()** action.

❑ Edit the **RBMGR.HPV** file and add the following statements after the last line in the file:

```
// Code not generated by the Visual Builder
Boolean bStarted;
```

❑ Save and close the file.

You have to make sure that this variable is initialized to false.

❑ In the Class editor enter **bStarted=false;** in the **User constructor code** entry field. Save and generate the Part source.

❑ Edit **RBMGR.CPV**. This file contains the stubs for all the Feature source generated.

You need to make a few changes to the logic required to make the part work. Begin with the **startHandlingEvents** action. This action is called once when the program starts. The **ready** event is used to initiate the call. The responsibility of **startHandlingEvents** is to initialize the class variables and to set the **bStarted** flag to true. The instance variable **iPreviousButton** is initialized to −1 indicating that there was no previous selection. The finished code looks like Code segment 27.

```
RBMgr& RBMgr::startHandlingEvents()
{
  iPreviousButton = -1;
  iCurrentButton  =  0;
  bStarted = true;
  return *this;
}
```

Code segment 27: Completed startHandlingEvents action

When the user selects a radio button you need to update the **current Button** attribute in your part. However, before you can do that you need to copy the present value of **currentButton** to the **previous Button** attribute and generate the proper events in the right sequence:

1. The previousButtonId event
2. The currentButtonId event

Refer to Code segment 28 and Code segment 29 to see how to code this correctly.

```
RBMgr& RBMgr::setCurrentButton(long
      aCurrentButton)
{
  if (!(iCurrentButton == aCurrentButton))
  {
    if( bStarted )
    {
      setPreviousButton( iCurrentButton );
      iCurrentButton = aCurrentButton;
      notifyObservers(INotificationEvent(
          RBMgr::currentButtonId, *this));
    }
  } // endif
  return *this;
}
```

Code segment 28: Code for setCurrentButton function

```
RBMgr& RBMgr::setPreviousButton(long
    aPreviousButton)
{
  if (!(iPreviousButton == aPreviousButton))
  {
    if( bStarted )
    {
      iPreviousButton = aPreviousButton;
      notifyObservers(INotificationEvent
          RBMgr::previousButtonId, *this));
    } /* endif */
  } // endif
  return *this;
}
```

Code segment 29: Code for setPreviousButton function

How the Radio Button Manager Works

First, the setCurrentButton member function checks to see if the new value, aCurrentButton, is different than the value in the instance variable iCurrentButton. If it is different, the function checks to see if the part has been started. If the part has indeed been started, the function calls setPreviousButton and passes as a parameter the value of iCurrentButton. The function setPreviousButton does some validation similar to setCurrentButton and if all is fine, assigns the value passed to the instance variable iPreviousButton, and sends a notification that the attribute changed by issuing the **notifyObservers** function call. This gives the program an opportunity to act on the fact that iPreviousButton has changed.

Notifications are handled synchronously, so any processing in the part waits until any other part interested in this event has acted upon it.

The function setPreviousButton returns to setCurrentButton, the new value held in aCurrentButton is assigned to iCurrentButton, and a notification is sent to inform interested parties that the value of currentButton has changed.

The previousButtonAsString and currentButtonAsString member functions simply create and return a temporary **IString** using the value of the corresponding long instance variable. See Code segment 30.

Since temporary variables are used and there is no set member function for these attributes (because they are read only), you can delete the declarations for iCurrentButtonAsString and **iPrevious Button AsString** in the RBMGR.HPV file. Delete the following:

❑ IString iPreviousButtonAsString;

❑ IString iCurrentButtonAsString;

Now you have a mechanism for detecting the selection of a radio button and signaling the appropriate events in the right sequence.

```
IString RBMgr::previousButtonAsString() const
{
   return IString (iPreviousButton);
}

IString RBMgr::currentButtonAsString() const
{
   return IString (iCurrentButton);
}
```

Code segment 30: Return current and previous button value

Using Persistent Data

The next part you need must be able to store and retrieve data. The information stored by this application is organized so that there is some data stored for each category. As a category is selected, the data for that category is accessed. A data structure which uses a key to access data is called a *map* or *dictionary*. In these data structures you have an association between a key (the selected radio button) and the data (the text in the MLE).

Fortunately, both Windows and OS/2 have a way to store this type of data structure. In Windows it is called the **Registry**, and in OS/2 it is called an **.INI** file. The Open Class Library implements access to both these type of files in a single class called **IProfile**. The IProfile class provides an operating system independent way to access persistent data commonly associated with applications.

Using the IProfile Class

There are two actions or member functions you use to get the data in and out of the file:

1. virtual IString elementWithKey(const char* key, const char* applName = 0)

2. virtual IProfile& addOrReplaceElementWithKey(const char* key, IString& data, const char* applName = 0)

Both of these functions take an application name as the last parameter. This is an optional parameter and you supply it directly to the object in the setting notebook of an **IProfile*** object in the Composition Editor. The first member function retrieves an **IString** when provided with a key and throws an exception if the key or the data for the key could not be found. The second function stores a data element, represented in an **IString** object in the location specified by the key.

The **IProfile** class requires the name of the file to be passed in the constructor of the class. This name can be entered right in the settings notebook of the **IProfile** object on the Composition Editor.

- ❏ Open the Composition Editor for the Reminder part.
- ❏ To add a part which is not on the palette, select **Options, Add part...** the **Add part** dialog opens as seen in Figure 140.
- ❏ Enter **IProfile*** as the **Part class** entry field and **reminder-Data** in the **Name** entry field; ensure that the **Part** radio button is selected.
- ❏ Press the **Add** push button and drop the part on the Composition Editor.
- ❏ Using the same steps, add an **RBMgr*** part to the free-form surface.
- ❏ Name this part **rbManager**. Figure 141 shows the Reminder application with the two nonvisual parts.

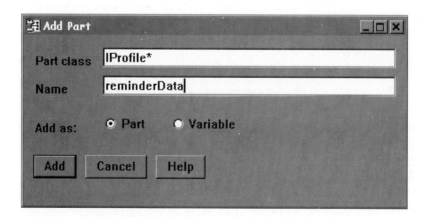

Figure 140: Add part dialog box

IProfile Settings

In order to improve the legibility and clarity of the figures representing screens, only the parts and connections currently being discussed are shown. However, be aware that no parts have been removed from the Composition Editor.

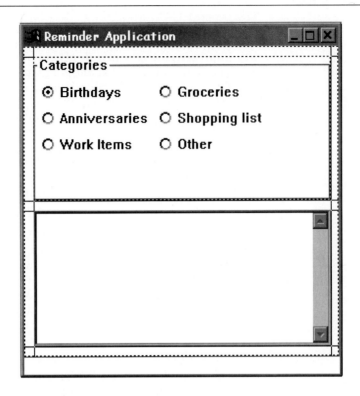

rbManager   reminderData

Figure 141: IProfile* and RBMgr* parts added

❏ Double-click on the **reminderData** part to open its settings notebook.

❏ Enter REMINDERS in the **defaultApplicationName** entry field. This name is used as the application name under RE-MINDER.INI to further identify the data from this application.

❏ Enter **REMINDER.INI** in the **name** entry field. This is the name which is used in the Windows Registry as the main key. In OS/2 it is used as the name of the .INI file.

❏ Press the **OK** button to save the changes.

From the requirements statement you know that when the program starts, the first radio button is selected and the data associated with that category is displayed in the MLE. As you remember, the **ready** event occurs after the part has been constructed and initialized, and before it becomes visible. This event only happens once. You can use the **ready** event to tell the **reminderData** object to retrieve the data element associated with the first radio button, which is radio button number 0. The radio button number is used as the key into the database. The term *database* is used loosely here, as neither the Windows Registry nor an INI file constitute a true database. Make the following connection:

❏ free-form (ready) event → reminderData (elementWithKey)

This is an incomplete connection as indicated by a dashed line. It needs a parameter and that parameter is the key to the data. For this connection the key is always 0.

Double-click on the connection to open its settings notebook. Note that when trying to open a connection you must take care not to double-click on the black handles of a selected connection, because the Visual Builder thinks you want to change the shape of the connection by dragging the handles. Double-click somewhere else along the line of the connection.

❏ Press the **Set parameters...** button.
❏ In the **key** entry field enter **0**. The **applName** parameter is not needed since you have already supplied a **defaultApplication-Name** which is used whenever an **applName** is required.
❏ Press **OK** in both dialogs to save.

From the function prototype, this function returns an **IString** containing the data associated with the key. In order to get the data into the MLE start the connection by:

❏ Select the connection

free-form (ready) → reminderData (elementWithKey)

❏ Right mouse click and connect

actionResult → mleReminder(text)

You also use the **ready** event to start the **rbManager** part. Connect:

❏ free-form(ready) → rbManager(startHandlingEvents)

These connections for the Reminder application are shown in Figure 142.

When a radio button is selected, the first thing you need to do is save the text in the MLE. This text is associated with the **previous-Button** attribute. As you recall from Code segment 29, selecting a new category causes two events to occur. First a **previousButton** event and then a **currentButton** event occurs. The **previousButton** event can be used to save the text currently in the MLE before it changes. The **currentButton** event can be used to retrieve the data associated with the button just pressed and put into the MLE.

As you have seen, there is more to a connection than just a line from source to target. Connections can also be made to:

❑ Pass parameters

❑ Catch exceptions

❑ Retrieve return values from an action

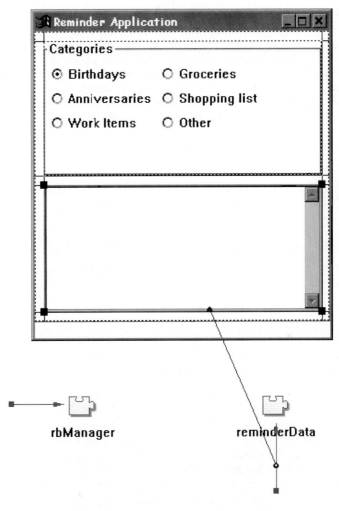

Figure 142: Both ready connections complete

When you press the right mouse button on a connection, a pop-up menu appears, much like the Preferred list for a part. This menu has the appropriate elements for this particular connection. When you are instructed to pass a parameter or retrieve a return value, you need to select the pop-up menu for the connection and go from there. You have already done this when you caught the divide by zero exception thrown by the Calculator application.

Overlapping Connections

If you are using the OS/2 version, very often when you connect a parameter to a connection, the line depicting the parameter is placed on top of the connection. If you made a mistake and you need to change or remove the parameter, it is almost impossible to select it once it has been placed. Most of the time you end up deleting the whole connection and starting over. If you are patient and have a steady pulse there is a way to separate the two lines using the following steps:

❑ Select the connection.

❑ Move the midpoint of the connection by dragging it to a point where the connection segment containing both the connection and the parameter is either perfectly horizontal or vertical.

❑ The lines separate.

Setting the IProfile Key

Let's continue building the application by connecting:

❑ rbManager (previousButton) → reminderData (addOrReplace-ElementWithKey)

❑ Parameters:

❑ rbManager (previousButtonAsString) → connection (key)

❑ mleReminder (text) → connection (data)

❑ rbManager (currentButton) → reminderData (elementWithKey)

Parameter:

❑ rbManager(currentButtonAsString) → connection(key)

Return value:

❑ connection (actionResult) → mleReminder (text)

Exception handling:

connection (exceptionOcurred) → mleReminder (removeAll)

If the key requested does not exist, or if there is no data for the particular key requested, the member function throws an exception. The application needs to catch the exception and clear the MLE contents, because there is no data for the selected category. The connection above takes care of that.

In order for the application to work, the **rbManager** object needs to know when a radio button gets selected. Connect:

❏ rbBirthdays (selected) event → rbManager (currentButton)

Parameter:

❏ rbBirthdays (selectedIndex) → connection (aCurrentButton)

Make sure you connect to the **selected** event, not the **selected** attribute. You should use the complete action, attribute, event list. The Preferred list provides the **selected attribute**, to get to the **selected** event you choose **More...** from the preferred list and then select **selected** from the **events** list box as shown in Figure 143 on page 228.

The next connection saves the text in the MLE when the program closes. Connect:

❏ frmMainWindow (closeEvent) → reminderData (addOrReplace-ElementWithKey)

Parameters:

❏ rbManager (currentButtonAsString) → connection (key)
❏ mleReminder(text) → connection(data)

Figure 144 on page 229 shows the Reminder application with the connections as it should appear at this point.

Compiling and Running

Save and generate the **Part source** and the **main() for part** for the application. Remember that generating the main() regenerates the make file, and you need to redo the changes to the make file to include the compilation of the Help file, refer to the previous chapter for details. In any case, you do not need to do this right away as the Help file should still be in good shape from the last time it was compiled.

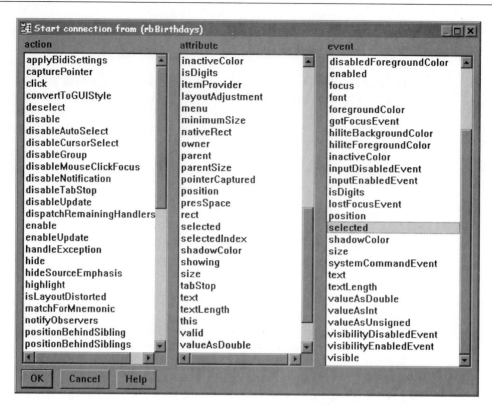

Figure 143: Selected event, not selected attribute

At a command prompt enter **nmake reminder.mak** to recompile the application. If you did not make any mistakes in the RBMGR user files the compilation should complete. Try running the completed application.

If you get errors from the compiler, make sure that all of the required files were loaded in the Visual Builder at the time you generated the code. It is possible that when you generated the code, the HELPHDR.VBB file was not loaded at that time. This is a common mistake, especially if you closed the Visual Builder after you finished the last example. The Visual Builder does not remember what files are needed for a specific project, so you must.

Testing the Reminder Application

The first time you run the program the main window should display with the first radio button selected and the MLE should be empty. Enter some text in the MLE and select a different radio button. Again, the MLE should be empty. Type a reminder for this category.

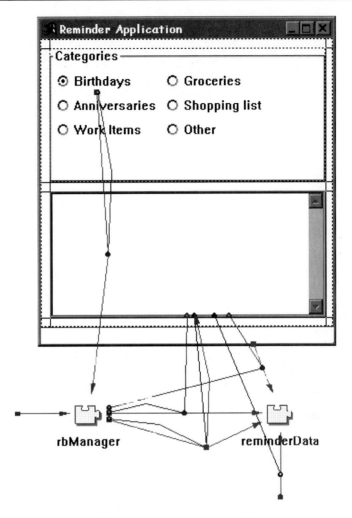

Figure 144: Completed data management connections

Now press the button for the first category and the text you typed initially should be in the MLE.

Exit the program and start it again. This time the first category is selected, and the text you previously entered the last time the application ran is in the MLE.

Continue testing by entering some real data for each category, exiting the program, and restarting it again. Whatever you entered should be saved. Verify that the user interface is still working properly and that the Help system works correctly.

Peeking into the Windows Registry

You may be interested in understanding how the data is being stored in the Windows Registry or the OS/2 INI file. First let's look at the Registry. Windows 95 comes with a utility called REGEDIT.EXE. This utility can be used to browse and edit the Windows Registry.

Extreme care should be taken when using this utility because you can accidentally corrupt the registry in such a way that Windows no longer starts. If you feel brave, start **REGEDIT**, select **Edit**, **Find**, and search for **REMINDER.INI**. If you have already run the program you should find an entry in the registry.

As you can see in Figure 145, REMINDER.INI contains REMINDERS which contains keys **0** to **5**, corresponding to the reminder categories represented by each of the radio buttons. In the window on the right, you can see the details and contents of each category. You can experiment by pressing the right mouse button on the entries for REMINDER.INI to see what can be done.

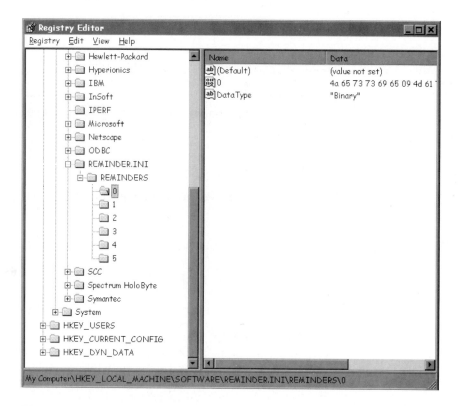

Figure 145: Windows Registry

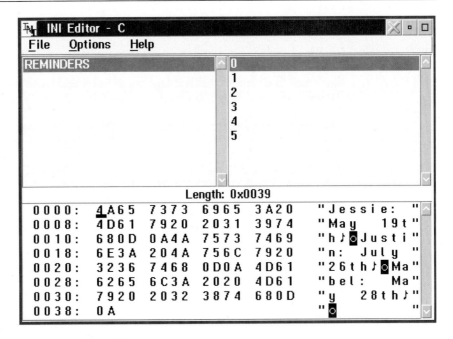

Figure 146: REMINDER.INI in INIE

Peeking into the OS/2 REMINDER.INI File

The OS/2 operating system does not provide you with any tools to peek into an .INI file. A utility called **INIE** is supplied on the CD-ROM with this book for this purpose. It can be found in the x:\VABOOK\TOOLS directory, where x: is the installation drive.

Start the INI editor by entering **INIE** at an OS/2 command prompt. At a command prompt, in the directory where REMINDER.INI can be found, enter **inie reminder.ini**. This is shown in Figure 146.

Chapter 8—Summary

You completed another fairly complex application. The Reminder List has a good combination of visual and nonvisual parts. In this chapter you:

❑ Completed the Reminder Application.

❑ Added the application logic by creating the RBMgr nonvisual part and combined it with the Open Class Library part IProfile.

❑ Ran the Reminder application which saved persistent data.

❑ Inspected the Windows Registry or OS/2 INI file.

What's in Chapter 9

In this chapter you develop a new application for calculating the status of a car lease. This application calculates the remaining miles on the lease, indicates whether the car has been driven too far, and any charge for extra usage. To do this you will:

❑ Build a reusable visual part based on the IMultiCellCanvas control.

❑ Build the MyDate part to get and display the current date.

❑ Build the LeaseCalc nonvisual part to perform calculations to determine whether the customer has exceeded the allowed distance and owes money to the car dealer.

❑ Use the IColor part to conditionally change the color attribute of a visual part.

9

Car Lease Application

In the following three chapters you build an application which calculates the current status of a car lease. The Lease application is based on the INotebook control and it uses a new nonvisual part to a read flat file which contains the data pertaining to car leases. The **INotebook** control is commonly used in many applications because it represents a real world object that users can easily recognize. Flat files are files which contain plain ASCII text and are commonly used for small applications and prototypes. This experience using the **INotebook** control and working with flat files will help you with future application development.

Application Requirements

When you lease a car there are many conditions to the lease which cover the cost of using the car. Leases can be very complex, but for this application you only need to understand the basic aspects which affect a simple car lease.

A car lease covers a specific period of time like 24, 36, or 48 months. The lease has a specific start date and a specific maximum of number miles or kilometers allowed for the duration of the lease. When the car usage exceeds the allowed amount, there is an additional charge for each mile, or kilometer, of usage over the allowed amount.

The Lease application solves a problem for a car dealership. Since there is a penalty when you drive more distance than allotted in the lease, at any time customers may want to know where they stand with their lease. The car dealer believes that a happy customer is one who does not have to pay extra at the end of the lease. A happy customer is more likely to lease again when the current contract is over.

When a customer contacts the car dealer, the customer provides their name and the current odometer reading on their car. The dealer can then easily calculate if the customer is over the allotted mileage for the lease.

It is difficult to find the lease information and enter all the data each time a customer calls for an update on their car lease status. The information for some sample leases is in a flat file for the Car Lease application. The flat file contains the lease information along with the customer name, car description, and other information.

The Lease application has three visual parts:

1. A CustomerCanvas with the detailed information for a specific customer.

2. A CustomerListCanvas with a list of customers.

3. A notebook with two pages, each containing one of the two canvases described above.

In this chapter you build a Car Lease calculating application, and in the next chapter you build an application which reads the contents of the flat file. Finally, you take the reusable parts from these two applications and combine them using a notebook. Start by constructing the visual part for the Car Lease application.

Making the CustomerCanvas

The detailed information for each lease and the calculated fields can all fit in a multicell canvas. By making a visual part with a base class of **IMultiCellCanvas**, you can reuse the canvas in different windows or applications. First create a new visual part, see Figure 147, using the following steps:

❑ Set the working directory to **x:\VABOOK\CARLEASE**.

❑ Enter **CustomerCanvas** for the Class name.

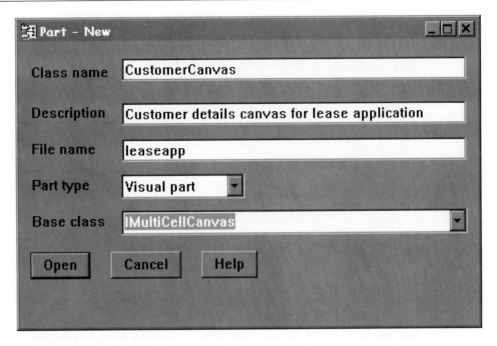

Figure 147: New CustomerCanvas visual part

❏ Enter **Customer details canvas for lease application** for the **Description**.

❏ Enter **leaseapp** as the File name. For this application you put all the part definitions in the leaseapp file.

❏ Keep the default Part type as **Visual**.

❏ Enter or select **IMultiCellCanvas** as the Base class.

❏ Press the **Open** push button to start editing the CustomerCanvas part.

Use the **IStaticText** control as a text label for each of the ten data fields in the CustomerCanvas. All the text labels should be right justified. This is a setting on the **General** page of the **IStaticText** control settings.

The application needs ten static text controls which identify the fields for the user. You could drop ten static text controls on the canvas, then individually edit each static text control to change the alignment and other settings, but that is a lot of tedious repetitive work. There is a feature of VisualAge for C++ that makes this faster.

Copying Controls

When you use multiple instances of a control, all with the same settings, first define one control. Use the **Edit**, **Copy** menu item in the Composition Editor to copy the control to the clipboard. Then create other instances of similar controls by selecting **Edit**, **Paste** and dropping a control on the multicell canvas. The Visual Builder automatically gives the new copy a unique part name and retains the modified settings of the control.

There is another way to duplicate a control and its settings using the keyboard:

1. Select the control you wish to copy. The control should be highlighted.
2. Press and hold the Ctrl key.
3. Press and hold the left mouse button while it is over the control (in OS/2 use the right mouse button).
4. Drag the duplicated control to a new location.

Both of these methods work for visual and nonvisual parts. You could use either one of these methods to place the ten **IStaticText** controls on the canvas. The instructions use a variation on the clipboard method using keyboard accelerators. Complete the following steps:

❏ From the **Data entry** category select an **IStaticText** part and drop it on the cell in row two and column two. This is the text for the first lease information field.

❏ Open the settings editor for the **IStaticText** control.

❏ Enter **txtToday** as the Subpart name.

❏ Enter **Today's date:** as the Text for the control.

❏ Select the right alignment radio button in the upper right corner of the **Alignment** group. See Figure 148.

❏ Press the **OK** button to save these changes.

Now that **txtToday** is set properly as seen in Figure 149, put the focus on the **Today's date** static text by placing the mouse over the control and pressing the left mouse button. While the static text control is selected, copy it to the system clipboard. Use one of the following methods outlined above, for example, from the menu bar, select **Edit** then **Copy**. Or you can press Ctrl+Insert.

The **Today's date IStaticText** control is now in the clipboard and can be copied to the other cells. You can not see what is in the clipboard unless you use a clipboard viewer that supports the Visual Builder's format. You can also try to paste from the clipboard. If you accidentally paste the wrong contents from the clipboard, use the

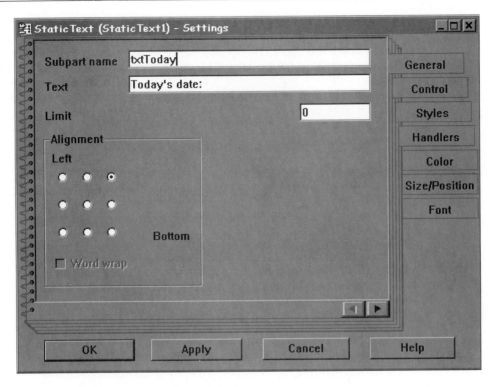

Figure 148: Settings notebook for Today's date

Undo function in the **Edit** menu item. Now you can easily make the rest of the labels for the Customer Canvas.

❑ From the menu bar, select **Edit**, then **Paste**. Or you can press Shift+Insert.

❑ The cursor is now loaded with the part from the clipboard. Move the mouse pointer to the cell in row 4, column 2. This is two rows below **Today's date**.

❑ Press the left mouse button to drop the part.

A copy of the **Today's date: IStaticText** control appears in the selected cell and it retains the right alignment setting. Repeat these steps until there are ten static text fields in the multicell canvas column 2. This is a lot faster than editing each static text control.

Adding Rows to a Multicell Canvas

You will run out of rows on the multicell canvas while you are copying from the clipboard. Just keep dropping the control on to the bottom row until there are ten controls. New rows are added automatically by the Visual Builder as needed. This places all the controls next to each other. It is not required, but it is a good idea to add blank rows between the controls. Directly add additional rows to the multicell canvas with the following steps:

❑ The mouse pointer must be pointing to an empty cell to get the multicell canvas pop-up menu. Place the mouse pointer over an empty cell on a row that holds a control. This way the mouse pointer is pointing to the multicell canvas and not a control on the canvas.

❑ Press the right mouse button and select **Rows**, **Add row after** to add an extra row between the controls.

❑ Repeat these steps so that each the static text control has a blank row between them.

Another way to add rows and columns to the **IMultiCellCanvas** control is through its settings notebook. On the General page of the notebook there are add and delete buttons for the rows and columns. Remember that you can only change the multicell canvas in one place at a time, either directly in the Composition Editor or in its setting notebook.

Directly edit the labels of the static text fields to read as follows:

❑ Customer name:

❑ Car model:

❑ Lease started:

❑ Allotment per year:

❑ Allotment to date:

❑ Odometer Reading:

❑ Difference:

❑ Rate for extra usage:

❑ Amount for extra usage:

It is not necessary to change the name of these controls because they are not used with any other parts. They are merely text labels for the fields on the canvas. Good programming practice encourages you to name them appropriately, but this is not necessary. For example you could name the **Today's date txtTodaysDate**. The CustomerCanvas should look like Figure 149.

Using Static Text to Display Data

You also need to display static lease data next to all the text labels except the **Odometer reading** field, which is a dynamic entry field. Use the **IStaticText** control for the static data fields. The static text

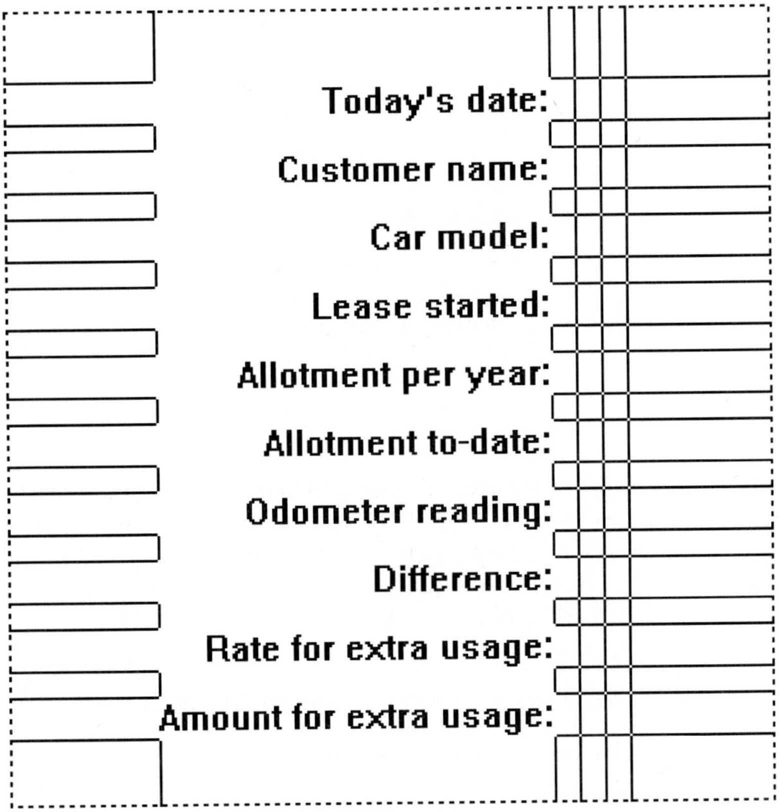

Figure 149: Customer Canvas IMultiCellCanvas control

control is good because it includes many conversions for different numeric formats and prevents editing its contents. An alternative would be to use **IEntryField** parts, but you would need to set each part's **readOnly** attribute to achieve the same result. Additionally, users find it confusing when an application has some entry fields that can be edited and some that are read only.

❏ Add an **IStaticText** control to the right of each of the labels added in the previous step.

These controls are used as output fields for the nonvisual parts. Make the following changes to the static text controls:

❏ Change the subpart names and text of all the static text controls according to Table 16.

❏ Add flyOverText to the static text fields you feel need explaining. For example, the one labeled **Difference** could use an explanation such as **Allotment distance to-date - Odometer**.

Table 16: Output text fields naming

IStaticText control name	Text
today	today
custName	custName
carModel	carModel
leaseStart	leaseStart
distancePerYear	distancePerYear
distanceToDate	distanceToDate
difference	difference
extraCost	extraCost
amountOwed	amountOwed

❑ In the Windows version, you need to drop an **IVBFlyText** control on the free-form surface of every part which has control that uses fly over text. This is due to a limitation in Windows.

❑ In OS/2 only one IVBFlyText control is needed per frame window. This factor comes into play when the dialog on a frame window is made up of several visual subparts.

Adding an Entry Field to the Multicell Canvas

The car dealer enters the current odometer reading of the car before calculating the status of the car lease. Add an **IEntryField** part for this field.

❑ Add an **IEntryField** part opposite the Odometer reading.

❑ Name the entry field **efOdometer**.

The canvas with the static text and entry field are shown in Figure 150.

The **Odometer Reading** entry field should only accept numbers to a maximum of six digits. You could use the same numeric only handler used in the Calculator application, but the odometer reading can only be a positive number. Use the **PosNumOnlyKbdHandler** which allows entering only positive numbers.

Users should not enter a negative number for the current odometer reading. It is a good design practice to prevent as much invalid data as possible at the source of the data, in this case the entry field. This makes your applications easier to use and less prone to errors due to invalid data.

❑ Load the KBDHDR.VBB file into the Visual Builder.

❑ Open the settings editor for the **Odometer Reading** entry field.

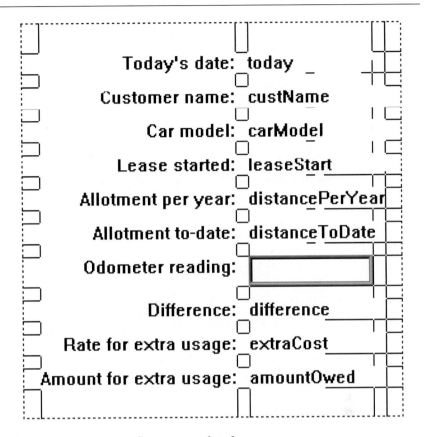

Figure 150: Customer Canvas completed

- ❏ Enter **6** in the **Limit** entry field.
- ❏ Select the **Handlers** page of the setting notebook.
- ❏ Enter **PosNumOnlyKbdHandler** as a handler for the part.
- ❏ Press the **Add after** button to add the handler.
- ❏ Press the **OK** button to save these changes.

Open the settings notebook for the multicell canvas, and set each text control on the right side so that they span two columns, 4 and 5, see Figure 151. This enables the entry field for the odometer reading to maintain its own size and not be governed by the width of the static text controls. Remember, the width of a column in a multicell canvas is determined by the width of the widest control in that column. If the static text controls did not span two columns, the entry field would be expanded to the size of the largest static text control in that column. This is a good example of why you need to do a little planning when using the multicell canvas.

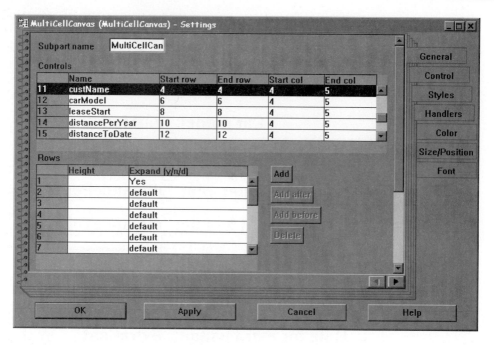

Figure 151: Expandable cell settings for the multicell canvas

Setting the Multicell Canvas as Expandable

A key feature of the **IMultiCellCanvas** control is the ability to resize rows and columns at runtime when a frame window is resized. This is very helpful when you want to see more information in an list box, but all the controls on the Customer Canvas are of fixed length. In this case, it is a good design to set the first and last rows and the first and last columns in the multicell canvas as expandable. With this setting, when the frame window is resized at runtime the controls stay centered in the window.

Set these rows and columns as expandable with the following steps:

❏ Open the settings notebook for the **IMultiCellCanvas** . Remember that you need to position the mouse pointer on an area of the multicell canvas that is empty or has no controls.

❏ Make sure the last row is empty. The last row may not be empty because you added a number of controls to the **IMultiCellCanvas**. If the last row is not empty because it has a control on it, add a new empty row at the end.

❏ Enter **y** in the appropriate fields to set the first and last rows and columns to expandable.

If you ever need to know the exact placement of a control on a multi-cell canvas, open the multicell canvas settings notebook and look in the first table called **Controls**. An example of this is shown in Figure 151.

❑ Now save the part and generate the **Part source** for the part.

Testing the CustomerCanvas

It is good practice to test the components of an application as you build them. This book has many places where you pause and compile the application. It is highly recommended that in practice you follow this *test as you go* method for developing applications. Even though the instructions in this book do not have a lot of iterations for each of the applications, you should feel free to generate and compile your project as often as you like.

Running a Canvas

Every application must have at least one frame window. If you compile and run a canvas without a frame window, you have an inaccessible multicell canvas on the screen. For example, you could generate the **Part source** and the **main( )** for the **Customer Canvas**, compile it, and run it. This application cannot receive any messages because it lacks a frame window. Do not try this unless you are curious. This fact is only good for betting other programmers on trivia.

Creating the TestView

Create a test application that uses the Customer Canvas by making a new visual part. Complete the following steps to make a test application as shown in Figure 152:

❑ Select **Part**, **New**.

❑ Enter **TestView** for the Class name.

❑ Enter **Test frame window for Customer Canvas** in the Description.

❑ By leaving the **File name** field blank, you let this part be saved in a separate file named TESTVIEW.VBB.

❑ Keep the default **Part type** as **Visual**.

❑ Keep the default Base class as **IFrameWindow**.

❑ Press the **Open** push button to start editing the **TestView** part.

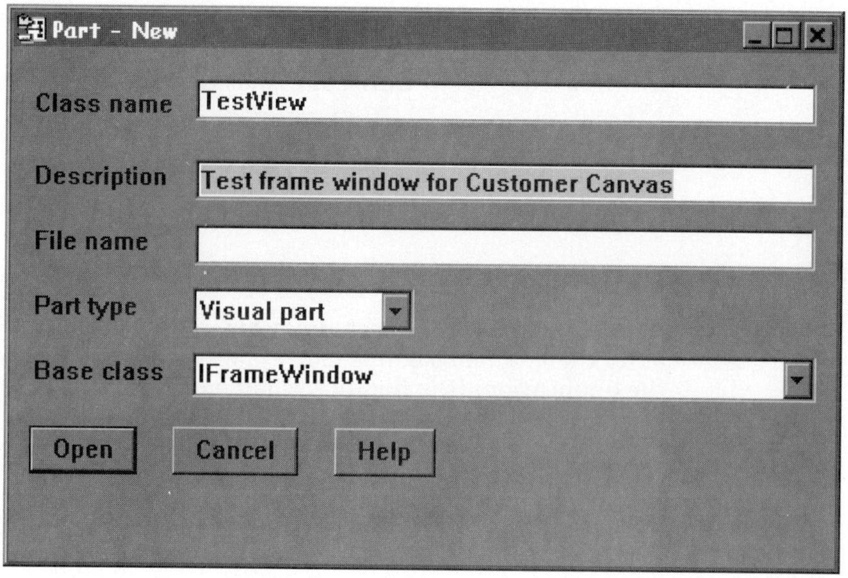

Figure 152: New TestView part

When the Composition Editor displays, complete the following steps:

- ❏ Delete the default **ICanvas** control in the **IFrameWindow**.
- ❏ Directly edit the frame window's title bar to read **Test Customer Canvas**.
- ❏ Add the CustomerCanvas* part to the frame window using the **Options**, **Add part...** menu items in the Composition Editor.
- ❏ Now the cursor is loaded with the **CustomerCanvas*** part, place it on the client part of the frame window.

The TestView application should look like Figure 153. This is a fast and easy way to test reusable canvases. Now generate the C++ code for TestView:

- ❏ Save and generate the **Part source** and the **main( )** for the TestView application.
- ❏ Compile the TestView application.

Running the TestView

Run the **TestView** application to test that the Customer Canvas is working correctly. The **TestView** application should look like Figure 154.

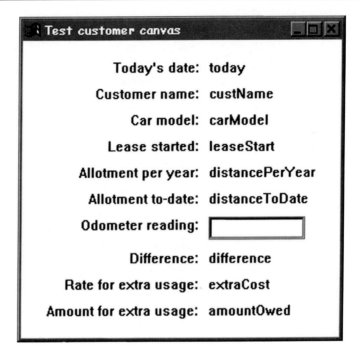

Figure 153: TestView frame window for Customer Canvas

Check for proper positioning and alignment of the static text fields. Test the positive integer numeric handler by attempting to enter something other than a positive number in the **Odometer reading** entry field. You should not be able to do that. Resize the frame window and all the controls should remain in the middle of the screen.

Making the LeaseCalc Nonvisual Part

The Customer Canvas is designed so that it holds the detailed information and calculated fields for each lease. By making a visual part with a base class of **IMultiCellCanvas**, you can reuse the canvas in different windows or applications.

Let's start to construct the nonvisual part that does the calculations for the lease. From the Parts Selector, refer to Figure 155 and create a new nonvisual part as follows:

❑ Enter **LeaseCalc** as the Class name.

❑ Enter **Calculates the difference and amount owed on a lease** in the description field.

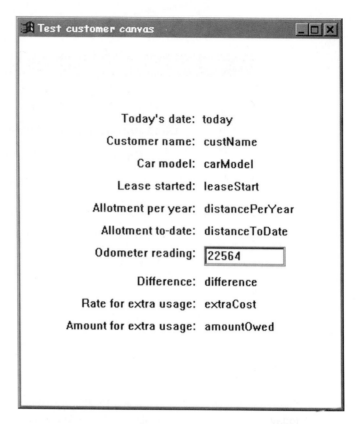

Figure 154: TestView with sized window and numeric input

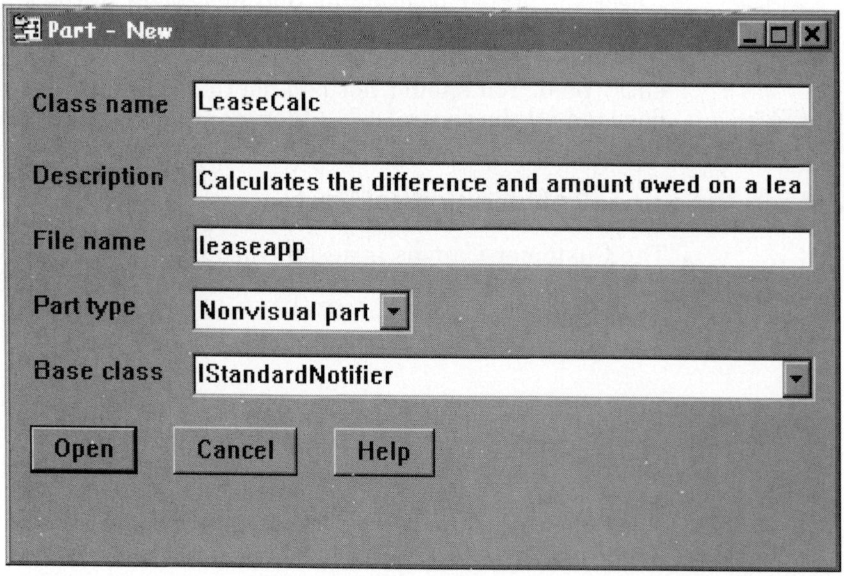

Figure 155: New LeaseCalc nonvisual part

❏ Enter **leaseapp** as the .VBB filename. This adds the LeaseCalc part definitions to the LEASEAPP.VBB file.

❏ Select **Nonvisual** as the Part type.

❏ Keep **IStandardNotifier** as the Base class.

❏ Press the **Open** push button to start editing the LeaseCalc part.

Defining the Attributes

Develop this nonvisual part as you did the nonvisual part in the Calculator application. The **LeaseCalc** part calculates whether the customer has driven over the distance allowed by the lease. To make these calculations, the **LeaseCalc** needs a number of attributes. Enter the attributes listed in Table 17 on the **Attribute** page for the part.

Table 17: Attributes for LeaseCalc

Attribute Name	Type	Description
differenceColor	IColor	If the customer does not owe any money the value is green, otherwise it is red.
leaseStartDate	IDate	The date when the lease started.
today	IDate	Today's date.
difference	int	The difference between the freeDistanceToDate and the odometerReading.
extraCost	int	The amount of money, in cents, per unit of distance. This is applied to calculate the amount owed on the lease.
freeDistancePerYear	int	The distance you are allowed to drive per year without incurring any penalty which is specified in the lease.
freeDistanceToDate	int	The calculated distance allowed free of charge from the leaseStartDate until today.
odometerReading	int	The distance driven to date.

Design Considerations

Some of the attributes are calculated inside the **LeaseCalc** part and their values are exposed in the public interface. These values should be prevented from being changed from outside the part. For example, **freeDistanceToDate** is calculated based on the **today, leaseStartDate** and **freeDistancePerYear** attributes. Another example is **difference**. These attributes are considered read only.

Attributes can be made read-only by removing their **Set member function** from the PIE. Complete the following:

❏ Return to the **Attributes** page of the PIE for the **LeaseCalc** part.

❏ Select the **freeDistanceToDate** attribute

❏ Remove its **Set member function** and press the **Update** button.

❏ Repeat for the **difference** attribute.

These steps are not required to make the application run properly, but this is one of many optimization techniques. When you remove the set member function from attributes, the generated code is smaller and the resulting application is smaller. In application development, smaller is usually better.

Defining the Actions

The **LeaseCalc** needs an action which calculates the amount that may be owed on the lease. Requirements for this action are listed in Table 18.

❏ Select the **Actions** page of the Part Interface Editor and add the **calculateAmountOwing** action.

It is helpful to add these part features in the Preferred connections list.

❏ Select the **Preferred** page of the PIE, and add all the new attributes to the preferred list.

Table 18: Actions for LeaseCalc

Actions	Description
IString calculateAmountOwing	Calculates the amount owing based on the formula below. amountOwing = difference * extraCost difference = odometerReading - freeDistanceToDate freeDistanceToDate = (freeDistancePerYear / 365) * (today - leaseStartDate) This value is zero if the "difference > 0".

❏ Now that the **LeaseCalc** part definition is complete, save the part and generate the **Part Source** code.

You need to generate the C++ **Feature source** code for these new features. The feature code is generated in the .HPV and .CPV files which are specified in the **Class Editor**. Remember you must specify the .HPV and .CPV filenames before you can generate the **Feature source**. Specify these files using **LASECALL** as the stem.

❏ Switch to the Class Editor for LeaseCalc and in **Required include files** enter:

  ❏ idate.hpp _IDATE_

  ❏ icolor.hpp _ICOLOR_

❏ Generate the feature source by selecting **File**, **Save and Generate**, **Feature source...** as seen in Figure 156.

❏ Press the **Generate all** button.

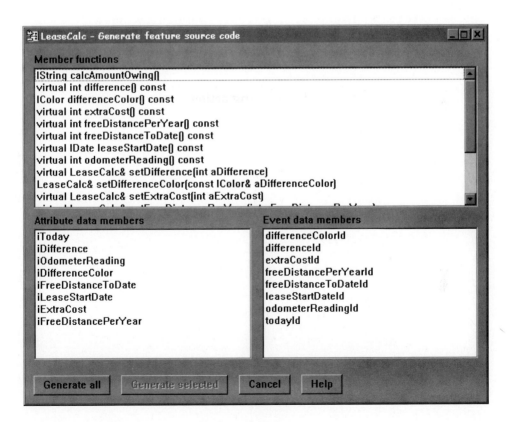

Figure 156: Generate All feature code for LeaseCalc

The LASECALC.HPV and LASECALC.CPV files are generated. The **E** in LEASECALC is dropped by the Visual Builder because it restricts file names to eight characters. This is because the Visual Builder is set to permit FAT file names in the Parts Selector **Options** menu.

Adding Logic to the LeaseCalc

Now you need to add the C++ code to the generated LASECALC.CPV file to actually perform the calculations needed to determine whether the distance driven exceeds the distance allowed to date and, if so, how much money is owed at this point in time.

❑ Open the LASECALC.CPV file in the **Program Editor**.

❑ Use the **Find** option of your editor to locate the **calculateAmountOwing** member function.

❑ Enter the code as shown in Code segment 31 to the **calculateAmountOwing** member function.

```
IString LeaseCalc::calculateAmountOwing()
{
IFUNCTRACE_DEVELOP();
IString strAmountOwing;
double dAmountOwing;
int aDifference = difference();
if( aDifference < 0 )
{
    aDifference *= -1; // change sign if negative
        double dDollarsOwing = aDifference * iExtraCost
                      / 100 * 100;
        double dCentsOwing   = ( aDifference *
                           iExtraCost ) - dDollarsOwing;

        IString strCentsOwing( dCentsOwing );
        if( strCentsOwing.length() == 1 )
{
        strCentsOwing += "0";
    } /* endif */
    strAmountOwing = ( "$ " + IString( dDollarsOwing /
        100 ) +"."+ strCentsOwing);
    }
    else
    {
        strAmountOwing = "$ 0.00";
    } /* endif *
return strAmountOwing;
}
```

Code segment 31: calculateAmountOwing member function

The **calculateAmountOwing** member function does the necessary calculations and produces a formatted string indicating how much money is owed. This string is the return value.

Whenever the **leaseStartDate** attribute changes the **LeaseCalc** part needs to recalculate the **freeDistanceToDate** value. Add the code in Code segment 32 to calculate **freeDistanceToDate**.

Notifications are sent when an attribute changes. This is accomplished using the **notifyObservers** function. Other parts get a chance to act upon the notification. When this happens, the data in the **LeaseCalc** part needs to update the text in the dialog box and indicate the new value. This happens using an attribute-to-attribute connection between visual and nonvisual parts.

```
LeaseCalc& LeaseCalc::setLeaseStartDate(const IDate&
    aLeaseStartDate)
{
if (!(iLeaseStartDate == aLeaseStartDate))
{
   iLeaseStartDate = aLeaseStartDate;
   notifyObservers(INotificationEvent(
   LeaseCalc::leaseStartDateId, *this));
   long lDaysElapsed = iToday - iLeaseStartDate;
      long lDistancePerDay = freeDistancePerYear() /
            365;
      iFreeDistanceToDate = lDistancePerDay *
            lDaysElapsed;
      notifyObservers(INotificationEvent(
            LeaseCalc::freeDistanceToDateId, *this));
   } // endif
  return *this;
}
```

Code segment 32: Calculating freeDistanceToDate

Using the IColor Class

There is another very nice feature in the **LeaseCalc** part. It sets the **differenceColor** attribute to red if the customer owes money, and to green if the customer owes nothing.

❑ Add the code in Code segment 33 to the setOdometerReading member function to get this function.

❑ Note the removal of the lines that check if the new value equals the old value of the odometer. This is because even if the odometer readings are the same for two customers you still need to calculate the other values.

❑ Save the modified LASECALC.CPV file so that the changes are compiled the next time you run the make file.

```
LeaseCalc& LeaseCalc::setOdometerReading(int
aOdometerReading)
{
  iOdometerReading = aOdometerReading;
  notifyObservers(INotificationEvent(
      LeaseCalc::odometerReadingId, *this));

  iDifference = iFreeDistanceToDate -
      iOdometerReading;
  notifyObservers(INotificationEvent(
      LeaseCalc::differenceId, *this));

  if( ( iDifference ) < 0 )
  {
     setDifferenceColor( IColor::red );
  }
  else
  {
     setDifferenceColor( IColor::darkGreen );
  }
  return *this;
}
```

Code segment 33: Setting the difference and its color

Completing the LeaseCalc Application

The **LeaseCalc** part is ready to be added to the **TestView** application. Open the Composition Editor for the **CustomerCanvas** part and add the **LeaseCalc** nonvisual part to the free-form surface.

❑ From the menu bar, select **Options, Add part....**
❑ Enter **LeaseCalc*** as the Part class.

The final application reads the required data for the **LeaseCalc** part from a flat file. To test the **LeaseCalc** part, you can put some default values in the part. You can enter initial values for a part in its settings editor.

❑ Open the settings notebook for the **LeaseCalc** nonvisual part.
❑ Enter default values for the attributes in Table 19.
❑ Save these new values by pressing the **OK** push button.

When you open the settings notebook of an object on the free-form surface, the first page of its notebook contains entry fields for all at-

Table 19: Initial values for LeaseCalc

Attribute	Value
extraCost	12
freeDistancePerYear	24000

tributes you have defined as read-write. These are the attributes which have both **get** and **set** methods. This notebook page is created dynamically from the part definition currently loaded into the Visual Builder. Values entered in this notebook are set by using the attribute's **set** member function in the constructor of the part which contains the object.

Making the MyDate Part

Many times applications need to show the current date. This can easily be done by using a static text field whose text attribute is connected to the **asString** attribute of an **IDate** part. Since this is a very common construct, design a composite part called **MyDate** to provide this function. The **MyDate** part is a combination of an **IStaticText** part and an **IDate** part. Follow these instructions and create a new visual part as seen in Figure 157.

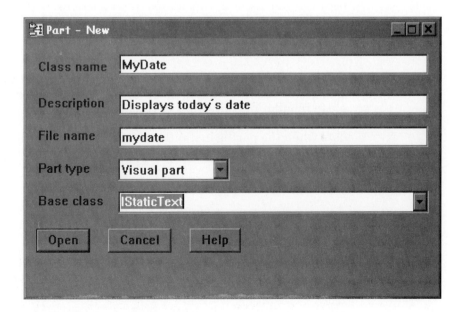

Figure 157: New MyDate part

❏ From the main Visual Builder dialog, create a new visual part.

❏ Name this part **MyDate**.

❏ Enter a suitable description like **Displays today's date**

❏ Under **File name** enter MYDATE.VBB.

❏ The **Base class** for this part is an **IStaticText** control. You must type **IStaticText** into the **Base class** entry field, since it is not one of choices of the drop down list box.

❏ Press **Open** and the Composition Editor opens with an **IStatic-Text** control on the free-form surface.

Define the **MyDate** part as shown in Figure 158 using the following steps:

❏ Directly edit the name of the **IStaticText** to something meaningful like **today**.

❏ Open its pop-up menu and select **Reset to default size**. Doing so sets the size of the control according to the text.

❏ From the menu bar select **Options, Add Part...** to add an **IDate***
part to the free-form surface. Name the part **todaysDate**.

❏ Connect the **asString** attribute of the **todaysDate** part to the **text** attribute of the **today** control.

When using the **MyDate** part, only the **today** text containing the current date appears in the application at development time. This is because you have encapsulated the functions within the MyDate part. The connections are not visible or editable when using the MyDate part. This is a good example of the proper use of C++ and the Visual Builder to support Object-Oriented development.

You can use the MyDate part in many applications. If you ever change the underlying implementation of the MyDate part it is simple to rebuild. You only need to recompile the MyDate part and relink the applications that use it. Currently the MyDate part holds the date when the part is instantiated. You may change the MyDate part to update itself every minute. This causes the part to change its date at midnight.

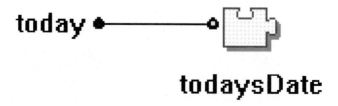

Figure 158: Composite MyDate part

Use the simpler MyDate part for this application and implement the refinements later. The users of this part benefit from these improvements by just relinking their applications. In fact, if you package the part into a DLL, they do not even need to relink their applications.

Promoting Part Features

When you use the MyDate part in an application, the only features available for connections are the features of the IStaticText control. This is because the MyDate part is a subclass of the IStaticText control. The features of the IDate part are not available. You need to promote any IDate features that you want exposed in the MyDate interface. You can promote the whole IDate part, by promoting its **this** attribute. You can also be more selective and promote one or more features to limit access to those features promoted. For this iteration promote the **today** attribute, see Figure 159.

❑ Open the pop-up menu for the IDate part

❑ Select Promote Part Feature....

❑ From the dialog that appears, select the today attribute.

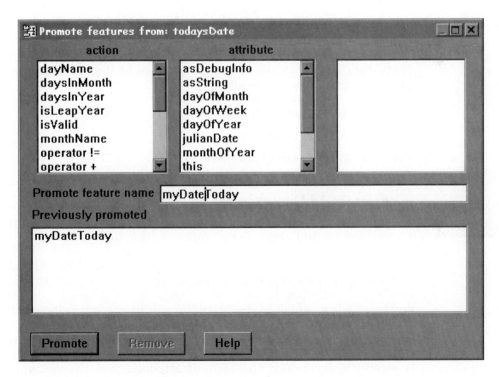

Figure 159: Promoting the today attribute

When promoting a part, the Visual Builder proposes a name for the promoted attribute. This is the name of the attribute preceded by the part name. For example,in this case the proposed name is **todays-DateToday**. Many times this name is either too long or inadequate to depict the attribute. If this happens you can override the proposed name by typing in your own, more meaningful name. Type over the proposed name with **myDateToday**.

If you find yourself promoting a lot of features in a part, you might be better off to promote the **this** attribute of the part. Promoting **this** effectively promotes the whole part. To use the features of a part, that has its **this** attribute promoted, you need to **tear off** the part in the Composition Editor.

Adding a Promoted Feature to the Preferred List

By default, promoted features do not appear on the Preferred list of the part. You can add the promoted feature to the Preferred list by switching to the PIE of the part, selecting the **Preferred** page and adding the promoted feature to the Preferred list. Remember you are looking for the new name of the feature; in our case, add **myDateToday** to the Preferred list as shown in Figure 160.

Completing the Application

In the CustomerCanvas, delete the **IStaticText** field opposite **Today's date** and in its place, add an instance of the **MyDate** visual part using the following steps:

❑ From the menu bar and select **Options**, **Add part...**.

❑ In the Add part dialog, enter **MyDate*** as the Part class.

❑ Enter **today** as the Part Name.

❑ Ensure that the **Part** radio button is selected.

❑ Press the **Add** button to load the cursor with the object.

❑ Move the loaded mouse pointer to row 2, column 4 of the multi-cell canvas and press the left mouse button to drop the part.

From the pop-up menu of the **today** object select **Tear-Off Attribute...** and another pop-up menu appears listing all the part attributes available to tear off. Scroll the list until you find **myDateToday**, which is the attribute you promoted. Selecting the attribute from the list loads the cursor, drop the **myDateToday** attribute on to the free-form surface. This attribute is of type **IDate** and all its features are available on the tear-off. Also, a connection is established between the torn-off attribute and the containing object.

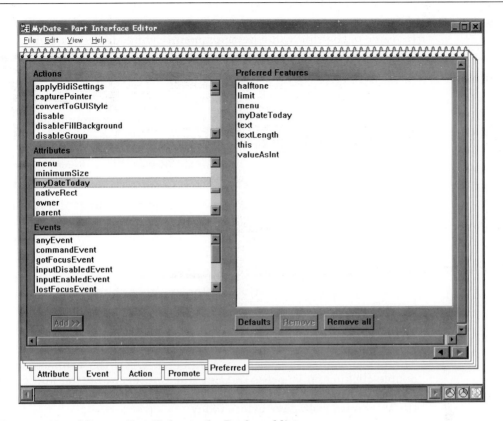

Figure 160: adding myDateToday to the Preferred list

There is a limitation in the current release of both the Windows and OS/2 versions of the product. Visual Builder attributes that have template declarations cannot be torn-off. If you use variables like this, the compiler complains because the code generation is incorrect.

Complete the CustomerCanvas with the following connections:

❑ myDateToday(today) → leaseCalc(today)

❑ leaseCalc (odometerReading) → efOdometer (valueAsInt)

❑ efOdometer (valueAsInt) → leaseCalc(calculateAmountOwing)

❑ above connection (actionResult) → amountOwed(text)

Make sure the connections above are made in the order indicated; otherwise, the amount owing is calculated for the wrong odometer reading.

The leaseCalc object calculates the amount the customer might owe every time the odometer reading changes. The calculateAmountOwing member function returns a formatted string indicating this value. In order to see this value on the amountOwing static text field, connect the **actionResult** from the connection to the text attribute of the amountOwing object. Continue by connecting:

- ❑ leaseCalc(difference) → difference(valueAsInt)
- ❑ leaseCalc(differenceColor) → amountOwed(foregroundColor)
- ❑ leaseCalc (differenceColor) → difference (foregroundColor)
- ❑ leaseCalc(extraCost) → extraCost(valueAsInt)
- ❑ leaseCalc(freeDistancePerYear) → distancePerYear(valueAsInt)
- ❑ leaseCalc(freeDistanceToDate) → distanceToDate (valueAsInt)
- ❑ Tear off the leaseStartDate attribute from the leaseCalc object
- ❑ leaseStartdate of leaseCal(asString) → leaseStart(text)

Three more connections are required to finish this part. In order to set the leaseStartDate attribute after the other values have been set, connect:

- ❑ free-form surface(ready) → leaseCalc(leaseStartDate)

The above connection needs a parameter. Open the connection by double-clicking on it, press the **Set parameters...** button and enter **IDate::today() - 45** in the **aLeaseStartDate** entry field. This sets the start date to 45 days before today.

Next, initialize the odometer reading to 0:

- ❑ free-form surface(ready) → leaseCalc(odometerReading)

The above connection needs a parameter. Open the connection by double-clicking on it, press the **Set parameters...** button, and enter **0** in the **aOdometerReading** entry field.

You may be wondering why the above two connections are being set by the **ready** event and not in the settings notebook of the **leaseCalc** part. The reason is that there is no way to control the sequence in which the values are set in the settings notebook. The **leaseStart-date** and the **odometerReading** must be set after the **freeDis-tanceToDate** and the **extraCost** values are set. The only way to guarantee the sequence is by using the ready event, which happens after the settings in the notebook have been set. In addition, the firing sequence of the connections from the **ready** event can be controlled using the **Reorder connections from** dialog box.

Lastly, connect:

- ❑ free-form surface(ready) → efOdometer(setFocus)

This connection will put the cursor on the entry field when the application comes up. Figure 161 shows the connections completed so far.

Running the LeaseCalc Test

❏ Save and generate the **Part source** for the CustomerCanvas.

❏ Generate the **main( )** for the TestView application as it needs a new make file which includes dependencies for the nonvisual parts added to the CustomerCanvas.

The **differenceColor** attribute of the LeaseCalc part is of type **IColor**. Objects of this type do not have a public constructor which takes no parameters; therefore, you have to provide a value for the object in the initialization list for the containing object **LeaseCalc**. Edit the LASECALC.CPP file, locate the constructor and change it to initialize the **iDifferenceColor** attribute to dark green:

```
LeaseCalc::LeaseCalc()
       :iDifferenceColor(IColor::darkGreen)
{
. . .
}
```

If you do not enter the above code you get the following error:

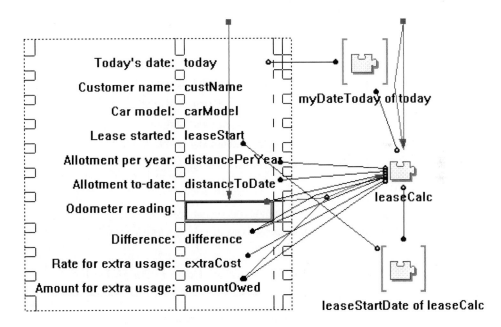

Figure 161: Connections in the CustomerCanvas

```
lasecalc.cpp(23:29) : error EDC3016: protected member
"IColor::IColor()" cannot be accessed.
```

The next time you generate the **Part source** for **LeaseCalc** you must reenter the initialization for **iDifferenceColor** in the .CPP and .HPP files because these files are rewritten every time you generate.

Running the Application

Compile and run the application to verify that it is working properly. The application should look like Figure 162. Enter an odometer reading. As you type the numbers the difference field is updated. The **Difference** and **Amount for extra usage** fields are dark green. Once the value of the odometer reading exceeds the number displayed in the **Allotment to-date** field, the **Difference** amount changes to a negative number, and the **Amount for extra usage** field shows the calculated amount. Both these fields are now red.

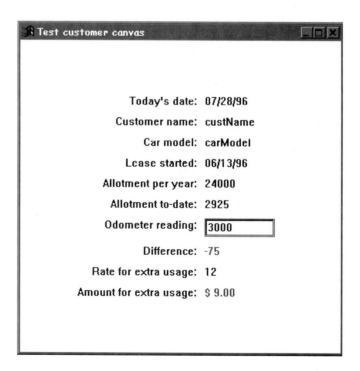

Figure 162: Completed application running

Chapter 9—Summary

In this chapter you built the first component of the Car Lease Application. You have:

❑ Built a reusable visual part based on the IMultiCellCanvas control. IStaticText controls were used for all the data fields needed to display the lease information.

❑ Built the MyDate composite visual part to get and display the current date.

❑ Built the LeaseCalc nonvisual part to perform calculations to determine whether the customer has exceeded the allowed distance and therefore owes money to the car dealer.

❑ Used the IColor part to conditionally change the foreground-Color attribute of a visual part.

What's in Chapter 10

In this chapter you develop the next part of the Car Lease application. This application reads lease information from a flat file containing sample data for a number of leases. To do this you will:

❑ Build a reusable canvas which will list the contents of the lease file.

❑ Use the **IListBox** control to display a list of customers.

❑ Create a **FlatFile** nonvisual part which provides the functions to open, close, read from, and write to a file.

❑ Create a **LeaseFileParser** nonvisual part which parses a string from a flat file and assigns fields to attributes.

10

Using Flat Files

In this chapter you build an application which displays the contents of a flat file in a list box. You will often find that you need to read or write data to a flat file. The nonvisual parts you develop in this chapter can easily be reused in your own applications. In fact, you will reuse these parts in the next chapter when you combine them with the **LeaseCalc** part.

The flat file CUSTOMER.DAT is included with the exercises, and it has sample data used in the Lease application. The flat file needs to be in the current directory when you run the application.

First, you build a reusable canvas which will allow you to see a list of the file contents, then make a **LeaseFileParser** nonvisual part to interface with the flat file, and then you combine the parts to make the application.

Making the CustomerListCanvas

To view the contents of the CUSTOMER.DAT file you need a control that will take a number of strings and display them in a list. The **IListBox** control is perfectly suited for displaying a list of strings. The IListBox is placed on an IMultiCellCanvas, so it will be sizable at

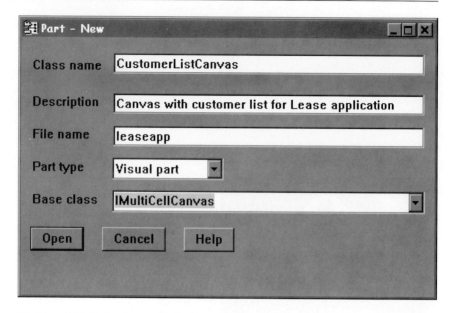

Figure 163: New CustomerListCanvas

runtime. First, create a new visual part as shown in Figure 163 using the following steps:

❏ Ensure that your current working directory is set to **x:\VABOOK\CARLEASE**. Load the LEASEAPP.VBB file into the Visual Builder.

❏ Enter **CustomerListCanvas** as the Class name.

❏ Enter **Canvas with customer list for Lease application** as the Description.

❏ Enter leaseapp for the File name or .VBB filename.

❏ Keep the part type as **Visual**.

❏ Enter or select **IMultiCellCanvas** as the Base class.

❏ Press the **Open** push button to start editing the **CustomerList-Canvas** part.

Using the List Box Part

This visual part needs a control to show the contents of the flat file. There are a number of controls in the Open Class Library that can be used to display text. One of the simplest controls to use for this is the **IListBox** control. The **IListBox** control allows you to add and re-move items from the list. You can select items from the list and pass the items in the list box to other parts for processing. The **IListBox** control has vertical and horizontal scroll bars that automatically become active when the list box is filled with more data than can be shown in its current size.

The scroll bars are helpful, but it is also helpful to have the **IListBox** expand both vertically and horizontally when a window is resized. This allows you to view more data in the list box. To get this behavior you need to put the list box on an **IMultiCellCanvas**, and set the column and row occupied by the list box as expandable.

❑ From the Lists category, drop an IListBox part on the multicell canvas in row 3 and column 2.

❑ Make the IListBox control larger by selecting one of the corners and stretching it.

❑ From the settings notebook of the multicell canvas set row 3 and column 2 as expandable.

The canvas should look like Figure 164.

The list box is a subpart of the canvas. Once the canvas is placed as the client of another control, like a notebook page or a frame window, the list box will not be accessible to users of that part. In order to be able to access and manipulate the list box from the containing part,

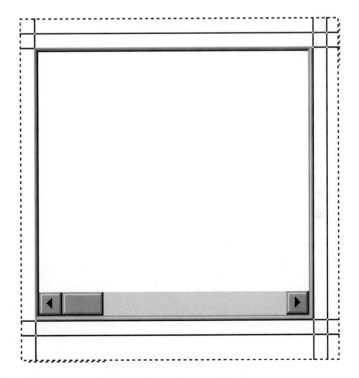

Figure 164: Resized IListBox control on multicell canvas

you must promote the list box object or some of its attributes. You can promote the whole list box by promoting the **this** attribute. You can later tear-off the list box attribute of the containing part and have access to all the list box attributes. A torn-off part appears like an original part placed on the free-form surface, but it is surrounded by brackets [].

❑ Position the mouse pointer over the list box and press the right mouse button to bring up the pop-up menu.

❑ Select **Promote Part Feature**.

❑ Select the **this** attribute of the list box to promote as shown in Figure 165.

❑ Enter **customerListBox** as the Promote feature name.

❑ Press the **Promote button** and close the dialog box.

❑ Open the PIE for the CustomerListCanvas part, select the Preferred page, and add the **customerListBox** attribute to the Preferred list.

Finishing touches

It would be good to provide a label for the list box so users will know what is in the list box. The **IStaticText** control will be fine as a label for the list box.

❑ From the data entry category, add an **IStaticText** control in the row over the **IListBox** control.

❑ Directly edit the text using Alt+left mouse button. The label should read **Select customer**.

❑ Save and generate the part source for the CustomerListCanvas. After you have saved the part, you can close this Composition Editor because you are finished editing the part, and closing it will save memory.

Testing the CustomerListCanvas

Now that you have built the **CustomerListCanvas**, you should test the application just as you did in the previous chapter. Create a temporary test frame window to test the CustomerListCanvas. From the Parts selector, create a new visual part:

❑ Enter **Testview2** for the Class name.

❑ Enter **Test frame window** for the Description.

❑ Leave the Filename field blank. This part is saved in a separate file named TSTVIEW2.VBB.

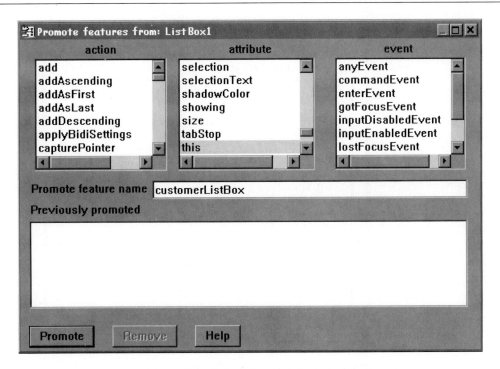

Figure 165: Promoting the this attribute of the list box

- ❏ Keep the default Part type as **Visual**.
- ❏ Keep the default Base class as **IFramewindow**.
- ❏ Press the **Open** push button to start editing the Testview2 part.
- ❏ Delete the default ICanvas control in the frame window.
- ❏ Directly edit the frame window title bar to read **Test Cus-tomerListCanvas**.
- ❏ Add the CustomerListCanvas* part to the frame window using the **Options, Add part...** menu item in the Composition editor. Place the CustomerListCanvas as the client of the frame window.
- ❏ Save and generate the Part source code for the Testview2 part.
- ❏ Generate the main( ) for the Testview2 part.
- ❏ From a command prompt, compile and run the Testview2 application.
- ❏ After the compile and link is finished, start the Testview2 application so you can see if it looks like Figure 166.

This is one of the simplest user interfaces you have constructed so far. You do not need a very complicated user interface to display data read from a flat file. Try resizing the frame window and you see the

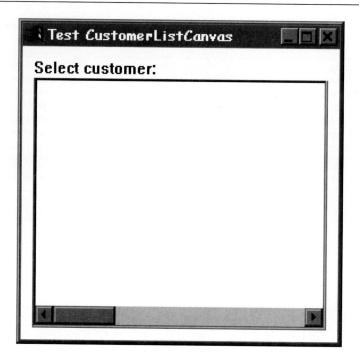

Figure 166: Running Testview2 testing application

list box expand and contract. Now that you know the user interface is fine, you are ready to start working on the nonvisual parts. Close Testview2 by selecting the system menu icon and then selecting the **Close** menu item.

Making the FlatFile Nonvisual Part

You need a nonvisual part to access the flat file which contains the sample data for your application.

A flat file is defined as a text file which only contains readable ASCII characters, and the organization of the file is that lines are separated from each other by carriage return and line feed characters. Operations such as read and write are performed one line at a time.

As you construct the flat file part, you should be thinking about how to make this part so it can be used in many applications which require manipulating flat files. You should make this part, and any other part, granular enough so it can be reused. That is the reason why this part only knows about flat files. It has no knowledge of a lease calculator, a customer list box, or the content of the files it will read from or write to. These are the attributes of a good design which make a part reusable.

❑ Start creating a new nonvisual part by selecting **Part**, **New** from the menu bar of the Visual Builder.

❑ Enter **FlatFile** as the Class name.

❑ Enter **Performs operations on ASCII flat files** as the **Description**.

❑ Enter FLATFILE as the .VBB filename.

❑ Select **Nonvisual** as the Part type.

❑ Keep **IStandardNotifier** as the Base class.

❑ The dialog should look like Figure 167. Press the **Open** push button to start editing the **FlatFile** part.

Defining the Attributes

By now you have a lot of experience defining nonvisual parts, so the instructions will be a little briefer. This part is responsible for performing operations on a flat file. The main function this part performs in the car lease application is reading data from a flat file. Each line in the file is read sequentially. Lines are terminated with a carriage return and a line feed. The attributes needed for the FlatFile part are listed in Table 20. Use this information to create the necessary attributes in the Part Interface Editor. Use the **Add with defaults** button to create the attributes.

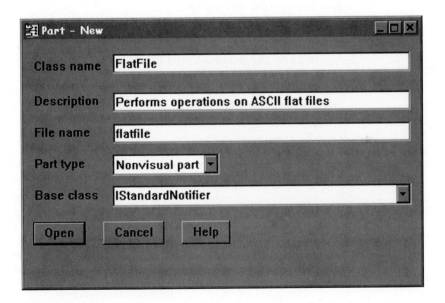

Figure 167: New FlatFile part

Table 20: Attributes for the FlatFile part

Attribute	Type	Description
fileName	IString	Contains the name of the currently opened file. If an **Open** action is executed without supplying a new filename, this attribute will be used to open the file.
currentLine	IString	Contains the last line read from the file.

Defining the Events

You need to add the events listed in Table 21 to the FlatFile part. Select the **Event** page of the Part Interface Editor and add these events using the **Add with defaults** button.

Table 21: Events for the FlatFile part

Event	Occurs
endOfFile	The next time a readLine action is attempted after the last line of the file has been read.
opened	After successfully opening a new file.

Defining the Actions

There are a number of actions needed for the FlatFile part to perform its responsibilities. Select the **Actions** page of the Part Interface Editor and add the actions listed in Table 22. Each action needs to have a type and return type of **FlatFile&**. Since you are not using the default return type you need to use the **Add** push button instead of the **Add with defaults**.

Table 22: Actions for the FlatFile part

Action	Description
close()	If a file is open, it closes it. The file is also closed when the part goes out of scope or is deleted, this is done on the destructor for the part.
open(IString newFileName = IString( ))	If a file is currently open it is first closed. It opens newFileName in read/write mode. If it fails an IAccessError is thrown.
readFile()	Reads the complete file a line at a time until EOF (end of file) is reached.
readLine()	Reads a line from the file into **currentLine**.
writeLine(IString aLine)	Writes **aLine** to the end of the file.

Switch to the **Preferred** page of the PIE and add all the new features to the Preferred list.

Generating the FlatFile Code

Now that you have specified all the events, actions, and attributes, the Visual Builder can generate the C++ code for the part. Just like all the other nonvisual parts, you need to specify the .HPV and .CPV filenames in the Class Editor.

❑ Switch to the Class Editor from the menu bar by selecting **View, Class Editor**

❑ Enter **FLATFILE.HPV** and **FLATFILE.CPV** in the appropriate fields in the **User files included in generation** section in the lower right section of the Class Editor.

❑ Enter **fstream.h** in the **Required include files** list. This include file contains the definitions required to perform file I/O and is part of the standard C++ library.

❑ On the Icon group box, enter **bitmaps** in the **DLL name** entry field and **8** in the **Resource id** entry field. This defines the icon to be shown on the Visual Builder whenever a **FlatFile** part is on the free-form surface.

❑ Select **File, Save and Generate, Part source** which will generate the C++ source code for the part.

❑ Select **File, Save and Generate, Feature source...** which brings up the Feature generation dialog. Press the **Generate all** push button and the Visual Builder will generate the code stubs for the public interface of the FlatFile part.

Adding Logic to the FlatFile Nonvisual Part

Once the public interface of the part has been entered and saved in the PIE, you can start using that part in the Visual Builder. In fact, you can use a part before you have entered the C++ logic in the .CPV file. The part interface, the events, actions, and attributes, is all you need to interface with a part by making connections in the Composition Editor. When developing your own parts, you may want to defer entering the C++ logic for your features until you have had a chance to try using the part and get a feel for the interface.

You need to add the C++ code for each of the following actions to the code stubs in the FlatFile part:

❑ open

❑ close

❑ readLine

❑ readFile

❑ writeLine

Defining the open Action

The **open** action has several responsibilities in addition to opening the file. First the **open** action performs a check to make sure that if a file is already open it will be closed using Code segment 34.

```
FlatFile& FlatFile::open(IString newFileName)
{
  // If a file is currently open, close it
  if( aFileIsOpen )
  {
    close();
  } /* endif */
  . . .
```

Code segment 34: If a file is open, close it

The next thing is to make sure that a filename is available. The filename can come from two places:

1. The fileName instance variable

2. Passed as a parameter in the open(IString newfilename) action

If there is no filename an exception is thrown by using Code segment 35:

```
  . . .
IString fileNameToOpen = newFileName;
  // Check to see if you have a file name
  if( fileNameToOpen.length() == 0 )
  {
    // if no name passed, attempt to use fileName
    fileNameToOpen = fileName();
    if( fileNameToOpen.length() == 0 )
    {
      // if fileName is also not set, throw exception
      IAccessError exc = IAccessError(
            "Need a filename to open" );
      ITHROW( exc );
    }
  }
  . . .
```

Code segment 35: Check to make sure there is a filename

So far, you have closed any previously opened file and are sure you have a filename to open. Next, you actually attempt to open the file and check for errors. If there are no errors, then the object is set to a good known state using Code segment 36:

```
. . .
// open file for read and append
  aFile.open( fileNameToOpen, ios::in | ios::app );
  // if the open worked, set proper state in object
  if( aFile.fail() == 0 )
  {
     eofReached = false;
     aFileIsOpen = true;
     setFileName( fileNameToOpen);

     // reset file position to beginning of file
     aFile.seekg( 0, ios::beg );

     notifyObservers(INotificationEvent(
       FlatFile::openedId, *this));
  } /* endif */
  // if the open failed, throw an exception
  else
  {
     IAccessError exc = IAccessError(
       "Could not open file: " + fileNameToOpen );
     ITHROW( exc );
  }
. . .
```

Code segment 36: open the file and check for errors

Finally, return a reference to this FlatFile object with Code segment 37:

```
. . .
  return *this;
}
```

Code segment 37: Return a reference to the FlatFile object

❑ Open **FLATFILE.CPV** in the Program editor and add these code segments to the **open** action stub.

You may have noticed three instance variables used that were not defined as part of the public interface in the PIE. These are private class variables and they need to be added to the **private:** definition section of the FLATFILE.HPV file. Open the file, locate the private definitions and add:

❑ `fstream aFile;`

❑ `Boolean aFileIsOpen;`

❑ `Boolean eofReached;`

Using the Close Action

The close action is very straight forward. You check to see if a file is indeed open and, if so, you close it and reset the state variables to the not opened state. Add the code with the **if** statement in Code segment 38.

```
FlatFile& FlatFile::close()
{
   if( aFileIsOpen )
   {
      aFile.close();
      aFileIsOpen = false;
      setFileName( "" );
   } /* endif */
   return *this;
}
```

Code segment 38: Close action for FlatFile

Defining the readLine Action

When reading a flat file you are actually reading strings of characters. The **IString** class has a member function which supports reading from a text file. The **lineFrom** member function is a static function which reads a line from a file and returns an **IString** object. After reading each line the state of the **aFile** object is checked to see if the end of the file has been reached. If it has, readLine sends an event to notify interested parties that this event has happened. The **endOfFile** event is usually used to close the file.

If the file has not reached its end of file, the string just read is assigned to the **currentLine** attribute using its set member function. As a side effect, setting the currentLine attribute generates an event which, in your case, will be used to add a line to the list box. This is done by virtue of a connection in the Visual Builder using Code segment 39.

```
FlatFile& FlatFile::readLine()
{
  IString strNewLine = IString::lineFrom( aFile );
  if( aFile.fail() )
  {
    eofReached = true;
    notifyObservers(INotificationEvent
        FlatFile::endOfFileId, *this));
  }
  else
  {
    setCurrentLine( strNewLine );
  }
  return *this;
}
```

Code segment 39: readLine action for FlatFile

Defining the readFile Action

The readFile action is nothing more than a loop which reads lines until the end of file is reached. Add Code segment 40 to get this function.

```
FlatFile& FlatFile::readFile()
{
  while( eofReached == false )
  {
    readLine();
  } /* endwhile */
  return *this;
}
```

Code segment 40: ReadFile action for FlatFile

Defining the writeLine Action

The writeLine action basically prepares an **IString** object by adding an end-of-line character at its end, and writes to the file using the standard C++ *shift* operator <<. Writing to a file changes its file position pointer to the end of the file. Before writing to the file, the current file position is saved; and after the write, it is restored to the original position. This moves the file position pointer to the beginning of the line just written. Add Code segment 41 to implement these functions.

```
FlatFile& FlatFile::writeLine(IString aLine)
{
  // save position pointer
  long mark = aFile.tellg();

  // write line ( always to end of file )
  aLine = aLine + "\n";
  aFile << aLine;

  // restore position pointer
  aFile.seekg( mark );

  return *this;
}
```

Code segment 41: writeLine action for FlatFile

This completes all the code that needs to be added to the FLAT-FILE.CPV and .HPV files. Save the FLATFILE.CPV and .HPV files so these changes can be used by the compiler.

There are two last details to look after:

1. When the FlatFile object gets constructed there are no files open. In order to properly initialize the object, enter the following in the **User constructor code** entry field in the Class Editor:

   aFileIsOpen=false; iFileName="";

2. When a FlatFile object goes out of scope or is explicitly deleted, the destructor code for the object must close the file. This is especially important if you have been writing to the file. In order to accomplish this, you have to switch to the Class Editor for the FlatFile part and add the following to the **User destructor code** entry field:

   if(aFileIsOpen) close( );

Save and generate the **Part source** from the Visual Builder.

Using the FlatFile Part

Go back to the Composition Editor for the **CustomerListCanvas** visual part. Drop a **FlatFile*** part on the free-form surface. Name the flat file object **file**.

The **open** action can be called with or without a parameter indicating the name of the file to be opened. Here are the rules for using the **open** action:

❏ If an **IString** is passed as a parameter, use it to open the file.

❏ If no parameter is passed, check the **fileName** attribute. If it is not empty, use its contents to open the file.

❏ If both no parameter was passed and the **fileName** attribute is empty, throw an exception indicating that no filename is available.

In building the second iteration of the TestView2 application you will use a file dialog box to select and supply the filename to the open function. Later, when you build the Car Lease application, you will hard code the filename because that sample application keeps all the data in one file, and there is no need to add the additional step for the users to select a filename when only one exists.

From the **Other** category, select an **IVBFileDialog** part and drop it on the free-form surface. Name this part **fileDialog**.

From the **Buttons** category, drop an **IPushButton** control in the cell at row 5 column 2 on the multicell canvas. Name the control **pbFile-Select**. Directly edit the text on the button to read **Select and open file**. Because the button is in an expandable column on the multicell canvas, it will grow in width as the list box grows. Normally, you would not put a button directly on a multicell canvas, you would use a set canvas instead and then place the set canvas on the multicell. However, this is just a tester application and you should not really be too concerned about how the test application looks, remember, the main objective is to test out the nonvisual parts you are developing.

From the **Other** category drop an **IMessageBox** part on to the free-form surface. Name this object **errorMessage**. In this message box you will display any error messages resulting from opening the file.

All the parts are now in place. To make them work together you need to make the following connections:

❏ pbFileSelect(buttonClickEvent) → fileDialog(showModally)

❏ fileDialog(pressedOkEvent) → file(open)

A parameter is required for the above connection, connect:

❏ fileDialog(fileName) → connection(newFileName)

from the above connection, connect:

❏ connection(exceptionOcurred) → errorMessage(showException)

Connect:

❏ file(opened) → file(readFile)

❏ file(opened) → list box(removeAll)

❑ file(currentLine) → list box(addAsLast)

❑ file(endOfFile) → file(close)

There are a few points to ponder about the above connections:

1. You can see how the events occurring in the flat file object are driving the object itself. The **opened** event causes the next action to occur, which is the **readFile**. After the file is read completely the **endOfFile** event causes the file to be closed. The fact that these connections can be done through the public interface is a sign of a well designed part, one with not many hard coded rules, which provides the part user enough flexibility not to be restricted by the design of the part.

2. There are two actions which are the result of the opened event:

❑ file(readFile)

❑ list box(removeAll)

The intent is to clear the list box before the file is read into the list box. You may be wondering how the sequence of the actions is controlled. The application needs to clear the list box before it reads the file. Connections are fired in the order in which they were made. In this case, the connection to **readFile** was created before the connection to **removeAll**. To change the order in which connections fire, bring up the pop-up menu for the object in which the connections originate; in your case, the **file** object. From the menu select **Reorder Connections From**.

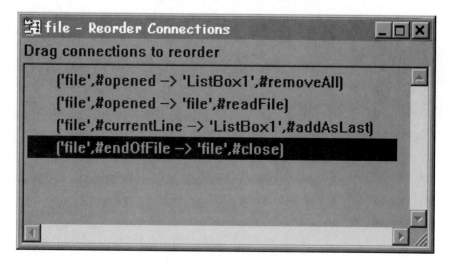

Figure 168: Reorder Connections dialog box

From this dialog shown, in Figure 168, you can rearrange or re-order the connections by simply dragging and dropping the connections into their proper sequence from top to bottom.

As the flat file is read, each line is put into the attribute **current-Line**. The **currentLine** attribute sends an event every time it changes. This event fires the connection to addAsLast on the list box.

Finally, it is a good idea to close the file after all records have been read and the EOF mark is reached. Figure 169 shows the completed connections.

Select **Save and generate**, **Part source** for the **CustomerList-Canvas**. Also, generate the **main() for part** for the TestView2 part. Switch over to a command prompt session and at the prompt enter **nmake tstview2.mak**.

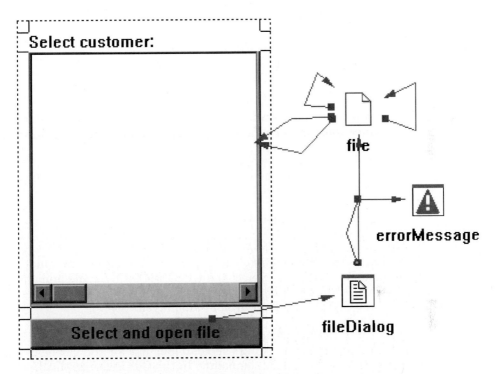

Figure 169: Completed connections to test the FlatFile part

Running the TestView2 Application

When you run the Tstview2 application (this is not a typo, you only get 8 characters if using FAT files), it looks like Figure 170. Test the application:

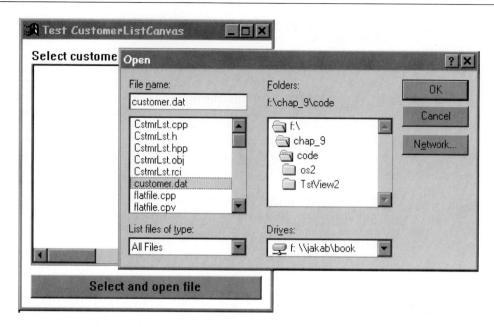

Figure 170: Opening a text file

❑ Press the **Select and Open file** button and the dialog box opens where you can select the file you want to read into the list box.

The file dialog box you see is provided by the operating system and is common to all applications running on that system, so its look and feel is familiar to the user.

❑ Select any text file available and press the **OK** button to open it.

The data from the file is automatically loaded into the list box. You can resize the frame window and you see the list box automatically expands and contracts. Select the CUSTOMER.DAT file and observe that the list box has been cleared of the previous file, and the contents of CUSTOMER.DAT are now displayed.

The data in the list box does not look very readable as seen in Figure 171. The flat file containing the customer list for the car dealership uses a # (pound sign) for comments. In the Car Lease application this data needs to be skipped. All the data fields appear unformatted in the list box, this is exactly as the data is stored in the flat file.

In order to format the data to the fields needed for the **Customer-Canvas** and **LeaseCalc**, you need to construct a nonvisual part that has knowledge of the final purpose of the data. In this case it needs to ignore comment lines and take each customer entry line, break it down into fields, and assign these fields to C++ attributes. This type

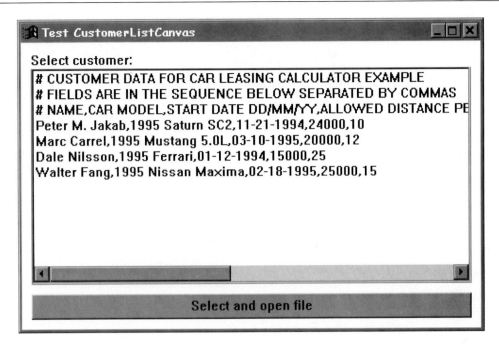

Figure 171: CUSTOMER.DAT displayed in list box

of function is called *parsing,* so the nonvisual part which you will build next, is appropriately called **LeaseFileParser**.

Making the LeaseFileParser

This part is responsible for converting lines which arrive from the FlatFile part into the format required by the application by parsing the line into fields. Lines from the file are received by the **inputLine** attribute. As lines are received they are parsed and stored in an internal collection.

❑ Ensure that the LEASEAPP.VBB file is loaded in the Visual Builder.

❑ From the Parts Selector, create a new nonvisual part, name this part **LeaseFileParser** and save it in the LEASEAPP.VBB file. Make the base class for this part **IStandardNotifier**.

Defining the Attributes

The **LeaseFileParser** part creates attributes that are derived by breaking down a line of text read from the flat file. These attributes are also used by both the **CustomerCanvas** and **LeaseCalc** parts. The attributes needed for the **LeaseFileParser** part are listed in

Table 23. Use this information to create these attributes in the Part Interface Editor.

Table 23: Attributes for the LeaseFileParser part

Attributes	Type	Description
leaseStartDate	IDate	The date when the lease started
carModel	IString	The model of the leased car
custName	IString	The name of the customer
inputLine	IString	The attribute which receives the line to be parsed. Parsing occurs automatically when this attribute changes.
extraCost	int	The amount of money, in cents, per unit of distance. Applied to calculate the amount owing in the lease.
freeDistancePerYear	int	The distance you are allowed to drive per year without incurring any penalty, as specified in your lease.

Defining the Events

You need to add the events listed in Table 24 to the **LeaseFileParser** part. Select the **Event** page of the Part Interface Editor and add these events using the **Add with defaults** button.

Table 24: Events for the LeaseFileParser part

Event	Occurs
lineAddedToCollection	Each time a new entry has been added to the internal collection.
lineParsed	Each time a line is parsed. At the time of this event all attributes have already been replaced with the ones just parsed.

Defining the Actions

There are a number of actions needed for the **LeaseFileParser** part to perform its responsibilities. Select the **Actions** page of the Part Interface Editor and add the actions listed in Table 25. Each action needs to have a type and return type of **LeaseFileParser&**. Since you are not using the default return types, you need to use the **Add** push button instead of **Add with defaults**.

On the **Preferred** page of the PIE add all the features of the part to the Preferred list.

Table 25: Actions for the LeaseFileParser part

Actions	Description
LeaseFileParser& elementAt(long Position)	Returns the element stored in the collection at Position and parses the line automatically.

Because this part has such a long name, the default filenames generated by the Visual Builder are meaningless. Switch to the Class Editor and enter the filenames listed in Table 26.

Table 26: Filenames for LeaseFileParser part

Entry field	Filename
C++ header file (.hpp)	parser.hpp _parser_
C++ code file (.cpp)	parser.cpp
User .hpv file	parser.hpv
User .cpv file	parser.cpv

There is one last detail to complete before you generate the code. You need to tell the Visual Builder which other header files need to be included to satisfy the compiler. Since you are using the ISequence, IStringParse, and IDate classes, you must enter the following lines in the **Required include files** area of the Class Editor:

❑ IDATE.HPP

❑ ISEQ.H

❑ ISTPARSE.HPP

Now the part definition is complete.

❑ Save and Generate the part source.

❑ Generate the Feature source for the part. You need to generate all the features you have defined for the LeaseFileParser part.

Adding Logic to the LeaseFileParser Nonvisual Part

The **LeaseFileParser** responsibilities are very simple. When a new line of text is available in the **inputLine** attribute, it is broken down into individual fields. The text in the inputLine attribute is expected to conform to a specific format. The file format uses the # (pound sign) to indicate comments. Any line that starts with **#** character is ignored. Any other lines are assumed to contain a series of fields separated by commas. Starting at the beginning of the line the fields are expected to be in the following order:

1. Customer name

2. Car model

3. Lease start date in dd-mm-yyyy format

4. Yearly distance allowance

5. Extra amount charged 0–99

Lines of text received from the file are stored in an ISequence collection class which is part of the Open Class Library. Elements can be added to the collection by the **addAsLast( )** member function and accessed by the **elementAt(position)** member function. For full details of the **ISequence** class, consult the Open Class Library Reference on-line book under **Sequence**. The reason a collection is used to save the lines read from the file is to improve the performance of the application. By using a collection, the file needs to be read only once. After that, valid lines from the file can be accessed directly from the collection without the overhead of rereading the file.

Coding the setInputLine Member Function

A good place to start coding the logic for the **LeaseFileParser** is at the point when a new line is available for parsing. The member function involved in dealing with a new line is the set function for the **inputLine** attribute.

❑ Open the **Parser.cpv** file in a text editor and modify the code as seen in Code segment 42.

```
LeaseFileParser&      LeaseFileParser::setInputLine(const
   IString& aInputLine)
{
   strNewLine = aInputLine;

   // do not handle blank lines
   if( strNewLine.strip().length() > 0 )
   {
      // make sure line is not a comment
      if( strNewLine[0] != '#' )
      {
         addToCollection();
         parseLine( );
         notifyObservers(INotificationEvent(
         LeaseFileParser::lineAddedToCollectionId,
*this));
      } /* endif */
   }
   return *this;
}
```

Code segment 42: setInputLine member function

The instance variables **strNewLine** and **strSequence** and the **add-ToCollection** and **parseLine** member functions need to be defined in the private section of the PARSER.HPV file. Open the file and add the following lines in the **private** declaration section:

❏ `LeaseFileParser& parseLine( );`

❏ `LeaseFileParser& addToCollection( );`

❏ `IString strNewLine;`

❏ `ISequence <IString > strSequence;`

As you can see from its declaration, the **strSequence** variable will hold IString objects. ISequences are template classes which can hold any type of object.

Looking at Code segment 42, you see that the line from the file is assigned to strNewLine. If the line is not blank, then you check to see if the first character of the line is a # (pound sign) indicating a comment line. If the line is not a comment, it is added to the collection, parsed, and a notification is sent indicating that a new line has arrived and is available in the collection.

Coding the addToCollection Member Function

The **addToCollection** member function simply calls **addAsLast**, passing the string read from the file. Add the member function code in Code segment 43 to the PARSER.CPV file.

```
LeaseFileParser& LeaseFileParser::addToCollection( )
{
  strSequence.addAsLast( strNewLine );
  return *this;
}
```

Code segment 43: addToCollection member function

Coding the parseLine Member Function

The parseLine member function uses the **>>** operator from the **IStringParse** class to break up the text contained in strNewLine wherever a comma (,) is found. This assigns the fields to temporary **IString** objects. One exception is the **leaseStartDate** attribute, which needs to create an **IDate** object when parsing **startDate** into month, day, and year.

Once you have parsed the line and constructed the temporary objects, they are used to set their respective attributes. Using the set member function rather than assigning the new values to the class attributes ensures that notifications are sent.

When parsing is completed and the attributes have been set, notification is sent to inform that the line has been parsed. Add the member function Code segment 44 to the PARSER.CPV file.

```
LeaseFileParser& LeaseFileParser::parseLine( )
{
  IString custName, carModel, startDate, distPerYear,
    extraCost;

  // parse line using the IStringParse class
  // >> operator, using commas as delimeters
  strNewLine >> custName >> "," >> carModel >> "," >>
    startDate >> "," >> distPerYear >> "," >>
    extraCost;

  // Use set fuctions so observers will be notified
  setCustName( custName );
  setCarModel( carModel );
  setFreeDistancePerYear( distPerYear.asInt() );
  setExtraCost( extraCost.asInt() );
  IString day, month, year;
  startDate >> month >> "-" >> day >> "-" >> year;
  IDate startDateAsIDate( IDate::Month(
    month.asInt() ), day.asInt(), year.asInt() );
  setLeaseStartDate( startDateAsIDate );

  notifyObservers(INotificationEvent(
    LeaseFileParser::lineParsedId, *this));

return *this;
}
```

Code segment 44: parseLine member function

Coding the elementAt Action

When you need to retrieve a line of text from the collection, you use the **elementAt** member function and supply the position in the line you need. The position is a zero based long integer. Add the code in Code segment 45 to the code stub in the PARSER.CPV file:

```
LeaseFileParser& LeaseFileParser::elementAt( long
    position )
{
  try
  {
    strNewLine = strSequence.elementAtPosition(
            ++ position);
    parseLine();
  }
  catch (IException& exc)
  {
    strNewLine = "";
  }
  return *this;
}
```

Code segment 45: elementAt member function

The position passed as a parameter is incremented before it is used to
retrieve the element from the collection. The position is incremented
because the position will come from the index of a selected item in a
list box. The index is zero based, but the parameter required for the
collection member function is one based, so the zero index of a list box
is the first index on the collection. If the element at this position exists it is parsed, just as if the line had come from the file. If the element does not exist, the collection will throw an exception, and as a
result of catching the exception, you set the **strNewLine** class variable to an empty string.

❑ Save these changes by saving the PARSER.HPV and CPV files.

Testing the LeaseFileParser Part

In the previous version of TestView2, you verified that the FlatFile
part was working correctly. You were able to open a file of your choice
and read the contents of the file into a list box. When you read the
CUSTOMER.DAT file it was treated just like any other file and the
information in the list box was correct but not really readable.

Now you have the LeaseFileParser part which will take care of parsing the CUSTOMER.DAT file. In order to test the part you iterate the
development of the test application.

Open the Composition Editor for the **CustomerListCanvas** visual
part and delete the following objects:

❑ pbFileSelect

❑ fileDialog

Notice how deleting the objects also deletes the connections attached to that object. You can delete an object by selecting it and pressing the **Delete** key or by opening the pop-up menu for the object and selecting **Delete**. These objects are being deleted because now the application will only be opening and reading from the CUSTOMER. DAT file.

❑ Open the settings notebook for the **file** part and enter CUS-TOMER.DAT in the **fileName** entry field. This will provide the default filename for the file object.

❑ Delete the following connection:

file(opened) → list box(removeAll)

Now add the **LeaseFileParser** part and make its connections with the following steps:

❑ Drop a LeaseFileParser* part on the free-form surface, call it **parser.**

❑ Move the connection from:

file(currentLine) → list box(addAsLast)

to

file(currentLine) → parser(inputLine)

To move a connection, select it by clicking on it, then drag the end of the connection you want to move to the new object. In this case, drag the end connected to the list box to the **parser** object and release the mouse button. The Preferred list for the parser displays, and you select **inputLine** as the attribute to complete the connection.

❑ Connect:

parser(lineParsed) → list box(addAsLast)

This connection needs a parameter to indicate what will be added to the list box.

❑ Connect:

parser(custName) → connection(text)

Finally, you need to read the file. The ready event can be used to trigger the **open** action of the file object. As you remember, the **ready** event occurs after the part in the Composition Editor has been constructed and initialized.

❑ Connect:

free-form surface (ready) → file(open)

❑ From the connection above connect:

connection (exceptionOccurred) → errorMessage (showException)

When this connection successfully opens the file, the **opened** event occurs. This event is used to trigger reading the flat file. This connection already exist from the previous iteration. All these connections are shown in Figure 172.

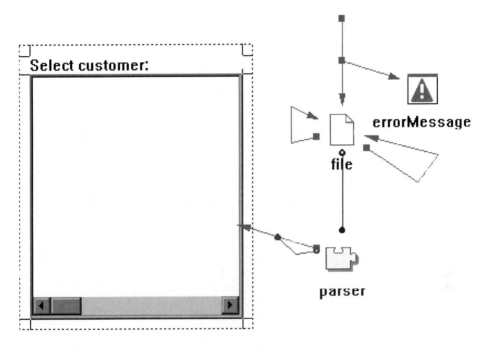

Figure 172: Connections for the CustomerListCanvas part

Running the Completed TestView2 Application

Now you can generate the code and test the application.

❑ Open the Composition Editor for the TestView2 part and generate the **main( )** for the part.

You need to do this because you have added new nonvisual parts to one of the parts, and the existing make file is not aware of these parts. By opening the part the Visual Builder, model gets refreshed, and the new make file generated will ensure that the **Lease-FileParser** part gets compiled.

❑ Also generate the Part source for the **CustomerListCanvas** part.

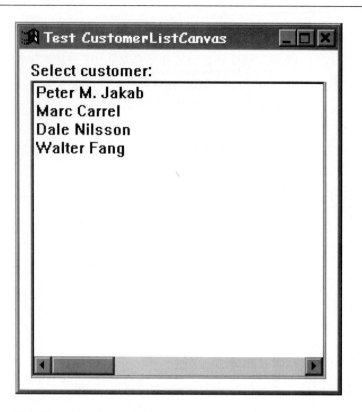

Figure 173: Running the completed TestView2 application

❑ From a command prompt enter **nmake tstview2.mak** to compile the new version of the TestView2 application.

❑ Start the application by entering **tstview2** at the command prompt.

As you can see in Figure 173, the list box only shows the customer name field of the record. Any other attribute from the parser can be displayed on the list box by changing the parameter passed in the connection from the parser (lineParsed) to the list box (addAsLast).

Chapter 10—Summary

You completed the second part of the Car Lease application. To do this you:

- ❑ Built a reusable canvas which lists the contents of the lease file.
- ❑ Used the IListBox part.
- ❑ Created a **FlatFile** nonvisual part which provides the facilities to open, close, read and write a file.
- ❑ Created a **LeaseFileParser** nonvisual part which parses a string from a flat file and assigns fields to attributes.
- ❑ Combined all of the above parts and tested them by building a simple test application.

You may not need a car lease program, but the ability to use flat files is very valuable. In the next application you will reuse the flat file parts, because they have a general purpose interface. Usually the first time you build an application, the parts are not very generic. As you continue to refine an application, you see ways to improve the part design.

What's in Chapter 11

In this chapter you complete the Car Lease application. You will reuse the composite visual parts created in he last two chapters. The completed application reads a car's lease information from a flat file; when you enter the current odometer reading, it calculates the status of the car lease. To do this you will learn to:

❑ Use the INotebook control.

❑ Add pages to the notebook.

❑ Use the IViewPort control.

❑ Add the CustomerCanvas and the CustomerListCanvas to the notebook pages.

❑ Use the IVBVariable part.

❑ Create a composite nonvisual part.

11

Finishing the Lease

Overview of the Lease Application

In the previous two chapters you built the components of the Car Lease Application and then tested them by inserting each of the components on to frame windows. This chapter combines both components into a single application and uses the notebook metaphor for its implementation. One page of the notebook contains the list of customers, the second page contains the details of the lease for the customer selected on the first page.

This application could have been implemented using a different design. For example, a main window could contain the list of customers, and when the user selects a customer a secondary window is created to show the details of the lease for that customer. That would also be a good design, but one of the objectives of this book is to expose you to as many techniques as possible. This chapter provides a good introduction to the **INotebook** control.

INotebook Control Considerations

When you use a notebook control, you should be aware of the performance considerations. Notebooks with a small number of pages are
recommended. How many pages is a small number? The number of
pages is relative to the complexity of the pages. For example, the settings notebook for applications in the operating system has about ten
well designed pages. These notebooks work fine and have acceptable
performance.

There have been a few attempts to design an entire application
around a notebook. These may seem practical because end users find
the notebook metaphor very easy to understand. Programmers find it
easier to use a notebook than to develop a screen hierarchy and navigation. However, large full screen notebooks with 20 or more pages,
with each page having nested multicell canvases and other complex
controls are destined to perform poorly. One software project actually
proposed a 100 page notebook as an application. Fortunately it was
never developed.

What is a Notebook?

A notebook is made up of several parts:

❑ The notebook itself

❑ The pages of the notebook

❑ Usually a viewport control in each page to handle scrolling of the
contents of the page

❑ The composite visual parts which are placed inside the notebook
pages (or on the viewport)

The default behavior of the notebook control in the current version of
the product constructs all notebook pages and their contents at the
time the notebook is constructed. This is regardless of whether the
pages are ever displayed by the user. In reality, only the first page of
the notebook needs to be completely constructed at the time the notebook is constructed. Pages other than the first page should be constructed, but left empty with no contents. This way the notebook page
tabs show and can be selected without incurring the cost of actually
instantiating the page contents. When the page is selected, the composite visual parts on the page are instantiated. For small notebooks
this is not a big problem, but for large, complex notebooks with lots of
pages it takes considerable time to construct the whole notebook.

Remember, there is overhead in constructing the actual contents of
the pages, and also in the initialization required to populate the page
with relevant data. This could include opening databases, reading
files, and so on.

Defining the Lease Notebook View

By now you should be familiar with the Visual Builder and how to save, generate, compile, and run applications. As you develop this application the instructions are not as detailed as the instructions in previous chapters, and there are fewer screen captures.

❑ Ensure your working directory is set to **x:\VABOOK\CAR-LEASE**. From this directory load all the .VBB files except **TESTVIEW** and **TESTVIEW2**.

❑ Create a new visual part.

❑ Name the Class **LeaseNotebook**.

❑ Use **IFrameWindow** for the **Base class**.

❑ Use **LEASEAPP** for the .VBB filename.

❑ Open the Composition Editor for LeaseNotebook.

❑ Delete the default canvas in the frame window.

❑ Directly edit the title of the frame window to read **Lease status calculator**.

❑ From the **Composers** category, add an **INotebook*** control as the client of the frame window.

❑ Open the settings notebook for the notebook.

For the purpose of consistency, this book uses the **pmCompatible** style for the notebook. This means that applications using this style look and behave the same in Windows and OS/2. If you are working exclusively on Windows developing your own applications, you may prefer not to set this style. If you use the native Windows notebook, your notebook looks the same as the notebooks in other Windows applications.

❑ Open the settings notebook for the INotebook control.

❑ On the **General** page enter the settings in Table 27.

❑ If you are developing in Windows, switch to the **Styles** page of the settings notebook and select **pmCompatible**.

Table 27: Setting for notebook control

Setting	Selection
Layout	Page tabs up
Binding	Spiral
Tab Shape	Square
Justification for Status area	Center
Justification for Tabs	Center

The settings notebook for the **INotebook** control provides many choices. If you want to experiment and see the visual result of the choices, you can select different settings, press the **Apply** button, and see what changed on the notebook on the Composition Editor. When you finish changing the notebook settings, the notebook should look like Figure 174.

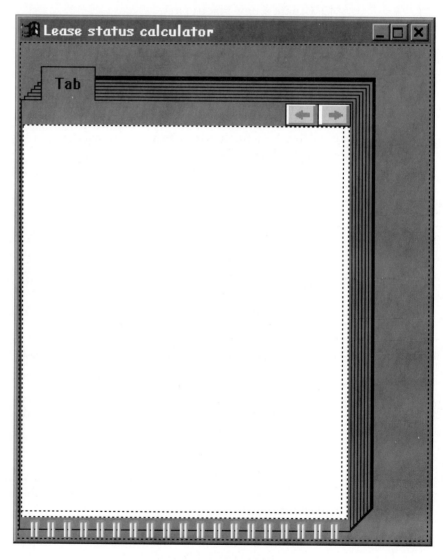

Figure 174: Notebook for the Car Lease Application

Selecting Notebook Parts

When you first drop an **INotebook** control it already has one page, and the page has an **ICanvas** control. The notebook page and canvas are provided by the Visual Builder. You need two pages in this notebook, one for each of the canvases you built in the previous chapters. Additional pages can be added from the pop-up menu for the **INotebook** control. You may find it difficult to display the correct pop-up menu for the notebook control, because there are three components occupying much of the same space on your screen

1. The notebook itself
2. The notebook page
3. The canvas

Refer to Figure 175 for suggested locations where you can place the mouse pointer to select the right component.

By far the hardest part to select is the notebook page, because it is hidden behind the canvas. To select it, place the mouse pointer between the two dashed lines on the inside of the notebook. Selecting the notebook page would be virtually impossible if this artificial area on the edge of the notebook page was not provided. This area is very thin, just a few pixels wide, and you need to be very careful when positioning the mouse pointer over it. This area is only seen in the Visual Builder and does not show at runtime.

❑ Select the pop-up menu for the notebook. You know you have the right pop-up menu when you see the **Add Page After** and **Add Page Before** menu items.

❑ Add a page after the current page to the notebook.

If you accidentally add too many pages to the notebook, you can delete them from the pop-up menu. You can also use the **Edit**, **Undo** menu item. Remember, Undo is your friend.

Notebook Page Settings

There are a few settings needed on the notebook page. The most important item to change is the default text on the tab on each notebook page. The Visual Builder automatically adds notebook pages with the generic **Tab** label. The text of the page tabs cannot be edited directly. You must change the text on the setting notebook for the notebook page with the following steps:

❑ Open the settings for the first notebook page.

❑ Enter **List** in the **Tab text** field.

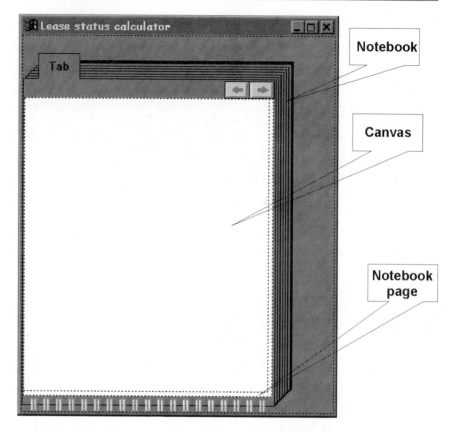

Figure 175: Mouse pointer locations

- ❏ Enter **Customer List** in the **Status text** field.
- ❏ Switch to the **Styles** page and select **statusTextOn**.
- ❏ Select the **OK** button to save these changes.
- ❏ On the Composition Editor, flip to the next page by selecting its **Tab**.
- ❏ Open the settings for the second notebook page.
- ❏ Enter **Details** in the **Tab text** field.
- ❏ Enter **Customer details** in the **Status text** field (see Figure 176).
- ❏ Switch to the **Styles** page and select **statusTextOn**.
- ❏ Select the **OK** button to save these changes.

If the text on the notebook tabs appears clipped, open the settings notebook for the notebook control and change the values under the **Page button and tab sizes** group box. Enter new values for both the Width and the Height in pixels, for example, 70 and 25 respectively.

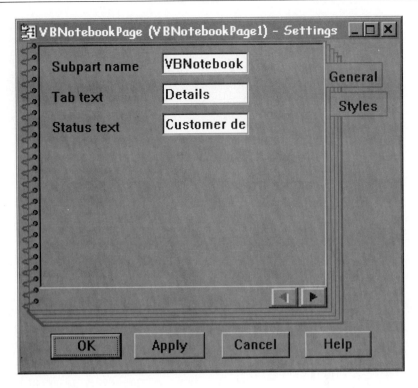

Figure 176: IVBNotebookPage Settings notebook

Using the IViewPort Control

Notebook controls take up quite a bit of screen real estate with the tabs, the pages, and the binding graphics. In addition, many times the users of your application may have a lower resolution monitor than the developer of the application. These factors result in a problem where all the contents of a notebook page do not fit on a notebook page, even when the notebook is maximized or full screen.

The **IViewPort** control is very well suited to solving this problems. It provides both vertical and horizontal scroll bars when needed by the client. It is a good design decision to replace the ICanvas control that the Visual Builder places on the notebook page with an IViewPort control.

❏ Delete the default **ICanvas** control from each of the notebook pages. Switch to the page, click on the canvas, and press the **Delete** key or select the **Delete** item form the pop-up menu.

❏ Add an **IViewPort*** part to each page of the INotebook.

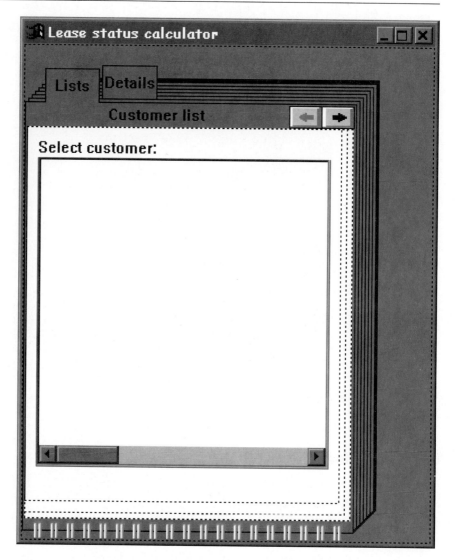

Figure 177: First page of the notebook

You may not see any scroll bars when you first place the viewport on to the notebook page, but the viewport control is on the notebook page. To confirm that it is actually on the notebook page you can place the mouse pointer in the middle of the page and select the viewport control by pressing the left mouse button. When it is selected the **IViewPort** control is listed in the information area at the bottom of the Composition Editor.

The next step is to reuse the two canvas parts you made in the previous chapters in the notebook pages:

❏ Add a **CustomerListCanvas*** part to the viewport on the first page of the notebook using the **Options**, **Add part...** from the Composition Editor menu bar.

❏ Size the **CustomerListCanvas** so that it fills most of the area on the viewport. Leave a few pixels of the viewport visible so it can be selected if needed. The notebook should look like Figure 177.

❏ Add a **CustomerCanvas*** part to the viewport on the second page of the notebook.

❏ Size the **CustomerCanvas** so that it fills most of the area on the viewport. Leave a few pixels of the viewport visible so it can be selected if needed. The notebook should look like Figure 178.

Viewport Considerations

The ICanvas control works fine with view ports because the viewport handles all the scrolling. There is a special consideration when using multicell canvas view ports. When the visual parts you are placing inside view ports are composed in a multicell canvas, the viewport must be told to size its client when its size changes. Without this setting, the multicell canvas does not behave as expected when placed on a viewport. For example, the scroll bars on the viewport does not show all of the hidden area of the multicell. The way to set up the viewport depends on whether you are running Windows or OS/2.

❏ In Windows the procedure is very straight forward. From the Styles page of the settings notebook for the **IViewPort** control, set the **expandableViewWindow** radio button to **on**.

❏ In OS/2 the viewport needs a special handler. Add an **IVBMinSizeViewPortHandler** on the **Handlers** page of the settings notebook for the **IViewPort** control.

The initial user interface is complete, so you can generate the code and test the application with the following steps:

❏ Save and generate the Part source code for the **LEASENB** part.

❏ Generate the **main()** for the **LEASENB** part.

❏ Switch over to a command prompt session and compile the Lease application. At the command prompt type **nmake lsntbook.mak**.

If you are getting linker errors at this stage, it is probably due to the fact that some files did not need to get compiled because they were from a previous compilation of your test programs. However, some temporary template resolution files are not in the right directories

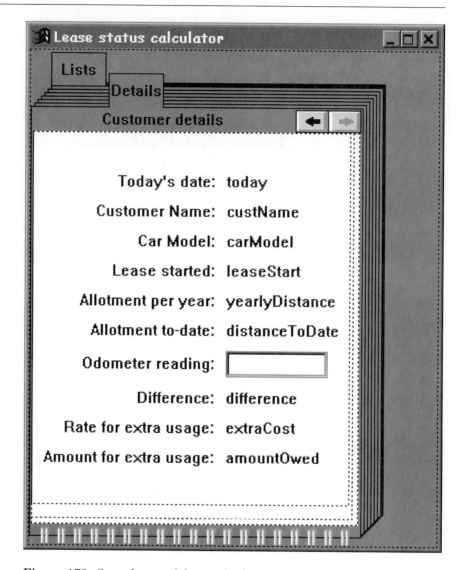

Figure 178: Second page of the notebook

for the linker to find them. To solve this problem you need to force a new compilation of these files. Delete the **.OBJ** files from your working directory and run **nmake** again. This time you should not get any errors.

❑ Start the Car Lease application by typing **lsntbook** at the command prompt to can see how it works.

When the Car Lease application starts you see a frame window with the notebook control as seen in Figure 179. You can resize the frame

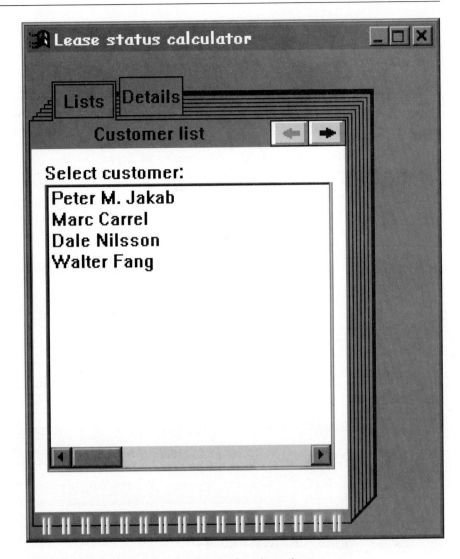

Figure 179: Running the Car Lease, first iteration

window, and the notebook control automatically expands and contracts because it is the client of the frame window. You can select the pages by pointing to the tabs and pressing the left mouse button. Close the program and continue developing the application.

Making a Composite Nonvisual Part

In the previous two chapters you built and used the FlatFile, Parser, and LeaseCalc nonvisual parts. All these functions are needed for the

Car Lease application. You tested the parts on their own by building some simple test applications. Now it is time to put it all together.

One way to provide the function required for the application could be to use the parts "as is" and interconnect them in the same Composition Editor as the visual parts. This would create a working part with a lot of function, as well as a lot of connections. Since these parts are used for a single purpose in this application, a better approach is to combine the nonvisual parts into a composite nonvisual part. This approach reduces the complexity of a part to the user by combining functions and reducing the number of connections.

Create a new nonvisual part to combine the functions of the FlatFile, Parser, and LeaseCalc nonvisual parts as shown in Figure 180:

- ❑ Enter **FileParserCalc** as the Class name.
- ❑ Enter **Composite nonvisual part for lease application** as the Description.
- ❑ Enter **LEASEAPP** as the .VBB filename. This adds the Lease-Calc part definitions to the LEASEAPP.VBB file.
- ❑ Select **Nonvisual** as the Part type.
- ❑ Keep **IStandardNotifier** as the Base class.
- ❑ Press the **Open** push button to start editing the LeaseCalc part.

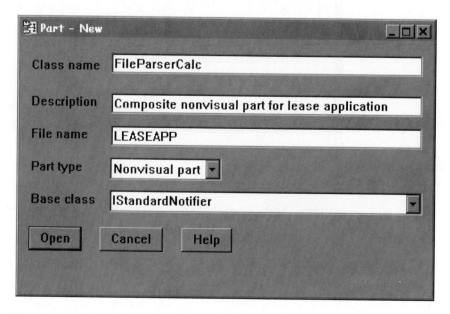

Figure 180: Creating the FileParserCalc

Defining the Attributes

Add the attributes specified in Table 28 to the **FileParserCalc** non-visual part.

This section covers composite nonvisual parts, and you may be wondering how you can combine the nonvisual parts in the Part Interface Editor. You can use the Composition Editor with nonvisual parts just like you have done with composite visual parts. Switch to the Composition Editor using the **View**, **Composition Editor** menu item.

You can simplify the Lease Notebook application by combining the nonvisual parts. To do this, add the following nonvisual parts to the free-form surface using the **Options**, **Add part...** menu item (see Figure 181):

- ❏ FlatFile* and name it **aFile**.
- ❏ LeaseFileParser* and name it **aParser**.
- ❏ LeaseCalc* and name it **aLeaseCalc**.
- ❏ IDate* and name it **today**.

Figure 181: Parts added to the Composition Editor

Table 28: Attributes for the FileParserCalc part

Attribute	Type	Description
leaseStartDateAsString	IString	The date when the lease started represented as an IString.
amountOwed	IString	The formatted amount owed represented as an IString.

Connecting the Nonvisual Parts

Make the following connections to open the flatfile:

❏ free-form surface(ready) → aFile(open)

❏ Open the settings notebook for **aFile**, select **Parameters** , enter **CUSTOMER.DAT** in the **fileName** attribute.

❏ aFile (currentLine) → aParser (inputLine)

❏ aParser (lineParsed) → aLeaseCalc (odometerReading)

Parameters for the above connection:

❏ Open the settings notebook of the above connection, select **Parameters**, and enter **0** in the **odometerReading** entry field.

The above connection enters a zero in the odometer reading attribute of aLeaseCalc every time a line is parsed. This resets the difference value and causes the amountOwed to be recalculated. Figure 182 shows these initial connections.

❏ aLeaseCalc (difference) → aLeaseCalc (calculateAmountOwing)

This connection calculates and updates the **amountOwed** field on the display every time the **difference** attribute changes. Connect the **actionResult** for the above connection:

❏ calculateAmountOwing(actionResult) → FileParserCalc (amountOwed)

To make the above connection you select the connection itself, bring up its pop-up menu, select **actionResult**, move the connection mouse pointer to the free-form surface and click. The two attributes you added in the PIE for this part appear in the pop-up menu. Select **amountOwed**. Figure 183 show the connections so far.

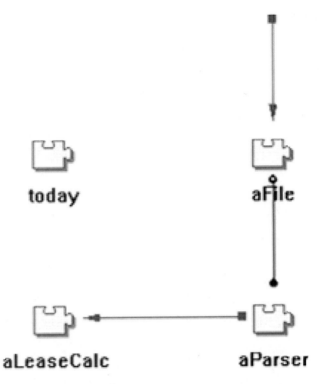

Figure 182: Initial connections for the FileParserCalc

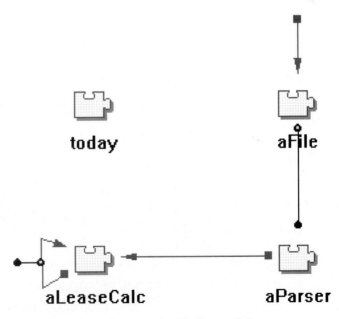

Figure 183: More connections for the FileParserCalc

Continue with the following connections:

- ❑ aParser (extraCost) → LeaseCalc (extraCost)
- ❑ aParser (freeDistancePerYear) → aLeaseCalc (freeDistancePer-Year)
- ❑ aParser (leaseStartDate) → aLeaseCalc (leaseStartDate)
- ❑ today(today) → aLeaseCal(today)
- ❑ Tear off the **leaseStartDate** attribute of the aParser part.
- ❑ leaseStartDate of aParser (asString) → FileParserCalc (lease-StartDateAsString)

Figure 184 shows the completed connections.

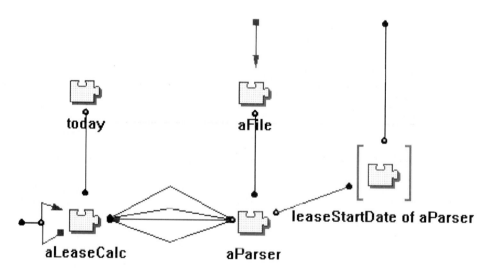

Figure 184: Completed connections for the FileParserCalc

Promoting Features

In order for this part to be usable when it is included in the rest of the application, you need to promote some of its features. By default all the features of the nonvisual subparts are be hidden and not available for connections.

- ❑ Switch to the PIE for the FileParserCalc.
- ❑ Select the **Promote** notebook page.
- ❑ From the **Subpart name** drop down list box select **aParser.**

❑ From the **Feature type** drop down list box select **attribute.**

❑ From the **Promotable Feature** drop down list box select **car-Model.**

❑ In the Promote feature name entry field enter **carModel**, press the **Add** push button.

❑ Repeat the steps above to promote the features in Table 29 as shown in Figure 185.

❑ Switch to the **Preferred** page of the PIE and add all the promoted attributes to the **Preferred Features** list box as shown in Figure 186.

❑ Save and generate the part source.

❑ Switch to the **Class Editor** and specify the .HPV and .CPV filenames. Use **FLPRSRCL.HPV** and **FLPRSRCL.CPV**.

❑ Generate the feature code for the FileParserCalc part.

Table 29: Features to promote in the FileParserCalc part

Promote Feature Name	Subpart Name	Feature Type	Promotable Feature
customerName	aParser	attribute	custName
extraCost	aParser	attribute	extraCost
freeDistancePerYear	aParser	attribute	freeDistancePerYear
leaseFileParser	aParser	attribute	this
freeDistanceToDate	aLeaseCalc	attribute	freeDistanceToDate
odometerReading	aLeaseCalc	attribute	odometerReading
difference	aLeaseCalc	attribute	difference
differenceColor	aLeaseCalc	attribute	differenceColor
readFile	aFile	action	readFile
todayAsString	today	attribute	asString

Completing the Lease Notebook Application

You will now modify the CustomerCanvas and the CustomerListCanvas parts you built in the previous two chapters. If you want to preserve these files, use the Copy feature of the Visual Builder to copy them under different names such as OldCustomerCanvas and OldCustomerListCanvas. You may save these copies in the same LEASEAPP.VBB file or in a separate file.

Delete all the nonvisual parts in both the CustomerCanvas and CustomerListCanvas parts. Their function is replaced by the new FileParserCalc you just finished building.

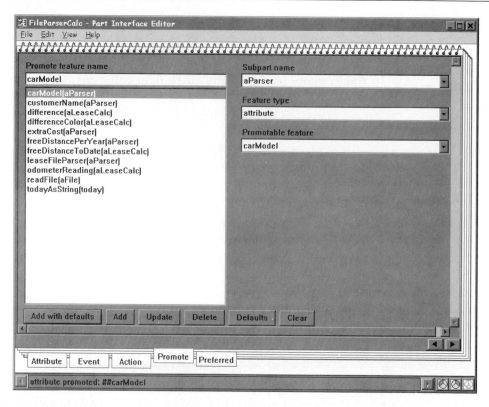

Figure 185: Promoting features on the FileParserCalc part

Finishing Touches to the CustomerCanvas Part

Perform the following steps to update the CustomerCanvas part to use the new **FileParserCalc** nonvisual part.

❑ Replace the **MyDate** part with an IStaticText control, name this control **today**.

❑ Add an **IVBFlyText*** part to the free-form surface to handle the bubble help for this panel.

❑ From **Options**, **part**... add a **FileParserCalc*** part to the free-form surface, and name it **leaseInfo**.

The data from the nonvisual part needs to be connected to the user interface. Make the following attribute-to-attribute connections so the Composition Editor looks like Figure 187:

❑ leaseInfo(todayAsString) →today(text)

❑ leaseInfo(customerName) → custName(text)

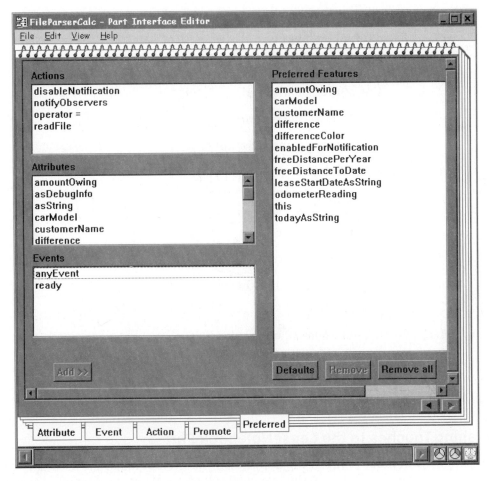

Figure 186: Adding promoted features to the Preferred list

❏ leaseInfo(carModel) → carModel(text)

❏ leaseInfo(leaseStartDateAsString) → leaseStart(text)

❏ leaseInfo(freeDistancePerYear) → distancePerYear(valueAsInt)

❏ leaseInfo(freeDistanceToDate) → distanceToDate(valueAsInt)

❏ leaseInfo(odometerReading) → efOdometer(valueAsInt)

❏ leaseInfo(difference) →difference(valueAsInt)

❏ leaseInfo(extraCost) → extraCost(valueAsInt)

❏ leaseInfo(amountOwed) → amountOwed(text)

❏ leaseInfo(differenceColor) → difference(foregroundColor)

❏ leaseInfo(differenceColor) → amountOwed(foregroundColor)

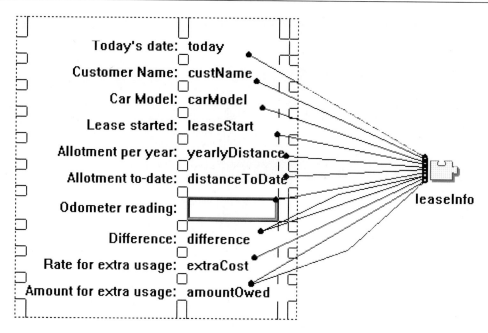

Figure 187: Connections in CustomerCanvas to leaseInfo

❏ free-form surface(ready) → efOdometer(setFocus)

❏ Save and generate the part source for **CustomerCanvas**.

Finishing Touches to the LeaseNotebook Part

In order to finish the application you need to make the necessary connections between the two notebook pages. When a customer is selected from the first notebook page, the information related to that customer is loaded into the attributes on the second page. When the user switches to the second page, the updated information is there and an odometer reading is typed into the odometer reading entry field. As numbers are typed, the difference between the Allotment to-date and the odometer reading is calculated and displayed in the Difference field.

There is a very subtle function used on the Amount Owing field. While the Difference amount is positive, the Difference and Amount Owing fields are a dark green color and display a 0 (zero). Once the **difference** becomes negative, the color changes to red and displays the calculated amount owed.

Using Variables with Notebooks

In order to communicate between the two pages, you need to have access to the list box in the **CustomerListCanvas** and the parser which is part of the **FileParserCalc** nonvisual part. These subparts can be accessed using an **IVBVariable** part. You can think of this part as a pointer to a part that already exists. Just like pointers in C and C++, they must point to valid objects before they can be used.

The **ready** event for the **LeaseNotebook** occurs after all its components have been constructed and initialized. This is a good time to initialize the **IVBVariable** parts, which are pointers to the list box and the parser.

- ❏ From the **Models** category add two **IVBVariable** parts to the free-form surface.
- ❏ Name them **parser** and **listBox**.
- ❏ Right click on the **parser** object to bring up its pop-up menu, select **Change type...**, and enter **LeaseFileParser*** in the **new part type** entry field.
- ❏ Click on the **listBox** object to bring up its pop-up menu, select **Change type...**, and enter **IListBox*** in the **new part type** entry field.

The icon for the list box variable changed to the icon for a IListBox control. That is because you changed the type of the pointer from **IStandardNotifier*** to **IListBox***. All the features of an **IListBox** control are now available through the variable part. The same is true for the **parser** object. So far, these pointers are not pointing to any real objects. They are known as "wild pointers." Connect the **ready** event to initialize the variables (or pointers):

- ❏ free-form surface(ready) → listBox(this)
- ❏ free-form surface(ready) → parser(this)

These two connections are incomplete, as noted by the dashed lines in Figure 188. A parameter is missing to specify the real objects for these variables. They are the actual customerListBox part from the CustomerListCanvas and the parser part from the FileParserCalc part. These features are not available right now on the LeaseNotebook. You must go back to the **CustomerCanvas** part and promote these features. Also, they should be added to the Preferred list of their respective parts to make them easier to find.

- ❏ Open the **CustomerCanvas** part. Click on the **leaseInfo** object to bring up its pop-up menu. Select **Promote Parts Feature...**. From the dialog box select the **leaseFileParser** attribute, change the **Promoted feature name** to **leaseFileParser**.
- ❏ Promote the **readFile** action. Change its name to **readFile**.
- ❏ Close the dialog to complete the promotion.

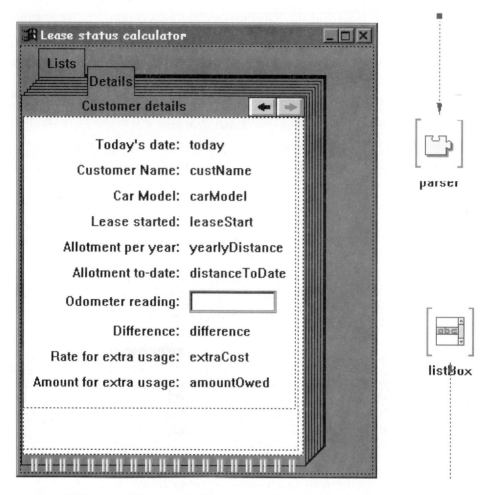

Figure 188: Adding two IVBVariables to the LeaseNotebook

❏ Switch to the PIE and select the **Preferred** page, add **lease-FileParser** and **readFile** to the Preferred list. Then **Save and Generate**, **Part source**.

The attributes you just promoted are now available for you.

❏ Switch back to the Composition Editor containing the **Lease-Notebook** part.

❏ Select the **List** tab of the notebook to select the first page.

❏ Click on the CustomerListCanvas and connect the customer-ListCanvas(customerListbox) attribute, as a parameter to the existing connection from ready to listBox variable(this).

❑ Select the **Details** tab of the notebook which flips to the second page as shown in Figure 189. Click on the CustomerCanvas and connect the customerCanvas(leaseFileParser) attribute, as a parameter to the existing connection from ready to parser variable(this).

These two connections properly initialize the variables so that when the ready event occurs they point to real objects inside the canvases.

When you select different pages on the LeaseNotebook, only the connections pertaining to the currently selected page are shown. The connections for the other pages are not shown, but they are still

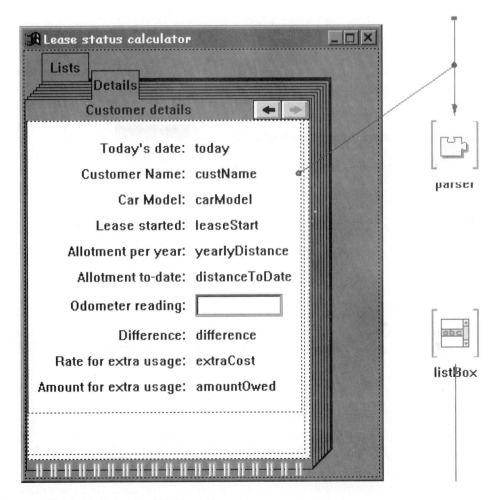

Figure 189: Initializing the IVBVariable parts

there. This is a feature of the Visual Builder which reduces the complexity of the connections to the notebook.

To complete the application a few more connections are needed. First, the list box needs to be filed with the list of customers. Next, when a user selects an entry in the list box the application needs to select the proper entry from the collection of customers in the parser. Make the following connections to fill the list box as lines from the file are being parsed:

❑ parser(lineAddedToCollection) → listBox(addAsLast)

As a parameter to this connection:

❑ parser(customerName) → connection(text)

To inform the parser when a customer is selected from the list box, connect:

❑ listBox(selection) → parser(elementAt)

As a parameter to this connection:

❑ listBox(selection) → connection(Position)

The next two connections read the file and select the first customer on the list when the application starts up. Switch to the **Details** page of the notebook. Use the **ready** event and connect:

❑ free-form surface (ready) → CustomerCanvas(readFile)
❑ free-form surface (ready) → listBox(selection)
❑ Open the connections settings notebook for the above connection by double-clicking it. Press the **Set parameters...** button and enter **0** in the **selection** entry field.

Figure 190 shows the completed connections.

Open the pop-up menu for the free-form surface; select the **Re-order connections from...**, and verify that the order of the connections is as follows:

1. free-form surface(ready) → listBox(this)
2. free-form surface(ready) → parser(this)
3. free-form surface (ready) → CustomerCanvas(readFile)
4. free-form surface (ready) → listBox(selection)

If the connections are not in this order, drag and drop the entries on the dialog and arrange them in this order.

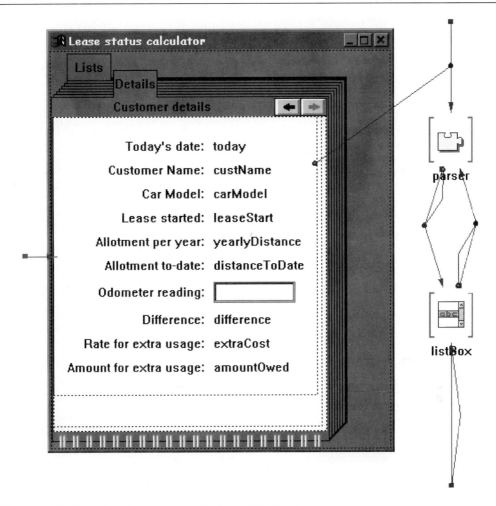

Figure 190: Completed connections for LeaseNotebook

Running the Lease Notebook Application

Save and generate the **main( )** and the **Part source** for the Lease-Notebook part. At the command prompt type **nmake lsntbook.mak** to compile and link the application. When the compilation completes, start the application. At the command prompt enter **lsntbook** to run the completed application. The Lease notebook should look like Figure 191.

Test the Car Lease Application by selecting different customers. Verify that the correct information is shown in the Details page and that the differences and amount owing values are calculated properly as shown in Figure 192.

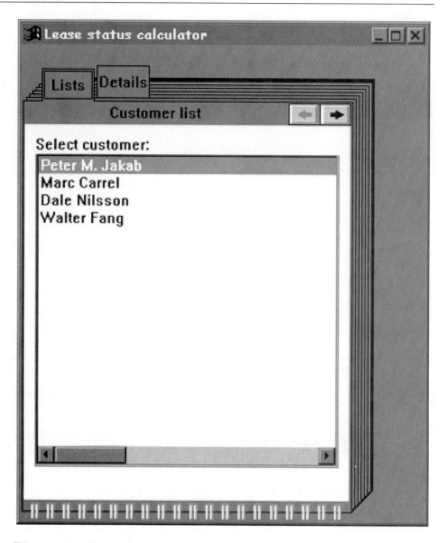

Figure 191: List page of the running application

If everything looks fine, you should pat yourself in the back. You have completed a fairly complex and involved application. If the application is not operating properly, check your connections and make sure you have not missed any. If you still have problems, this is a good opportunity to recompile the application using the Trace options and follow the sequence of events which leads to the notebook displaying on the screen. The file should open, its contents read and displayed in the list box, as each line was parsed from the file. When a selection is made in the list box the correct entry is selected from the collection in the parser. It is parsed and the new values are updated in the Details page. The odometer reading field is set to zero.

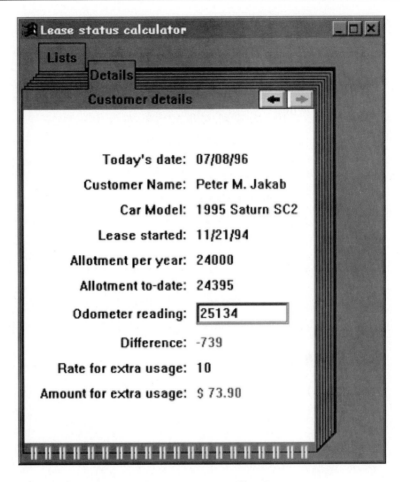

Figure 192: Details page of the running application

Chapter 11—Summary

In this chapter you completed the Car Lease application. You reused the composite visual parts created in Chapters 8 and 9 and combined the nonvisual parts into a composite nonvisual part. You have also learned to:

❑ Use the INotebook control.

❑ Add pages to the notebook.

❑ Use the IViewPort control.

❑ Use the IVBVariable part.

❑ Create a composite nonvisual part.

What's in Chapter 12

In this chapter you will build a Data Viewer application called DB-Viewer. To build this application you will use the Data Access Builder to create the nonvisual parts. You do not need to do any C++ coding in this chapter. In making the DBViewer application you will do the following:

❑ Build a simple application that interacts with a database.

❑ Use the Data Access Builder to map relational database tables to C++ classes.

❑ Generate C++ classes in the Data Access Builder.

❑ Import class definitions into the Visual Builder.

❑ Use the data access nonvisual parts to build an application for viewing the contents of the database. This database contains tables with information on contacts, including name, area, and phone number.

❑ Use the IDatastore class to open a database.

❑ Use the Container control and Container columns to display a details view.

12

Making a
Data Viewer

In this chapter you use the data access nonvisual parts to build an application which is refined using the iterative method. This application manages a table with information about contacts, including their name and phone number.

Building the Contact Database

You need DB2 installed on your system in order to complete this application, see the installation instructions at the beginning of the book if you have not yet installed DB2.

The Open Class Library data access classes support DB2 Version 1.2, Version 2.0, and Version 2.1. DB2 Version 2.0 is required for the Windows NT operating system and Version 2.1.1 is required for the Windows 95 operating system.

At the time of printing, only the Windows version of VisualAge for C++ supports ODBC (Open Database Connectivity), which gives you access to most of the leading databases. To use ODBC you need an ODBC driver provided by the database supplier. A try-and-buy version of DB2 Version 2.1 is included on the CD-ROM included with the book. An ODBC driver is supplied with DB2.

The database used in this example is built by running a .BAT file on Windows or a .CMD file on OS/2. This file contains command line calls to DB2. Create the database using the **CONTACT.BAT** file (or **CONTACT.CMD** IN OS/2) which is installed in the **x:\VABOOK\DATABASE** directory. The **Contact** database is installed on the drive you specify as the parameter to the command file.

❑ In Windows, open a **DB2/2 Command Window** session by selecting **Start**, **Programs**, **DB2 for Windows**, **DB2 Command Window**.

In OS/2 any command prompt session will do.

❑ At the command prompt enter:

contact x

The version of DB2 included with the CD-ROM in this book is 2.1.1. If you already have DB2/2 version 1.X installed in your system use the CONT1X.CMD file to create the database instead of CONTACT.CMD.

This command file installs the **Contact** database on drive x:. Be careful, there is no colon (:) after the drive letter in the parameter you specify. The command file executes the following functions:

1. Starts the database services.
2. Deletes the Contact database if it already exists.
3. Creates the Contact database.
4. Connects to the Contact database.
5. Creates the Contact table.
6. Adds data to the Contact table.
7. Creates the Area Table.
8. Adds data to the Area Table.
9. Creates the Contview view.
10. Commits the database.
11. Resets the database connection.

In OS/2 the security for the database is managed by the User Profile Management (UPM) application. If necessary, you are prompted to enter the userid and password of the local database administrator (usually USERID = USERID and PASSWORD = PASSWORD).

If you do not have a USERID user with a password of PASSWORD with administrator authority, please use UPM to create one to perform this exercise. This is the default administrator setup when you first installed DB2/2.

In Windows NT, start the Administrative Tools, User Manager application and add a user named **USERID** with a password of **PASSWORD**. Give this user administrator access. Also, from the Control Panel, Services folder, ensure that the DB2 Security Server is started.

In Windows 95, just logon to Windows as USERID with a password of PASSWORD. Windows 95 automatically creates the new user for you.

Data Access Builder

Start the Data Access Builder by selecting the associated icon in the VisualAge C++ folder.

  In the Windows version you can change the **working directory** in the Data Access Builder. If you do not change the working directory the code is generated in the default directory **x:\IBMCPP\WORKING**.

You can also start the Data Access Builder from a command prompt in the directory where you want the files generated.

❑ Open a command prompt and change the directory to **x:\VABOOK\DATABASE**.

❑ Start the Data Access Builder by entering **IDATA** on the command line.

Variations on Starting the Data Access Builder

  In OS/2 there are a few variations to starting the Data Access Builder. The icon for the Data Access Builder is in the **Tools** folder within the VisualAge C++ folder, so you must go into the **Tools** folder to start the Data Access Builder by selecting the associated icon.

Also, the OS/2 version does not have an option in the Data Access Builder to change the path of the generated files. One technique to manage this limitation is to generate the data access files, then copy or move them to your build directory. If you want to change the path where the generated files go, start the Data Access Builder from a command prompt in the directory where you want the files generated.

❑ Open a command prompt and change the directory to **x:\VABOOK\DATABASE**.

❑ Start the Data Access Builder by entering **ICSDATA** on the command line.

You can achieve the same result by changing the working directory in the settings notebook for the icon representing the Data Access Builder before starting the program by double-clicking the icon.

Mapping the Database Table to C++ Parts

When you start the Data Access Builder a Startup window appears as shown in Figure 193. You have the option to permanently discard this window by selecting the checkbox labeled **Display this window on startup**.

Proceed mapping the database tables to C++ classes by the following steps:

❑ From the Startup window, select the **Create class...** push button to work with the database tables. If the startup window does not show, select **File**, **Create class...** from the menu bar.

❑ Select the **CONTACT** database in the **Database** list box.

❑ If you are running in Windows, select DB2 Version 2.X from the **Database Type** list and **TABLE**, **VIEW** from the **Table Filter**, **Type** list.

❑ Select the **Connect** push button. If you are running on OS/2 and you have not logged on the database, UPM prompts you with the logon dialog at this point.

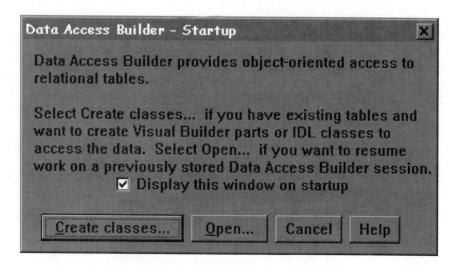

Figure 193: Opening screen of the Data Access Builder

❏ Select all the tables in the Contact database by selecting the **Select all** push button as shown in Figure 194. This selects:

USERID.CONTACT table

USERID.AREATABL table

USERID.CONTVIEW table

❏ Select the **Create classes...** push button to start the mapping process.

Figure 194 shows the Data Access Builder for Windows dialog box. The OS/2 version of the dialog is very similar, without the Database Type and Table Filter areas.

The Windows product is newer than the current OS/2 version. There are improvements introduced in the Windows version reflected in the figures in this book. If you do not see DB2 listed in the **Database type** list you probably installed VisualAge for C++ before you installed DB2. You need to Register DB2 as an available database before you can proceed. Select **Options, Register Database** from the menu bar.

There are subtle differences in the screen you see in OS/2 version. However, the instructions to build the exercises work in both platforms.

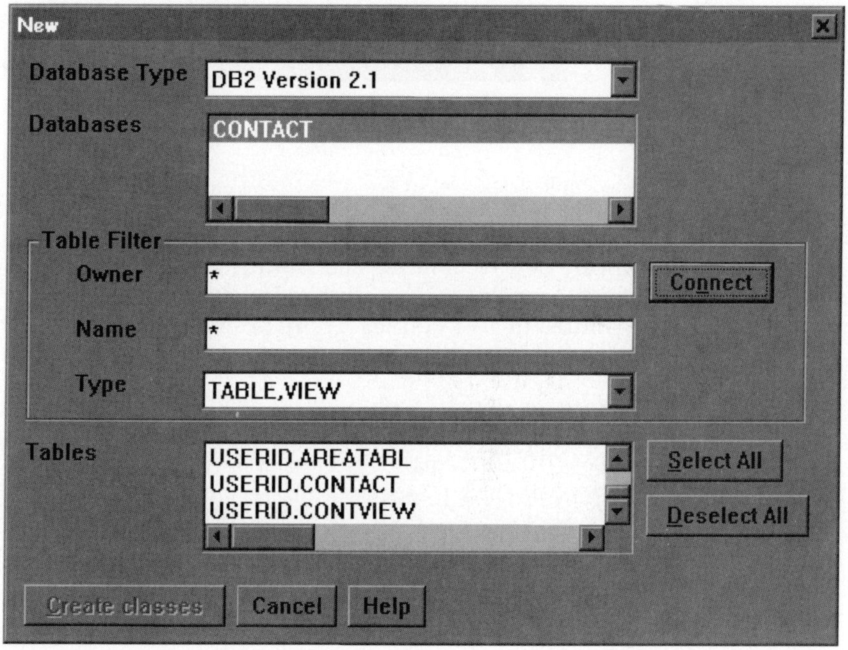

Figure 194: Create classes dialog box

In Windows, after you select the **Create classes** push button the Create Class Options dialog box appears. This dialog gives you a chance to select your generation and data access method options, as seen in Figure 195.

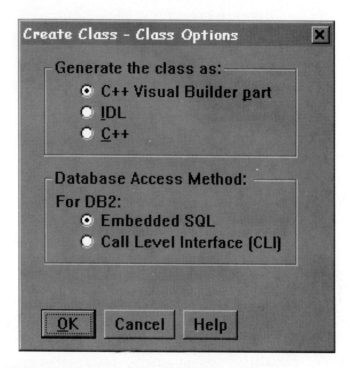

Figure 195: Create Class - Class Options dialog

Any references to database tables in this book apply to both tables and views. The mapping process runs automatically and the tables are mapped to C++ objects. The Data Access Builder reads the table definitions, translates the columns in the tables, and maps the columns to attributes in C++ classes. There are two tables and one view which are mapped to the following classes as shown in Figure 196:

AREATABL CLASS

CONTVIEW CLASS

CONTACT CLASS.

Creating Additional Mappings

The classes generated by the Data Access Builder contain all the columns in the table as attributes in the class. You may not need all the columns in the class, or you may want to optimize the size of the

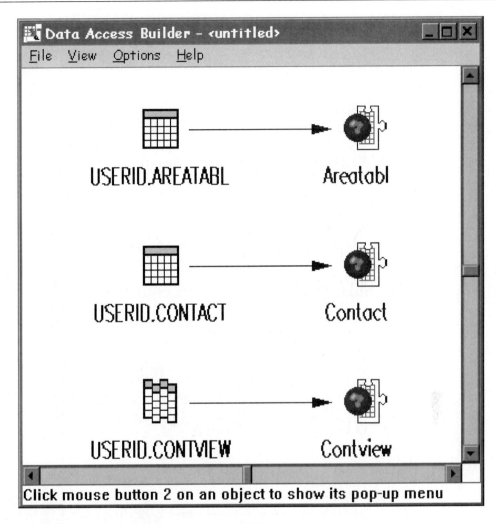

Figure 196: Class Mapping for the CONTACT database

class. To do this you can create additional table mappings and then delete selected attributes which are not required by your application from the class. This section shows how to make additional mappings, and the section *Viewing Table Mappings* shows you how to delete attributes in the class.

❑ Click the right mouse button on the **CONTVIEW** table icon. The pop-up menu allows you to access the table settings and to create additional C++ classes which map to the table.

❑ From the pop-up menu, select **Create class** and another class is created as shown in Figure 197.

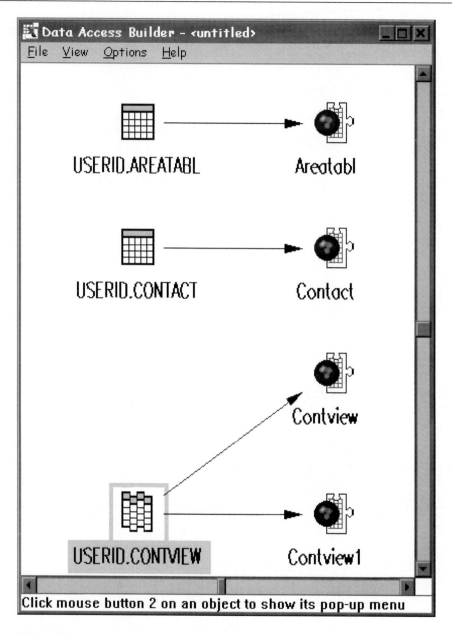

Figure 197: Additional mapping for CONTVIEW

The Contview1 mapping is not used in this application. After you finish experimenting with it you can delete it.

Viewing the Table Mappings

The Data Access Builder appears similar to the Composition Editor in the Visual Builder, but there are a number of differences. The Data Access Builder is a static view of the table mappings. You can not reposition the icons which represent the tables or classes. The arrows indicate that there is a mapping relationship between a table and a class. These arrows are not like the connections in the Visual Builder. Let's look at the part the Data Access Builder created with the following steps:

❑ Press the right mouse button on the blue sphere to access the pop-up menu for the class.

❑ Select **Open Settings** to view the mapping data where you can view the following:

1. On the **Names** page you can modify the filename used for the generated files.

2. On the **Attributes** page you can view the mapping for the attributes. For example the database **varchar** attribute is mapped to the Open Class Library **IString**.

3. On the **Members** page (**Part Methods** in OS/2) you can view the declaration of the methods defined to access the database.

4. In OS/2 there is an **IDL Methods** page that displays the methods in the SOM (System Object Model) generated classes. This application only uses the Visual Builder parts, so you can ignore this page for now.

The contact part settings are shown in Figure 198.

Generating the Data Access Code

The Data Access Builder can generate the C++ code for the classes that are mapped from the database tables. The OS/2 version supports imbedded SQL only, and the Windows version additionally supports SQL CLI (Call Level Interface). When you generate the C++ code for the classes you are prompted to select the type of file you want generated. The Data Access Builder can also generate the files required for SOM classes. This option is not used with this book. The default generation option for the Data Access builder generates C++ classes and the export file for the Visual Builder. Generate the data access classes with the following steps:

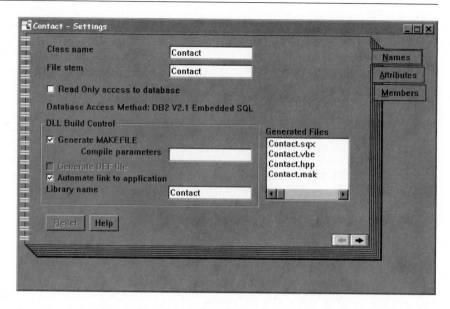

Figure 198: Settings for the CONTACT part

❑ From the **Contact** class pop-up menu, click on **Generate** to create the files for that class. When the code is generated the class icon changes.

❑ Repeat this same step to generate the C++ files for the **Areatabl** and **Contview** classes.

The Data Access Builder generates a number of files for each class. The files generated for the **Contact** class are listed in Table 30.

The OS/2 version of the Data Access Builder appends either **v** or **y**, depending on the file type, to the generated file name. This imposes a seven character limit to the filenames you choose for the classes. In OS/2 the .VBE file is CONTACTV.VBE.

Table 30: Files generated by the Data Access Builder

Filename	Description
CONTACT.HPP	Header file for the classes Contact and ContactManager
CONTACT.CPP	Contact and ContactManager classes definition
CONTACT.DEF	Definition file for compiling the DLL
CONTACT.SQX (.SQC in OS/2)	SQL code to access the database that includes the code for the class methods
CONTACT.VBE	Export file to import the class definition in to the Visual Builder
CONTACT.MAK	Make file which compiles contactv.cpp and produces a contact.dll and a contact.lib

After the code is generated a new option is added to the pop-up menu of each class. You can click on **View source** to browse the code generated. You can save the mapping as a **.DAX** file using the **File**, **Save** item on the Data Access Builder menu bar.

❑ Close the Data Access Builder.

Compiling the Data Access Parts

The generated files include a .MAK file which is used for compiling the data access parts. The .MAK file includes compiler options which make the Data Access Parts into Dynamic Link Libraries or .DLL files. One of the output files from the compile is a .LIB file which is required by the linker for parts that use the data access .DLL.

The compile process runs **IDATAPRE (SQLPREP** in OS/2) which requires that the database engine be running. To start the database, on Windows enter **db2start** at a command prompt; on OS/2 enter **startdbm** at a command prompt. If the database was already running when you attempt to start it, you get an informational message from DB2 indicating so. You may safely ignore that message.

Now you are ready to run **nmake** on the make files generated by the Data Access Builder. At the command prompt enter the following commands:

❑ nmake contact.mak

❑ nmake areatabl.mak

❑ nmake contview.mak.

If you are running OS/2 and you are not logged on the database, you are be prompted to logon. Enter **userid = USERID** and **password = PASSWORD**. The make file for the Contact part produces the files listed in Table 31.

Table 31: Files generated by nmake

Filename	Description
contact.dll	The executable dynamic link library for the contact object
contact.lib	The library file needed when you compile application that uses the contact.dll
contact.bnd	The bind file for the contact.dll
contact.cxx (.c in OS/2)	The result of the SQL precompiler
contact.obj	Object code for contact.cxx

Viewing a .VBE File

The Data Access Builder generates a .VBE file which enables you to import the parts into the Visual Builder. An excerpt of the CONTACT.VBE file is shown in Code segment 46.

```
//VBBeginPartInfo: ContactManager,  "ContactManager -
// mapped from USERID.CONTACT"
//VBParent: IStandardNotifier
//VBIncludes: "Contactv.hpp" _CONTACT_
//VBPartDataFile: 'Contactv.vbb'
//VBComposerInfo: nonvisual,6003,cppods3u
//VBAction: refresh,"retrieve all objects in
datastore", ContactManager&, ContactManager& refresh()
//VBAction: select,"select objects from datastore",
   ContactManager&, ContactManager& select(const
IString& clause)
//VBAttribute: items, "collection of Contact*",
   'IVSequence <Contact*> *',IVSequence <Contact*> *
   items() const, , itemsId
//VBPreferredFeatures: items, refresh, select
//VBEndPartInfo: ContactManager
```

Code segment 46: ContactManager definition in CONTACT.VBE

Importing parts and classes into the Visual Builder is done through the use of .VBE files. If you have some existing C++ code that you want to use in the Visual Builder, you first have to write a .VBE file. Then use the **Import part information** feature in the Visual Builder to import the .VBE file. For complete information on .VBE file format, consult the on-line book *Building Parts for Fun and Profit*.

Importing the Data Access Parts

Now that you have generated the data access parts, you can use these parts in the Visual Builder.

❑ Open the Visual Builder and set the working directory to **x:\VABOOK\DATABASE**.

❑ Select **File**, **Import part information...** on the menu bar.

❑ Select the three .VBE files generated by the Data Access Builder:

AREATABL.VBE

CONTVIEW.VBE

CONTACT.VBE

When these files are imported into the Visual Builder, the Visual Builder creates binary part files. The names of the binary part files is specified in the .VBE file.

AREATABL.VBB

CONTVIEW.VBB

CONTACT.VBB

Each **.VBB** file defines a number of classes. For the examples in this book you use the class that models a row of the table and the class that models the entire table. To start working with the data access parts, you need to load the nonvisual part **IDatastore** which is used to model the connection with the database:

❑ In the Parts Selector, load the file **VBDAX.VBB**. If you are in Windows this file can be found in the **x:\IBMCPPW\IVB** directory. In OS/2 it is found in the **x:\IBMCPP\DDE4VB** directory.

In this chapter and the next, you use the data access parts that the Data Access Builder generated to construct two applications:

1. DBViewer

2. DBAddRecord

The answers are in the **x:\VABOOK\DATABASE\ANSWERS** directory in the **DBASE.VBB** file.

Constructing the DBViewer

Now that the data access parts are available, you can start building the DBViewer application. The purpose of this application is to display the data in the database using a container control.

❑ Ensure that the working directory is set to **x:\VABOOK\DATABASE**.

❑ From the Parts selector, create a new visual part.

❑ Make the Class name **DBViewer**.

❑ Enter **Contact database viewer with Container control** in the **Description** field.

❑ Leave the Part type as **Visual**.

❑ Make the Base class **IFrameWindow**.

❑ Enter **DBASE** in the **File name** entry field.

❑ Press the **Open** button to start building the part.

❑ Change the title bar text of the frame window to read **Database viewer application**.

❑ Delete the default canvas inside the frame window.

❑ Place an IMultiCellCanvas as the client of the frame window.

The Database viewer should look like Figure 199.

Using the Container Control

The **IContainer** control is one of most complex controls in the Open Class Library. And you thought the IMultiCellCanvas and the INotebook controls had a lot of settings!

You are familiar with list boxes because list boxes are commonly used in many applications. Even though they are still used today, in many applications they can be considered the predecessors of the container control. List boxes can only accommodate a single column of data, and no provisions exist for putting a title on the column. But the biggest limitation is that list box controls can only accept a very limited amount of data, a maximum of 64K. This limit includes all the overhead of managing the data. Depending on how many bytes you display for each entry, you are able to display a maximum of a few thousand entries.

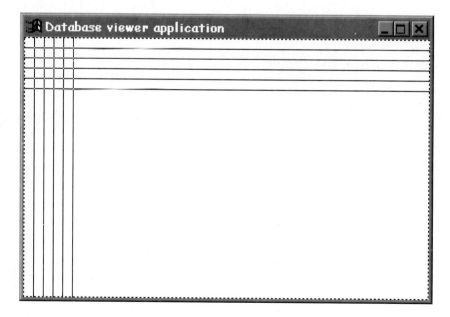

Figure 199: DBViewer so far

The container control virtually removes all these restrictions. In the container details view you can have as many entries as you have memory and hard disk space to support. There are mechanisms for staging data in and out of the container to reduce the burden of filling a container with millions of entries. The container can have multiple columns and each column can have its own title. The container itself can have a title. The titles do not scroll off the screen as the data moves. There are other nice things about the container; for example, column and title separators, and run time user sizable panes.

The container control can be used to display different views of the same data. These views include, among others, an icon view, a tree view, and a details view.

In Windows you have the choice of using the native container or the OS/2 PM compatible container supplied by the Open Class Library. For the purpose of consistency between the two platforms, this book uses the OS/2 PM Compatible container.

The Visual Builder uses the **IVBContainer Control** which is a sub-class of IContainer. Complete the following steps to add an IVBContainer control to the DBViewer:

❏ From the Lists category add an **IVBContainerControl*** to the multicell canvas column 2, row 2.

❏ Open the settings notebook for the multicell canvas and set column 2 and row 2 as expandable.

❏ Size the container so that it occupies most of the client window.

❏ Open the settings notebook for the container control.

❏ Under subpart name enter **cnrDBApp**.

❏ Give a title to the container, for example, **Contact listing**, and check both the **show title** and **show title separator** check boxes.

❏ Select **centered** as the title alignment.

❏ Select **showDetailsView** in the **View type** list box. This view produces a multi-column capable control.

The container part must know the type of the objects it contains. If you do not enter the type in the container, the Visual Builder displays an error dialog when you try to generate the C++ code. The container type is statically set when the application is compiled.

❏ In the **Container item attributes** group box, enter the **Item type** for the container. The type is the data access part **Cont-view***.

After you enter the type, the **Text** list should not be empty. If it is, you have entered an invalid part type. Since you are only using the details view, you do not need to select any attribute from this list.

❑ If you are developing in Windows switch to the **Styles** page and select the **pmCompatible** radio button.

❑ Press **OK** to save the changes.

Figure 200 shows the DViewer with the container inserted.

Using Container Columns

The container needs three container columns to display the data from the CONTVIEW table.

❑ From the Lists category, add three **IContainerColumns** controls in the container. One for **Name**, another for **Phone**, and the last one for **Location**.

❑ For each container column, open the settings notebook and complete the following as shown in Figure 201.

1. Enter Subpart names, for example **cnrcolName**, **cnrcolLocation** and **cnrcolPhone**.

2. Enter **Heading text** which describes the contents of the column.

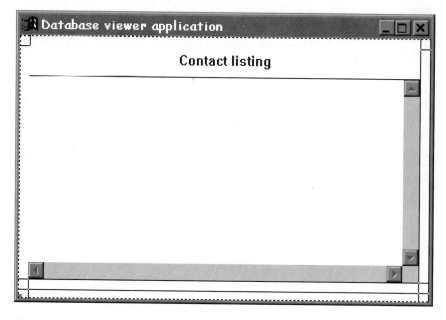

Figure 200: Inserted container and title for the DBViewer

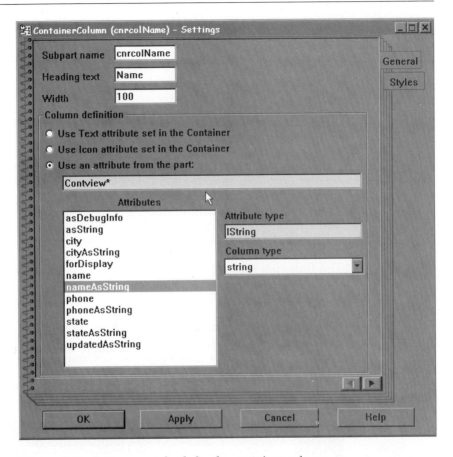

Figure 201: Settings notebook for the container column

3. You may have to try different values in the **Width** entry field so that all of the contents of the field are shown. This value changes with the resolution of the display and the font used. You can start with the default width and adjust once you see how the running application looks.

4. In the Column definition group box, select the **Use an attribute from the part** radio button.

5. Select the type which appears in the **Attribute** list box for each column.

6. Look in the **Styles** page of the container column notebook for options you can select. For example, all tree columns could use the **horizontalSeparator** style and the first two columns the **verticalSeparator**.

7. Press the **OK** push button to save these settings.

❏ Make the column and row which contains the container control in the multicell canvas expandable.

Testing the DBViewer

You have now completed the user interface part of the application. As always, it is a good idea to test the user interface before going on to add the logic for the application.

Save and generate the **Part source** and the **main()** for the DB-Viewer part. At the command prompt enter **nmake dbviewer.mak** to compile the application. Run the application by entering **db-viewer** at the command prompt. It should like Figure 202. Because of the multicell canvas you should be able to expand and contract the frame window and the container control resizes as necessary.

The link step in the compilation process takes a lot longer now than in the previous exercises. This is caused by the parts generated in the Data Access Builder. These classes and the container classes are template classes, which creates and additional step called "template resolution." In this step the compiler and linker have a very heavy workload. Even in the fastest machines this process is comparatively slow. The good news is that in most cases, unless you change the data types of the container, template resolution only happens once.

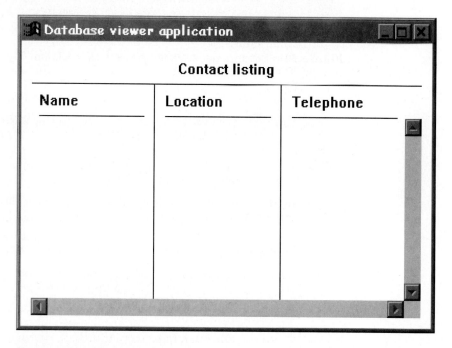

Figure 202: DBViewer running

Using the IDatastore Part

The final step is adding the nonvisual parts that provide the business logic to connect the database and display its contents:

- ❏ Add a **ContviewManager*** part to the free-form surface. Call it **contactViewMgr**.

- ❏ Add an **IDatastore*** part to the free-form surface. This part represents a database connection. These parts are not on your pallet, so you use the **Options, Add part...** menu item in the Composition Editor.

- ❏ Directly edit the **IDatastore** part with the name **DBConnection**.

- ❏ Open the settings notebook for the **DBConnection** part and enter **CONTACT** as the **datastoreName**.

- ❏ Enter **USERID** as the **userName** and enter **PASSWORD** as the **authentication**. Both of these fields must be entered in upper case. If you are running Windows NT, you may leave these fields blank, as you are automatically logged on to DB2 when you log on to the system.

Figure 203 shows the settings editor for the IDatastore part. The Visual Builder does not prevent lower case characters in these fields, but at runtime the database does not recognize lower case entries for the **userName** or **authentication**. The **CONTACT** database name is hard-coded as a default for this application. When you build your own applications you should probably not hard-code these values. Instead you can get them from the user at runtime or from other data attributes in your program such as entry fields, list boxes, or attributes in other nonvisual parts.

There are very few connections to get the DBViewer displaying the data from the database. The first connection connects to the database. It is convenient to use the **ready** event for this purpose. Connect:

- ❏ free-form (ready) → IDatastore (connect)

A successful connection to the database results in the **Connected** event. Use it to refresh the contents of the contact table.

- ❏ DBConnection(Connected) → contactViewMgr(refresh)

The refresh action causes the **items** attribute in the table to change. The **IVBContainerControl** has been especially designed to connect to parts which contain collections of items. The manager parts generated by the Data Access Builder have a collection and an **items** attribute. The container also has an **items** attribute. Make the following connection:

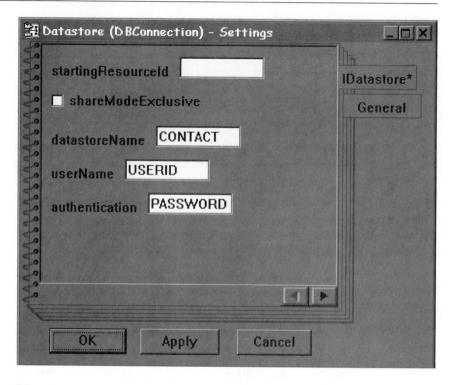

Figure 203: Settings notebook for the IDatastore

❏ contactViewMgr (items) → cnrDBApp (items)

The last action required is to disconnect from the database when the application closes. The closeEvent of the frame window can be used to signal that the application is closing.

❏ framewindow(closeEvent) → DBConnection(disconnect)

Figure 204 shows the current connections for the DBViewer.

Running the Finished DBVIEWER Application

❏ Generate the **main()** for part and the Part source.

❏ Compile the application by running **nmake dbviewer.mak**.

If you are having problems with the link step of the nmake, delete the subdirectory **DBVIEWER** and its contents. This subdirectory is created by the compiler, and it contains left over and most likely obsolete template files generated by a previous compilation.

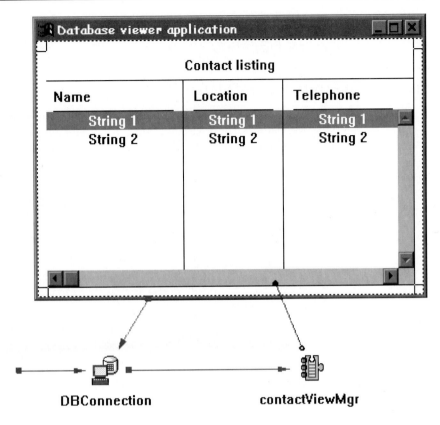

Figure 204: Complete connections for the DBViewer part

Run the application by typing **DBVIEWER** at the command prompt. You may also think that it takes longer for this application to start up. Consider what is happening before the main window opens:

1. If you just finished compiling, the compiler and linker are being swapped out of memory.

2. The **DBViewer** application starts.

3. The Data Access Builder DLLs are loaded.

4. The CONTACT database is opened.

5. The CONTVIEW table is updated from the database.

6. The container is updated to display all the names in the database.

7. The application becomes visible and gets focus.

You can scroll through the entries of the database and resize the frame window. This is an excellent example of how the multicell canvas provides you with a way to show more information by changing the size of the frame window and resizing the control which holds the data, see Figure 205.

Distributing Programs which use DB2

If you plan to distribute executable files which access a DB2 database, you should be aware of certain considerations with respect to the components shipped. In addition to the executable program you

Figure 205: Finished DBViewer application running

created and any DLLs which are required by the program, you must also distribute the DLLs created by the Data Access Builder.

Binding the executable files to the database

The bind files (.BND) created by the Data Access Builder, must also be distributed with the program and must be bound to the database before the program can access the data. In order to Bind your program to the database you run the **BIND** command in DB2 Version 2.1 or higher or the **SQLBIND** program in DB2 1.1 and 1.2.

In the **x:\VABOOK\DATABASE\ANSWERS** directory you find a file called: **DOBIND.BAT** for Windows or **DOBIND.CMD** for OS/2.

```
@echo off
@if .%1 == . goto error
db2 connect to contact
db2 bind areatabl.bnd
db2 bind contact.bnd
db2 bind contview.bnd
db2 bind %1:\ibmcppw\bnd\cppwacl2.bnd
db2 connect reset
@echo .
@echo If all return codes where zero the bind
@echo operation was successful
@echo .
goto theend
:error
@echo .
@echo This file MUST be run from a DB2 Command Window
@echo Syntax is: DOBIND X, where X is the drive where
@echo VisualAge is installed
@echo .
:theend
```

Code segment 47: DOBIND.BAT binds executables to database

Before you can run the completed database exercises provided with this book you need to install the database and run the DOBIND file. In Windows start a DB2 Command Window and type DOBIND X, where X is the drive where VisualAge for C++ is installed. In OS/2 any command prompt session will do.

The completed exercises, in the **x:\VABOOK\DATABASE\ANSWERS** directory, from chapters 12 and 13 will only run properly when using the version of VisualAge for C++ from the CD-ROM which came with this book, and after running the DOBIND command file. This is because of different levels of runtime DLLs available in different versions of the products. If the completed programs do not run in your machine, you will have to load the VBB files from the answers directory into the Visual Builder and regenerate the Source code for the different components and recompile the application. You will also need to regenerate and recompile the Data Access DLLs.

Chapter 12—Summary

In this chapter you built a data viewer. To do this you learned to:

❑ Build a simple application which interacts with a database.

❑ Use the Data Access Builder to map relational database tables to C++ classes.

❑ Generate C++ classes in the Data Access Builder.

❑ Import the class definition into the Visual Builder

❑ Use the data access nonvisual parts to build an application for viewing the content of the database. This database contains tables with information on contacts including name, area, and phone number.

❑ Use the IContainer control and IContainerColumn to display a details view.

What's in Chapter 13

In this chapter you will improve the DBViewer application with the function to add new records to the database tables. To do this you will:

❑ Develop a secondary window.

❑ Use factory objects to allow dynamic memory allocation for secondary windows.

❑ Use an IVBVariable with a factory object.

❑ Delete dynamically allocated windows.

❑ Implement double promotion of part features.

❑ Incorporate the secondary window with the DBViewer application.

13

Adding Database Records

The purpose of this chapter is to refine the DBViewer by providing function to add records to the database. The name of the new application is DBAddRecord. You will build the necessary function in the application so that when the user selects the **Add** button a data entry window displays. This window is created dynamically and destroyed when the operation is completed. The user can choose to add the record to the database or to cancel the operation. There are a lot of new concepts and good programming techniques to learn in this chapter.

Building a Reusable Canvas

Whenever you have a nonvisual part that encapsulates data and the operations which act upon that data, you should also build a **view** object to represent the data to the user. It is common to use this view in more than one panel. For example, a row in the database is represented by the **Contact** nonvisual part. Typical operations on databases include add, delete, and update. All of these operations need to display the same data, but the panels used for these operations are different from each other. It makes sense to build a visual part that contains the data elements needed and then reuse it in all the panels which need the data represented.

Following this advice is very easy when using the Visual Builder to build visual parts. You will first create a canvas part which is not in a frame window. In this canvas you will place the user interface elements corresponding to the data in the database. Start by following these steps to build the **ContactCanvas**, which will be used in the **ContactAddView** of the DBAddRecord application. The **Contact-Canvas** part can also be reused to build a **ContactUpdateView** and a **ContactDeleteView**.

Copy the following files from the **x:\VABOOK\DATABASE\AN-SWERS** into the **x:\VABOOK\DATABASE** directory:

❑ KBD*.*

❑ PH*.*

❑ MY*.*

Start the Visual Builder and:

❑ Set the working directory to **x:\VABOOK\DATABASE**.

❑ Load all the **.VBB** files in this directory into the Visual Builder. Also load the **VBDAX.VBB** file. These are the **.VBB** files that should have loaded:

1. areatabl

2. contact

3. contview

4. dbase

5. kbdhdr

6. mydate

7. phone

8. vbdax

9. vbbase

❑ From the **Parts Selector**, create a new visual part as shown in Figure 206.

❑ Make the Class name **ContactCanvas**.

❑ Enter **User interface to contact objects** in the **Description** field.

❑ Enter **DBASE** as the **File name**.

❑ Leave the Part type as **Visual**.

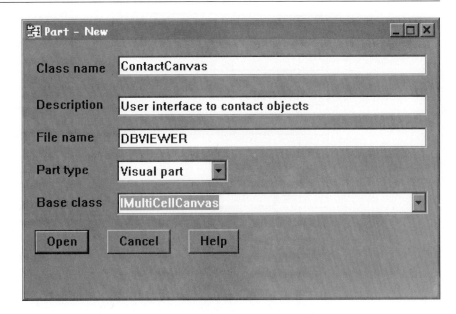

Figure 206: New ContactCanvas part

☐ Make the Base class **IMultiCellCanvas**.

☐ Select **Open** to open the Composition Editor.

Constructing the ContactCanvas

The ContactCanvas is based on an IMultiCellCanvas. In previous chapters you have placed individual controls in a multicell canvas cell. It is possible to place other canvases in a cell of a multicell canvas. This is done to accommodate more than one control in one cell. As you remember, a multicell canvas only allows a single control per cell; but if that control is another canvas, multiple controls can be placed on that second canvas. This is a good technique, for example, for placing buttons on a multicell canvas. It is not recommended that you layer multicell canvases more than two or three deep. The performance of your application will degrade if you add many layers of canvases. The ContactCanvas is built with a multicell canvas and a set canvas. Refer to Figure 207 to see the layout of the controls.

The Contact part has four attributes which need to have a user interface representation. You need to add the appropriate controls to the IMultiCellCanvas for the attributes in Table 32.

☐ Add rows to the multicell canvas, as necessary, to fit and space the controls.

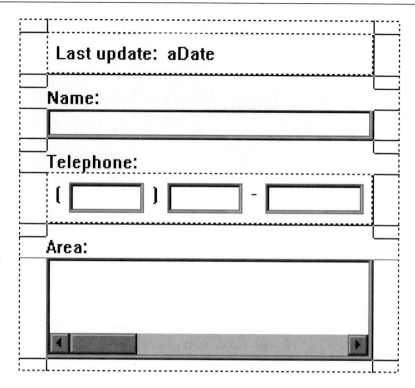

Figure 207: Multicell canvas for CustomerCanvas

Table 32: Active user interface components

Attribute	Control	Description
efName	IEntryField	This field holds the first and last name of each contact. The name is the key, so it must not be blank or contain duplicate entries.
lbArea	ICollectionViewListBox	This list box provides a choice of cities from the Areatabl table of the database.
dateUpdated	MyDate	Shows the date this entry was last updated. On a new entry the current date is used.
phoneNumber	PhoneEntry	A part supplied in the CD-ROM which handles formatted phone number entry fields entry fields.

❑ Add an **ISetCanvas** control to row 2, column 2 of the multicell canvas.

❑ Add an **IStaticText** control to the set canvas and label it **Last update:**.

❑ From the **Options, Add part...** menu bar item, add a **MyDate*** part to the set canvas. Name this object **lastUpdate**.

❑ Add an **IStaticText** control to row 4, column 2 of the multicell canvas. Label it **Name:**.

❑ Add an **IEntryField** to row 5, column 2 of the multicell canvas.

❑ Name the entry field **efName**, open its settings notebook, and change the **Limit** to only accept 20 characters. This is the length of the **NAME** field in the database.

❑ Add an **IStaticText** control to row 7, column 2 of the multicell canvas. Label it **Telephone:**.

❑ Make sure the **PHONE.VBB** file is loaded in Visual Builder. Add a **PhoneEntry*** control to row 8, column 2. Name the object **phone**.

❑ Add an **IStaticText** control to row 10, column 2 of the multicell canvas. Label it **Area:**.

❑ From the Lists category add an **ICollectionViewListBox** to row 11, column 2 of the multicell canvas. Name the object **lbArea**.

❑ Open the settings notebook for the lbArea and in the **Item type** entry field enter **Areatabl***.

❑ Set tabbing order appropriately.

Promoting the ContactCanvas Features

The **ContactCanvas** is a subpart which can be used in a number of other views or even other applications. Some of the attributes in the controls need to be promoted as part features to allow connections to the data. Use the pop-up menu for each part to promote the features listed in Table 33.

Table 33: Promoted features on ContactCanvas

Subpart Name	Feature	Promoted Feature Name
lastUpdate	text	dateText
efName	text	efNameText
lbArea	items	areaItems
lbArea	selectedCollectionPosition	areaCollectionPosition
phone	phoneAsString	phoneText

- ❏ Open the settings notebook of the multicell canvas and set the first and last columns and row 2 as expandable. Row 2 is the row with the list box.
- ❏ Open the PIE and, in the **Preferred** page, remove all the current preferred features and then add all of the promoted features in Table 33 to the Preferred list.
- ❏ Save and generate the part source for the **ContactCanvas**.
- ❏ Close the **ContactCanvas** Composition Editor.

Double Promotion

A key aspect of Object-Oriented languages is data encapsulation. In the **ContactCanvas** you promoted the text attributes of the entry field controls as features so you can access these features when ContactCanvas is used in other parts.

As a further example, in ContactCanvas you used the prefabricated part **PhoneEntry**. This part is a composite visual part. The visual part combines three entry fields on a set canvas with some static text controls as delimiters for the entry fields. This composite part has a nonvisual part which combines the entry field contents into a single string. It also does the reverse, taking a string in the format (AAA)PPP-NNNN and breaking it into three components, the Area code, Prefix, and Number. There is also a keyboard handler attached to each of the entry fields which allows only positive numbers. The PhoneEntry part encapsulates and hides all this complexity from the user. Only the **phoneAsString** attribute of the component is needed in the application. It was promoted when the part was built and is available in the part interface.

The **PhoneEntry** part is a subpart of the **ContactCanvas** part, which will be used as a subpart of the **ContactAddView** part, which you will build next. In order for the **phoneAsString** attribute to be available in **ContactAddView** at the next level of encapsulation, it must be promoted again. This is called *double promotion*. The second time the attribute was promoted, it was given **phoneText** as the promoted name. This name is more explicit and simplifies the interface; even with a different name, it is still the same attribute.

As subparts are further combined, you need to continue to promote the attributes, actions, and events needed by the containing part. On the surface this may seem cumbersome, but it serves a very useful purpose. As the subparts are combined, the composite parts become more and more complex. By requiring feature promotion, the composite parts have a simplified interface with only their base features and the chosen promoted features.

Constructing the ContactAddView

Now you can test the **ContactCanvas** in a frame window. Follow these steps to implement the **ContactAddView** window:

- ❏ Create a new visual part from the **Parts Selector**. Name it **ContactAddView** with a Base Class of **IFrameWindow**. Use **DBVIEWER** as the file name. Open the Composition Editor.
- ❏ Delete the default **ICanvas** in the frame window.
- ❏ Add an **IMultiCellCanvas** as the client of the frame window.
- ❏ From the **Options**, **Add part...** menu bar item, add the subpart **ContactCanvas*** to row 2 and column 2 of the multicell canvas. Name the object **contactCanvas**.
- ❏ Directly edit the title of the frame window to read **Add contact**.
- ❏ Open the settings notebook of the multicell canvas and set the first and last columns and row 2 as expandable.
- ❏ Generate the **Part source** and the **main()** for the **Contact-AddView** part.

Now you are ready to compile the **ContactAddView** as a standalone test application. At a command prompt enter **nmake cntctddv.mak**. Run the **ContactAddView** application to test it. Enter **cntctddv** at the command prompt. The test application looks like Figure 208. You can size the window, and the controls stay in the middle of the frame window and the list box height changes. The **Last Update** date is showing. It is just the user interface, but you are just getting started developing the **ContactAddView**. Close the test application and continue building the application.

Finishing the ContactAddView User Interface

The **ContactCanvas** has no buttons or other controls for the user to trigger events. This gives the developer using this canvas the flexibility to use the appropriate controls for the task, such as toolbar buttons, push buttons, or custom controls.

The design for the **ContactAddView** calls for two push buttons on the canvas which are **Add** and **Cancel**. Because of the canvas layout, adding two push buttons directly on the multicell canvas would not look very good. The buttons would either be too far apart from each other, in columns 2 and 4 or if the buttons were in columns 1 and 2, the button on column 2 will be very large because its size is determined by the width of the **ContactCanvas**. You can overcome this problem with an **ISetCanvas** control as you did before. Follow the steps below and add the buttons to the **ContactAddView**

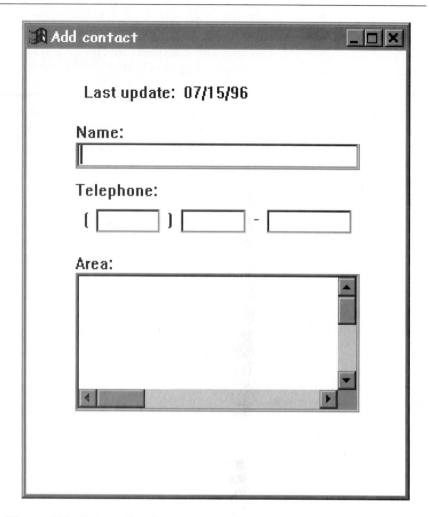

Figure 208: Test application running

❑ Add an **ISetCanvas** control to row 4, column 2 of the multicell canvas.

❑ Add two **IPushButton** controls to the set canvas

❑ Open the settings notebook for the first push button, change the subpart name to **pbAdd**, and change the text to **~Add**. Make it the **default** button.

❑ Open the settings notebook for the second push button, change the subpart name to **pbCancel**, and change the text to **~Cancel**.

❑ Make a connection from the **Cancel** push button **buttonClick-Event** to the frame window close action.

❑ Set the tabbing so that the buttons will be accessible from the keyboard.

The **ContactAddView** part should look like Figure 209.

Save and generate the Part source, compile and run **ContactAdd-View** again. Confirm that the buttons look good and that you can close the window by pressing the **Exit** button.

If everything works fine, continue with the instructions below and modify the DBVIEWER part so that it will use the **ContactAdd-View** part. Later in this chapter you will return to work on the

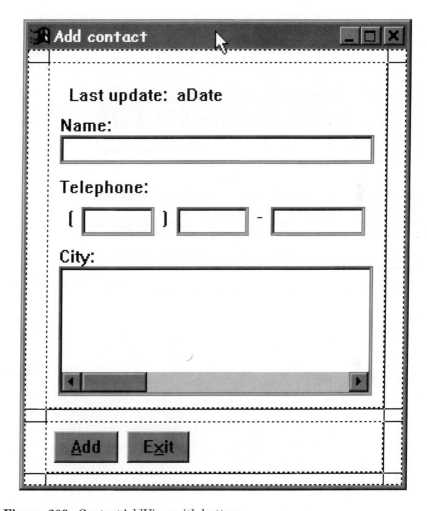

Figure 209: ContactAddView with buttons

ContactAddView part and complete the logic which adds the record in the dialog to the database.

Improving the DBVIEWER Part

The next step involves changing the DBViewer part you built in the previous chapter so it supports the add record function. Since you already have a great deal of time invested in building **DBViewer**, you will use it as the starting point for a new part called **DBAddRecord**.

- ❏ Make sure the **DBASE.VBB** file is loaded in the Parts Selector.
- ❏ The working directory should be **x:\VABOOK\DATABASE**.
- ❏ Select and press the right mouse button on the **DBViewer** visual part to display its pop-up menu.
- ❏ Select the **Copy** function to rename and save this part. Use the name **DBAddRecord.** Copy the new part to the **DBASE** file.

You are using a copy of the DBViewer part as a starting point for this application. This application is a variation of the DBViewer, which worked just fine and is fully tested. It is a good idea to preserve the original DBViewer by copying this part as the new DBAddRecord, instead of just renaming DBViewer.

Using Commit and Rollback

When you perform operations on a database it is a good design to provide the **Commit** and **Rollback** functions. As records are added to a database they are not added permanently until a Commit command is issued. Until a Commit is issued the user can send a Rollback command to the database. Rollback restores any changes to the database since the last Commit.

The user interface for DBAddRecord supports Add, Commit, and Rollback. Follow the steps below and add buttons for these functions:

- ❏ Open the Composition Editor for the **DBAddRecord** part.
- ❏ From the frame extensions category, add an **IToolBar** to the frame window.
- ❏ Delete the **IToolBarButton** control that is on the tool bar.
- ❏ Add three **IPushButton** controls to the tool bar.
- ❏ From the settings notebook of each push button, adjust the settings as shown in Table 34.

Add another container column to the container object cnrDBApp, call it **cnrcolLastUpdate**. This column will hold the date a record was

Table 34: Push button settings

Function	Subpart Name	Label
Add	pbAdd	~Add
Commit	pbCommit	~Commit
Rollback	pbRollback	~Rollback

last updated. Open the settings notebook for the container column and use the **updated** attribute from the **ContView*** object is used. Label this column **Last update**. Set the proper separator styles for the **Telephone** and **Last update** columns. Your part should now look like Figure 210.

Setting the detailsViewSplit

The container control can have a vertical line which splits the container. This line can be moved with the mouse at runtime to change the visible width of a column; it is called the **detailsViewSplit**. The line appears after a specified column and a specified distance from the left side of the container. Make the following connection to the container:

❑ free-form surface (ready) → cnrDBApp (detailsViewSplit)

This connection needs as a parameter, the column before the split line appears. Connect as a parameter to the above connection:

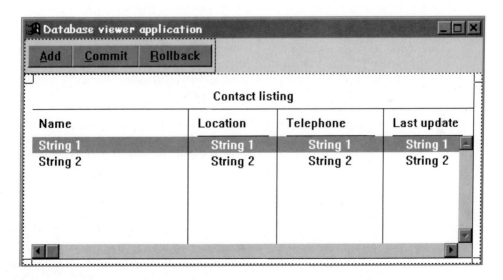

Figure 210: Toolbar with buttons added

❏ cnrColName(this) → connection(detailsViewSplit)

❏ Open the settings for the connection, press the **Set Parameters...** button, and enter a value indicating the position in **pixelsFromLeft** where the line should appear. Try 180.

When the application runs, there will be a double vertical line on the container after the **Name** column. You can move this line to the left and right, which reveals more or less of the **Name** column.

What are Factories?

C++ classes are allocated and instantiated in memory with the **new** statement. By default the classes used in the Visual Builder are allocated and instantiated when the application is started. The Visual Builder generates the **new** statement for each part. This is fine for a one screen application that takes minimal resources; but as you begin to make a real application with many screens and many nonvisual parts, you will encounter a number of problems:

1. It is difficult fitting all the visual parts on the free-form surface.

2. Larger applications will take a long time to start because of the time to allocate and construct all the classes.

3. If you delete an object, there is no way to start a new instance of that object.

4. All windows for an application are started when the application starts, whether or not they are eventually shown or not.

Most good C++ programmers would not tolerate these restrictions. The Visual Builder has a special part which allows you to directly instantiate a part. The **IVBFactory** control is used to create new instances of a specific type. The type must be set at development time in order for the Visual Builder to generate the proper C++ code. This is really no different than coding a **new** statement by hand, you must know the type of the object being creating.

It is better if you think of the IVBFactory part as an object factory. This is because factory objects are not of a unique class; rather, they are a mechanism for dynamically instantiating objects of any class.

Using Object Factories

Object factories provide a very useful function for application developers. In this application a factory object is used to instantiate the **ContactAddView** panel at runtime. You can trigger the allocation of a new ContactAddView object by an event, for example, when the **Add** push button is pressed. Add an **IVBFactory** part to the **DBAddRecord** part using the following steps:

- ❏ Open the Composition Editor for the DBAddRecord part.
- ❏ From the models category, add an IVBFactory object to the free-form surface.
- ❏ Name it **addViewFactory**.
- ❏ From the pop-up menu for the **addViewFactory**, change its type to **ContactAddView***. Do not forget the asterisk (*), without it, the Visual Builder will reject the type as unknown.

Now make the connection that causes the addViewFactory to instantiate, or **new** a **ContactAddView** part at runtime. Use the **Add** push button to start the following connection as seen in Figure 211:

- ❏ pbAdd (buttonClickEvent) → addViewFactory (new)

Inspecting the Object Factory

All object factories can do is instantiate a new object of a class. Let's inspect the **addViewFactory** object and see what it contains:

- ❏ From the addViewFactory pop-up menu, select **Browse Part Features...**.

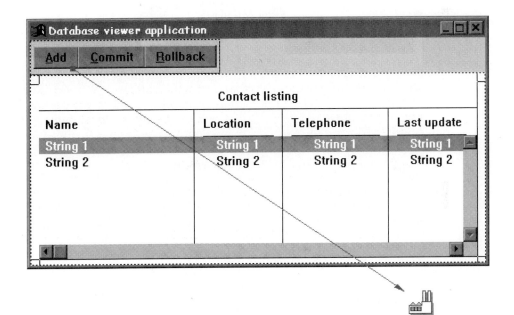

addViewFactory

Figure 211: Connection to addViewFactory

In the **Feature implementation browser** you can see all the actions, attributes, and events for the factory object as shown in Figure 212. The **addViewFactory** object has only one action **new**, and only one event **newEvent**.

❏ Select the **activeColor** attribute to view its detail information.

As shown in Figure 212, the attribute type and the description are shown, but there are no **get** or **set** functions. This means that you can not get or set any of the attributes in the factory object.

The factory object does not represent the object it creates; it is merely the mechanism that creates it. To access the features of the object factory you need an **IVBVariable** object connected to the factory object. Any constructor parameters can be set at the factory. Close the **Feature Implementation Browser** dialog box and continue implementing the application.

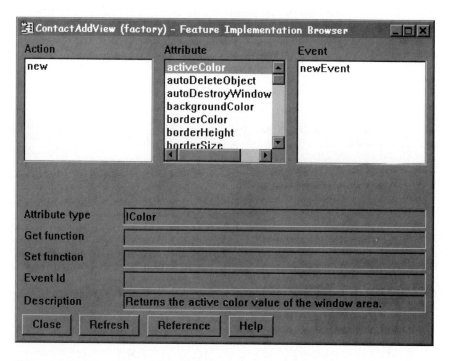

Figure 212: Browsing part features of a factory object

Using Variables with Factories

As you can see, the **IVBFactory** part only has one member function, the **new** action, which allocates and constructs the part at runtime. You have already made a connection that instantiates a new **Contact-AddView** object when the user presses the **Add** button. If you compile and run the application as it stands, when you press the **Add** button nothing will happen. The ContactAddView is a frame window, and windows have to be shown before they become visible. But the factory object has no **show** member function, see Figure 212. To access all the features of the object just created, represent the object on the free-form surface with an **IVBVariable** part:

❑ From the model category, add an **IVBVariable** to the free-form surface.

❑ Name it **addView**. This variable will point to the **Contact-AddView** part with the information given by the user.

❑ From the pop-up menu for the **addView** variable, select **Change Type...** and set the type to **ContactAddView***. After the type of the variable is set, its icon changes to show the part type.

The final step is to associate the variable with the factory object. The variable represents the new **ContactAddView** object created by the factory, so it must be set after the factory executes the **new** of the **ContactAddView**. The factory **newEvent** occurs after the **new** concludes, and the **newEvent** can be used to set the variable object, as shown in Figure 213.

❑ addViewFactory (newEvent) → addView (this)

Making Modal Windows

Modal windows have specific behavior which is different than modeless or normal windows. They are commonly used as special purpose secondary windows like message boxes and error windows because they take the focus away from the rest of the application. In this application this means that while the **ContactAddView** is active, the main view of **DBAddRecord** is not accessible until the secondary window closes.

The DBAddRecord application design allows only one database operation at a time. Showing the **ContactAddView** window as a modal secondary window is a good way to enforce this design. Make the following connection to display the **ContactAddView** window:

❑ addViewFactory (newEvent) → addView (showModally)

There is another aspect to modal secondary windows. They are dependent on, or tied to the primary window. When the primary window is closed the secondary window is automatically closed. As shown in Figure 214, make the following connection, which provides an owner for the constructor of the **ContactAddView** window:

❑ frame window (this) → addViewFactory (owner)

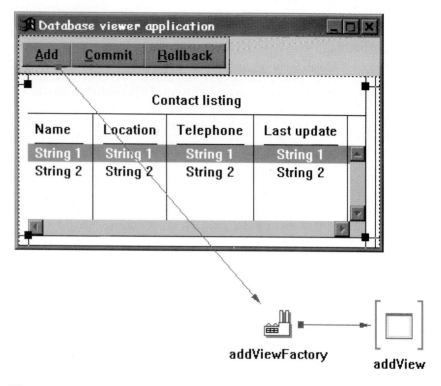

Figure 213: Connection to IVBVariable

What is Auto Delete?

There is a very important consideration when using secondary windows which are dynamically allocated. You need to consider how to delete and deallocate the memory used by the window and underlying objects when the window is closed. When the **new** action is executed, memory is allocated for the C++ object and memory is allocated for the presentation object. When the secondary window **close** action executes, the operating system frees the memory for the presentation object. When this happens the C++ object memory is still allocated but is not accessible. This causes a serious problem of memory fragmentation and memory leaks. As long as the application is running, the use of that memory is lost to all applications in the system. Repeatedly creating and closing modal windows causes additional memory leakage, until eventually the program or the system crashes.

When the main window of the application is closed, all memory used by the process is freed by the operating system. This is acceptable for applications that are only used for a short time and then closed, but inadequate for applications that are intended to stay running for long periods of time with lots of user interaction. The solution is to set the

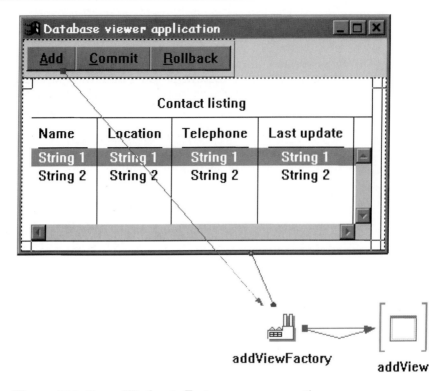

Figure 214: FrameWindow to Factory owner connection

Auto delete attribute of the factory object. When **Auto delete** is set on, the C++ object will automatically be destroyed right after the presentation object is destroyed. Make this change to the **AddViewFactory** object with the following step:

❑ On the **addViewFactory** settings notebook **General** page, select the check box labeled **Auto delete**. Press the **OK** button to save.

Before Fixpak CTO304 for the VisualAge for C++ for OS/2 Open Class Library, selecting the Auto delete setting causes the application to trap or crash when the window is closed. This problem only occurs with modal windows. If you use an OS/2 version of VisualAge for C++ which does not have Fixpak 304 installed, do not set the **Auto delete** option. To delete modal windows before installing the Fixpak you need to connect:

❑ addViewFactory (newEvent) → ContactAddView (deleteTarget)

This connection is needed to delete the actual C++ object, pointed to by the variable, when the window returns from the **showModally** action. Make sure this connection is after showModally. Use the **Reorder connections from...** dialog to verify the correct sequence.

The version of VisualAge for C++ for OS/2 in the CD-ROM does not have Fixpak 304 installed, you must therefore use the alternate method described above, instead of selecting the Auto delete option in the factories.

If you choose to show your window modeless, by using the **show** action instead of the **showModally** action you must use the Auto delete option of the factory to eliminate memory leaks.

Testing the Secondary Window

At this point you should test the DBAddRecord application and make sure that the secondary window displays and is deleted properly.

❑ Save and generate the Part source and the main() for the DB-AddRecord part.

❑ Compile the DBAddRecord application at a command prompt enter **nmake dbddrcrd.mak**.

❑ Run DBAddRecord, press the Add button and the **Add contact** window should display and look like Figure 215.

There are two ways to verify that the C++ object is being properly deleted:

1. Compile the program with debug information. Run the program under the debugger and set a breakpoint in the destructor for **ContactAddView**. Make sure the program stops at the breakpoint after the secondary window is closed.

2. Add an IFUNCTRACE_DEVELOP( ); statement after the opening brace in the destructor for **ContactAddView**. Compile the program with trace information. Make sure that the ICLUI_TRACETO environment variable is set to STDOUT (see the Debugging chapter for details). Start the program by entering **dbddrcrd > trace.out**. Make sure you open and close the secondary window. Close the program. Look in the **TRACE.OUT** file for a line indicating that the destructor ran.

Adding a Record to the Database

To make the ContactAddView window functional you need to add some parts and make some more connections.

❑ Open the Composition Editor for the **ContactAddView** part.

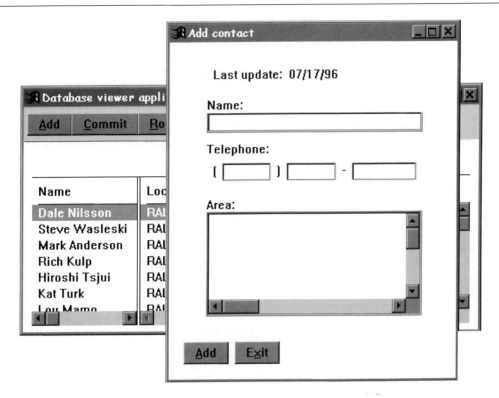

Figure 215: Add contact secondary window

☐ From the **Options**, **Add part** menu item add the **Contact*** part to the free-from surface and name it **contact**.

☐ Add the **AreatablManager*** to the free-form surface and name it **areaTableMgr**.

One of the steps in adding a contact to the database involves selecting a city from the list box **lbArea**. The database contains all the areas which are valid for this application in the table called **Areatabl**. The **AreatablManager** part created by the Data Access Builder represents this table. Make the following connections to see all of the entries from the table in the list box:

☐ free-form surface (ready) → areaTableMgr(refresh)

☐ areaTableMgr(items) → contactCanvas(areaItems)

It is customary to preselect the first item in a list box. To do it connect:

☐ free-form surface (ready) → customerCanvas(collectionPosition)

❏ This connection needs a constant parameter indicating what position to select. Open the settings for the connections, press the **Set parameters...** button, enter **1** in the **collectionPosition** entry field, and check the **select** check box.

Select the pop-up menu for the free-form surface and select **Reorder connections from**. Ensure that the order is as seen in Figure 216.

Next you need to deal with the actions that need to happen to add the record to the database when the **Add** button is pressed in the ContactAddView object:

1. The current date needs to be transferred to the **contact** object.

2. The text entered in the entry fields needs to be transferred to the **contact** object.

3. The index of the **Area** selected in the list box needs to be transferred to the **contact** object. This technique of using the selected index of the list box as the actual area number works because the key of the area table is in the same order and in the same sequence as the cities in the table. The first city has a key of one, the second city a key of two and so on. If the keys were not in step with the order of the cities in the table this technique would not work. Another more complex method of matching positions in the list box to keys in the database must be devised. This is a more advanced topic and is not dealt with in this book.

4. The now properly initialized **contact** object needs to be added to the database.

Implementing all of the steps above is accomplished through connections from the **Add** push button. Connect the **pbAdd(buttonClick-Event)** to each attribute of the **contact** object, then pass the attributes from **ContactCanvas** to the respective connections as shown in Table 35.

In OS/2, the name of the parameter in the connection is simply called **a**. This name has changed several times in different Fixpaks, and it

Figure 216: Connection order of the free-form surface

Table 35: Connections to contact object

Contact Attribute	Parameter to Connect
updated	dateText
name	efNameText
phone	phoneText
area	areaCollectionPosition

will probably change again. In Windows, the name is more descriptive. For example, the parameter name for the **pbAdd → phoneText** connection is **aPhone**.

Now that the **contact** object has been updated with the data in the dialog box, you need to actually add the record to the database. Connect:

❏ pbAdd(buttonClickEvent) → contact(add)

It is very important that the add action happens after the content of the dialog box has updated the **contact** object. Select the Add button, right mouse click, which displays the pop-up menu for the button; and select **Reorder connections from...** in the dialog box displayed, ensure that the order of the connections is as in Figure 217.

It is possible for the **add** action to fail, in that case an exception will be thrown. You should catch this exception and present a message box showing the exception codes returned by the database.

From the other category drop an **IMessageBox** part on to the free-form surface. Call this object **addFailedMsg**.

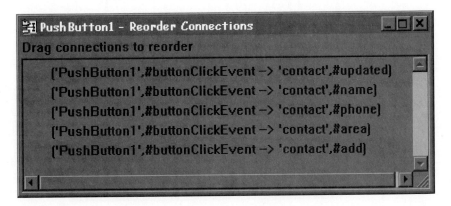

Figure 217: Reordered connections for pbAdd

From the last connection: pbAdd(buttonClickEvent) → contact(add), connect:

❑ connection(exceptionOccured) → addFailedMsg(showException)

❑ Open the PIE for the **ContactAddView** part.

❑ Switch to the **Preferred** page and add the **closeEvent** to the Preferred list.

❑ Save and generate the Part source for the **ContactAddView** part.

This completes the first iteration of the **ContactAddView** part. Save and generate the Part source. Your connections should look like Figure 218.

Open the Composition Editor for the DBAddRecord part and connect:

❑ addView(closeEvent) → contactViewMgr(refresh)

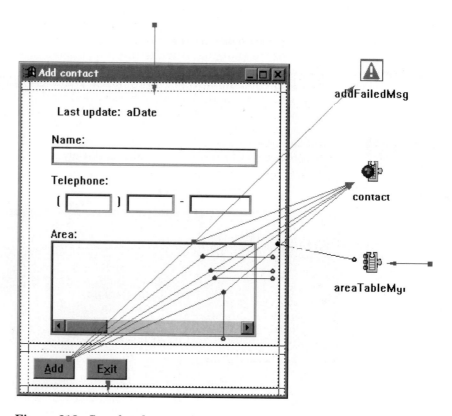

Figure 218: Completed connections for ContactAddView

This connection is required to force a refresh of the container so that the new entries will be displayed. Without this connection the new entries are in the database, but are not visible in the container. There is a setting for the container control called auto update. This is a costly setting because any change in the container refreshes the screen. The auto update can cause excessive refreshes and screen flickering. It is better to explicitly refresh the container, and this is easy to control with a modal design.

Testing the Add Records Function

Now you are ready to recompile the program, test the application, and try adding records to the database.

❑ Save and generate the Part source and the main() for the **DB-AddRecord** part.

❑ Compile the **DBAddRecord** application at a command prompt enter **nmake dbddrcrd.mak**.

❑ Run the DBAddRecord application to test it. Enter **dbddrcrd** at the command prompt.

❑ Once the application is running, press the Add button, which creates a new **Add contact** window as shown in Figure 219.

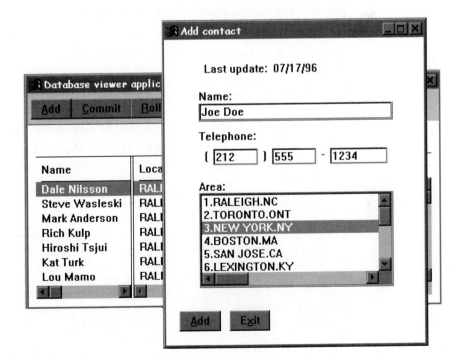

Figure 219: Inserting John Doe into the database

Table 36: Sample data for new contact

Attribute	Value
Date updated	Supplied by the system
Name	John Doe
Phone	(212) 555-1234
Area	Select **New York**

❑ Enter the data from Table 36 for a new contact.

❑ Select the **Add** push button to add the contact to the table. Repeat with another entry if desired.

❑ Select the **Exit** button when you have finished.

❑ Verify that **John Doe** is added to the contact list.

Implementing a String Generator

When you first select a city from the **Add contact** window, the contents of the list box are not quite what you would expect. The city names are displayed, but there is also more information. The list box also shows a number and the state/province of the city separated by periods. These are all the columns of the Areatabl table as shown in Figure 220.

The default **items**-to-**items** connection between the **areaTableMgr** and **lbArea** parts does not provide for any formatting of the data. To display only the city part of the Area table, you need to define a string generator for the ICollectionViewListBox.

❑ Open the Composition Editor for the **ContactCanvas** part.

❑ Open the settings notebook for the **lbArea**, and in the entry field labeled **String generator**, enter the following:

```
IStringGenerator<Areatabl*>( new IStringGenera-
torForAreatablFn())
```

❑ Switch to the Class Editor for the **ContactCanvas** part and, in the **Required include files**, enter **strgen.hpp**.

The **STRGEN.HPP** is a file you create to define a subclass of the Open Class Library class **IStringGeneratorFn**. This class has a pure virtual function **stringFor**, which you override to provide your implementation which returns only the **city**.

Use your favorite editor and create a new file called **strgen.hpp** with the lines in Code segment 48.

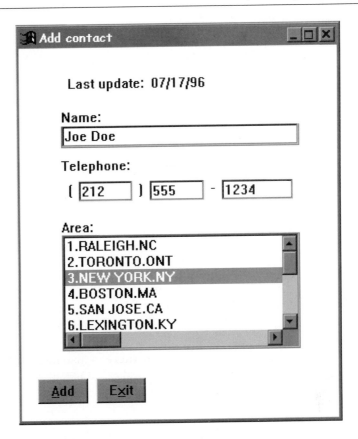

Figure 220: Area list box

Save and generate the Part source for the ContactCanvas part. Recompile the DBAddRecord application by running the make file and run the program. Add another record to the database and observe the contents of the list box; only the city names are now showing, as seen in Figure 221.

Connecting Commit and Rollback

When you close the application, all the data needs to be permanently incorporated in the database tables. Make the following connection:

❏ main frame window(closeEvent) → DBConnection(commit)

Make sure you connect to the **closeEvent** event, not to the **close** action. The **close** action appears in the Preferred list for the frame window, so you must go the **More ...** option to get the complete list of actions, attributes, and events. This is a good example of the difficulty in finding the correct name of a part feature.

```
/* * * * * * * * * * * * * * * * * * * * * * * * * * * * * * * * * * * * * * * * * * * * * * *
*
/*  Class required to provide a string generator    */
/* * * * * * * * * * * * * * * * * * * * * * * * * * * * * * * * * * * * * * * * * * * * * * *
*
#include "areatabl.hpp"    // Use this line in Windows
// #include "areatabv.hpp" // Use this line in OS/2
#include <istrgen.hpp>

class IStringGeneratorForAreatablFn: public
IStringGeneratorFn<Areatabl*>
{
public:
IStringGeneratorForAreatablFn() {};
virtual ~IStringGeneratorForAreatablFn() {};
virtual IString stringFor(Areatabl* const&  pAreaTable
)
{
IString generatedString(
   pAreaTable->city());
   return generatedString.stripTrailing();
  }
};
```

Code Segment 48: String generator class in strgen.hpp

The connection to **commit** must fire before the connection to **disconnect**. Open the **Reorder connection from** dialog for the main frame window and ensure the proper order of the connections, as seen in Figure 222.

Commit commands can be issued at any time by pressing the **Commit** button. DB2 has another very useful feature which is accessible through the IDatastore object. The **rollback** action allows data just added to be backed out of the database tables. Added rows to tables will be rolled back to their state when the last commit was completed. Make the following connections to implement commit and rollback in the DBAddRecord application:

❑ pbCommit (buttonClickEvent) → DBConnection(commit)

❑ pbRollback (buttonClickEvent) → DBConnection(rollback)

❑ pbRollback (buttonClickEvent) → contactViewManager (refresh)

The completed DBAddRecord part should look like Figure 223.

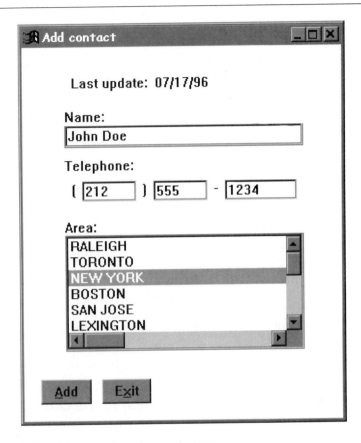

Figure 221: List box with string generator

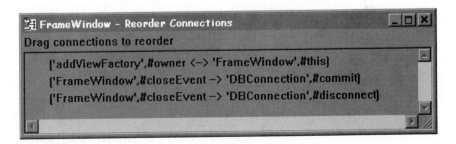

Figure 222: Order of connections for closeEvent

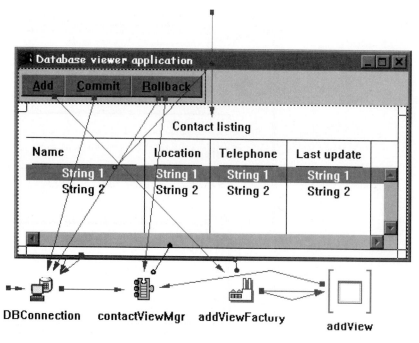

Figure 223: Completed DBAddRecord part

 ### *Binding the Application to the Database*

On an OS/2 system the commit and rollback functions will not work properly until you *bind* the **DAXSCL.BND** file with the **CONTACT** database. If using the OS/2 version, at a command prompt enter:

❑ sqlbind x:\IBMCPP\BND\DAXSCL.BND contact

Testing the Completed DBAddRecord Application

All the parts are now in place, and all the connections are complete. It is time to do the final compile and test of the finished application:

❑ Save and generate the **Part source** for DBAddRecord.

❑ Generate the **main( )** for DBAddRecord.

❑ Compile the DBAddRecord application.

❑ Start the DBAddRecord application.

❑ From the main window, select the **Add** push button.

❑ Enter the data in Table 37 in the **Add contact** window.

❑ Select the **Add** push button to add the new contact to the database. Press the **Cancel** button.

Table 37: A test contact entry

Attribute	Value
Last updated	Supplied by the system
Name	Sue Jones
Phone	(919) 555-9876
Area	Select **Raleigh**

❏ Verify that the entry for Sue Jones is indeed in the container list. You might have to scroll the list to reach the bottom.

❏ Press the **Rollback** button. Sue's entry should be gone from the list.

❏ Enter the data again; this time, press **Commit**. Now press the **Rollback** button again. Sue's entry is still in the list because rollback can only back out the data entered since the last commit.

❏ Enter your own name and phone number. Select an area where you would like to live. Select the **Exit** button. Your name should not be in the list.

❏ Enter your information again. This time press the **Add** button. Verify that your name is in the container list.

❏ Exit the application. Exiting the program committed the database. Start the program again, and your name should still be there.

If you have problems when running the application, use the many techniques you have learned to solve them. You can use a message box to catch exceptions and you can use tracing to see how the connections are processed at runtime.

Final Considerations

There are a few usability items that can be improved when running the DBAddRecord application. For example, when selecting the **Commit** or **Rollback** buttons, you may want to display a warning dialog giving the user a chance to change their mind. Also, there are no provisions for preventing entry of blank fields in the database. These improvements would be easy to implement and would improve the completeness of the application. Adding error detection and correction, application help, and warning dialogs are elements of a complete application design. These improvements are left for the reader to implement. A possible solution implementing some of the above suggestions and the Update and Delete operations can be found in the **x:\VABOOK\DATABASE\ANSWERS\4DREADER** directory.

You managed to build this entire application by coding only the string generator used with the area list box. The rest of the coding was done by connecting to visual and nonvisual parts. This was possibly due to the depth of the Open Class Library and the advanced code generation in the Data Access Builder and the Visual Builder. Taking the time to learn the Open Class Library is time well invested and will yield excellent payback in your career programming with VisualAge for C++.

Chapter 13—Summary

In this chapter you enhanced the DBViewer application by providing the function to add new records to the database tables. You learned to:

❑ Use an existing part as a starting point for a new part.

❑ Develop a secondary window.

❑ Use factory objects to allow dynamic memory allocation of objects.

❑ Use the Auto delete feature of the factory object to avoid memory leaks.

❑ Use variables with factory objects.

❑ Incorporate a secondary window with the DBAddRecord application.

❑ Implement a string generator to improve the usability of a collection view list box control.

❑ Implement the Add, Commit, and Rollback database functions.

This is all you will do with this application. A real database application has far more complexity and includes functions like update, delete, and sorting. Adding these functions is not hard, if you apply the principles and techniques you have learned.

What's in Chapter 14

In this chapter you will learn some additional techniques for completing applications. The following subjects are covered:

❑ Making a DLL

❑ Making a Resource DLL

❑ Using the class Browser

❑ Learning how to pass parameters to a program

❑ Making a Smart Window

Finally, this chapter briefly discusses some of the more advanced topics in application development.

14

Wrapping It Up

There are a number of aspects to developing applications that have been mentioned already in this book but not fully explained. For example, the use and construction of the DLLs used in the Calculator, and other examples, to handle keyboard input and to supply icons and bitmaps. You will probably want to make new DLLs and modify the ones supplied with this book for your own applications.

Making DLLs

In this book you have used a number of keyboard handlers to control what characters are allowed in a text control such as an IEntry-Field control. These handlers are provided in a DLL named **KBDHDR.DLL**. This DLL is made from several object files, which are the result compiling the source files containing the actual code to handle the keyboard strokes.

The code in the source files is very similar whether used in a .DLL or an .EXE file. The only difference in making a .DLL rather than an .EXE is that you must decide which member functions and events need to be exposed to the user of the .DLL. For the keyboard handlers this was not too difficult, because there is only one member function in each object file and there are no events.

The mechanism for exposing a member function or event is called exporting the feature. Features that are not exported are not accessible to the program using a .DLL. All **constructors** and **destructors** must be exported. Exporting can be done in a number of ways.

The compiler directive **#pragma export** can be used to export member functions. For example, the NumOnlyKbdHandler can be exported as shown in Code segment 49. Note that the whole definition of the member function needs to be entered twice. You can not use **#pragma export** to export data members; it can only be used to export member functions.

```
#pragma export (NumOnlyKbdHandler::characterKeyPress(
    IKeyboardEvent& event))
Boolean NumOnlyKbdHandler::characterKeyPress(
    IKeyboardEvent& event )
{

}
```

Code segment 49: Using #pragma export

The next way to export features is to include the **_Export** keyword in the member function declaration. This method requires a little less typing. The same function, NumOnlyKbdHandler, can also be exported as shown in Code segment 50.

```
Boolean _Export NumOnlyKbdHandler::characterKeyPress(
    IKeyboardEvent& event )
{
    . . .
}
```

Code segment 50: Using _Export

Any features not explicitly exported by one of these methods must be exported in a .DEF file. This is cumbersome and not recommended for C++ because you have to use the mangled names generated by the compiler. The utility CPPFILT and the library utility in Windows, ILIB, can be used to generate a .DEF file. For more details on exporting or generating .DLL files, consult the on-line *User's Guide* and/or *Programmer's Reference*.

When you use a DLL, the object code for the functions in the DLL is not included in the executable file. This gives the benefit of smaller executables and also the ability to share the code in the DLL with more than one program. The code in the DLL is dynamically loaded and linked with the rest of the program at execution time, hence the name Dynamic Link Library.

When making an executable file that references a DLL, these references must be resolved by the linker. The linker must know the name of the import library that contains the information on the contents of the DLL. **Import libraries** are generated by the **ILIB** library utility on Windows and its counterpart, **LIB**, in OS/2.

You can explicitly include the name of the import library in the link statement in the make file, or you can include a reference indicating which library file to use in the header file that is included by parts using the functions in the DLL. To implement this last method, include a #pragma library statement in the header file. For example, notice that the KBDHDR.HPP file has this implemented as shown in Code segment 51.

```
. . .
#ifndef __NO_DEFAULT_LIBS__
  #pragma library("kbdhdr.lib")
#endif
. . .
```

Code segment 51: Using the #pragma library

The statements in Code segment 51 are included in the object file generated by the compiler. The linker recognizes the **#pragma library** statement and uses the indicated file as an import library to resolve references to functions in the **DLL**.

Make Files for DLLs

The make file that generates a DLL is very similar to the one used to generate an executable. The main difference is in the compiler flags and in the generation of the import library. The /GE compiler flag is needed to compile the code as a DLL. The on-line reference book defines this flag as shown in Code segment 52.

```
/Ge<[+]|-> /Ge+: Use the version of the runtime
    library that assumes an EXE is being built.
/Ge-: Use the version of the runtime
    library that assumes a DLL is being built.
Default: /Ge+
```

Code segment 52: Definition of the /Ge compiler flag

Note that either a hyphen or slash can be used to define a compiler flag. Thus, **-Ge-** is the equivalent to **/Ge-**.

```
. . .
GCPPFLAGS= -Gm+ -Tdp -Gd+ -I. -Ge-

.obj.lib:

kbdhdr:    kbdhdr.dll kbdhdr.lib

kbdhdr.lib:  pnumdec.obj numonly.obj uckeybd.obj \
    hexonly.obj pnumonly.obj lckeybd.obj numdec.obj
      copy << kbdhdr.def
      LIBRARY kbdhdr
      DESCRIPTION 'KEYBOARD HANDLERS DLL'
      EXPORTS
<<
      cppfilt -b -p $** >> kbdhdr.def
      ilib /FREEFORM /Q /GENI:kbdhdr kbdhdr.def

kbdhdr.dll:   numonly.obj pnumonly.obj uckeybd.obj \
    hexonly.obj lckeybd.obj numdec.obj pnumdec.obj
 icc $(GCPPFLAGS) /Fekbdhdr.dll numonly.obj \
    pnumonly.obj uckeybd.obj hexonly.obj numdec.obj \
    lckeybd.obj pnumdec.obj kbdhdr.def

numonly.obj:   numonly.cpp {$(INCLUDE)}kbdhdr.hpp
         ICC -c $(GCPPFLAGS)  numonly.cpp

pnumonly.obj:   pnumonly.cpp {$(INCLUDE)}kbdhdr.hpp
         ICC -c $(GCPPFLAGS)  pnumonly.cpp
. . .
```

Code segment 53: Windows make file for KBDHDR.DLL

The Windows make file in Code segment 53, shows the step where the
CPPFILT utility is used to make a **Module Definition File** (.DEF)
file using the information in the .OBJ files mentioned in the dependency list for the .LIB file. The next step is to use **ILIB** to generate an
import library based on the information in the .DEF file just created,
see Code segment 54. You can browse the **KBDHDR.DEF** file in Windows to see why it is not recommended that you code it by hand.

```
         .

    GCPPFLAGS= -Gm+ -Tdp -Gd+ -I. -Ge-

    .obj.lib:

    #kbdhdr:    kbdhdr.dll

    kbdhdr.dll:    numonly.obj pnumonly.obj uckeybd.obj \
        hexonly.obj lckeybd.obj numdec.obj
        icc $(GCPPFLAGS) /Fekbdhdr.dll numonly.obj \
          pnumonly.obj uckeybd.obj hexonly.obj numdec.obj \
          lckeybd.obj kbdhdr.def
     IMPLIB /NOLOGO kbdhdr.LIB kbdhdr.DLL

    numonly.obj:    numonly.cpp {$(INCLUDE)}kbdhdr.hpp
         ICC -c $(GCPPFLAGS)  numonly.cpp

    pnumonly.obj:    pnumonly.cpp {$(INCLUDE)}kbdhdr.hpp
         ICC -c $(GCPPFLAGS)  pnumonly.cpp
         .
```

Code segment 54: OS/2 make file for KBDHDR.DLL

The OS/2 make file is somewhat simpler. The **IMPLIB** utility can take an existing .DLL file and create an import library from the information in it. The .DEF file in OS/2 can easily be coded by hand since it does not need as much information as the Windows file. See Code segment 54 for the complete OS/2 KBDHDR.DEF file.

```
LIBRARY KBDHDR INITINSTANCE TERMINSTANCE
PROTMODE
DATA MULTIPLE NONSHARED READWRITE LOADONCALL
CODE LOADONCALL
DESCRIPTION 'KEYBOARD HANDLERS FOR VA C++'
EXPORTS
```

Code segment 55: DEF file for OS/2

You should consider packaging code which can be used by multiple applications in a DLL. If you package and distribute VisualAge for C++ parts as DLLs you must also supply the corresponding .LIB, .HPP, .VBB and .DLL files. Otherwise, the users of your parts can not integrate them in their application.

Making a Resource DLL

Resource DLLs are one of the components that can be used when developing applications. You must compile the resource DLL in order to

use bitmaps and icons in your applications. In the Calculator you used a resource DLL for the bitmaps on the tool bar buttons. The instructions for building a resource DLL were not included in the Calculator application in order to keep the instructions focused. It is not very difficult to make a resource DLL once you have sample files to use. You can add your own bitmaps and icons to the existing BITMAPS.DLL, or you can create your own resource DLL.

There are several different files needed to make a resource DLL. These files are listed in Table 38. The .RC and .DEF are text files which are developed and modified in a text editor. The bitmaps and the icon for the Calculator application were drawn using the icon editor in OS/2, then converted for Windows. Remember that icons are different from bitmaps. Bitmaps are a single image, while icon files can contain multiple formats and a hot spot.

The format for the .RC file is different in OS/2 and Windows. The resource file used to make the Windows DLL is shown in Code segment 56, and the OS/2 file is shown in Code segment 57. The RC file is fairly self explanatory. Code segment 58 show a sample .DEF file.

```
1 BITMAP   PLUS.BMP
2 BITMAP   MINUS.BMP
3 BITMAP   TIMES.BMP
4 BITMAP   DIVIDE.BMP
5 BITMAP   CLEAR.BMP
6 ICON     TRAIN.ICO
7 ICON     NOTEBOOK.ICO
8 ICON     FLATFILE.ICO
```

Code segment 56: Windows Resource file

```
BITMAP   1 PLUS.BMP
BITMAP   2 MINUS.BMP
BITMAP   3 TIMES.BMP
BITMAP   4 DIVIDE.BMP
BITMAP   5 CLEAR.BMP
ICON     6 TRAIN.ICO
ICON     7 NOTEBOOK.ICO
ICON     8 FLATFILE.ICO
```

Code segment 57: OS/2 resource file

```
LIBRARY bitmaps
DESCRIPTION 'BITMAP RESOURCE DLL'
```

Code segment 58: Sample DEF file

In both the Windows and OS/2 versions, you use an object file to link the resource DLL. To get this object file you only need the simplest

Table 38: Resource files

File	Description
.BMP	The bitmap file is a binary representation of an image or picture.
.RC	The resource text file specifies resources with their type, content, and id. The id can be a reference name or an ordinal.
.DEF	This is a text file that is required for the linker.
.RES	This file is an output from the resource compiler.
.C	The resource file in OS/2 must link to an object. The initial release for the Windows platform also requires an object for the resource DLL.

program. See Code segment 59, for one of the smallest, most error-free programs possible.

```
void emptyPlaceHolder()
{
   ;
}
```

Code segment 59: Sample C file

```
bitmaps.dll: bitmaps.obj bitmaps.lib bitmaps.res\
     bitmaps.c
                   icc /Gd- /Ge- /I. /Tdc /B"/DLL /NOE" -
Fm$(@B).map  /Febitmaps.dll \
             bitmaps.exp \
             bitmaps.obj \
             bitmaps.res

bitmaps.lib: bitmaps.obj bitmaps.res
       copy << bitmaps.def
       LIBRARY bitmaps
       DESCRIPTION 'BITMAP RESOURCE DLL'
       EXPORTS
<<
       cppfilt -b -p $** >> bitmaps.def
       ilib /FREEFORM /Q /GENI:bitmaps bitmaps.def

bitmaps.obj: bitmaps.c
   icc -c+ bitmaps.c

bitmaps.res: bitmaps.rc  plus.bmp minus.bmp times.bmp
divide.bmp train.ico notebk.ico flatfil.ico
  irc -r bitmaps.rc
```

Code segment 60: Make file for a resource DLL

The last file needed is a make file as shown in Code segment 60. The make file in the Windows version uses **irc** as the resource compiler, and the OS/2 version uses **rc**. To see the OS/2 make file look at the **x:\VABOOK\BITMAPS\BITMAPS.MAK** file. You can make the resource DLL by running the make file. At a command prompt, enter **nmake bitmaps.mak**.

When the compile and link completes, you can use the BITMAPS.DLL file in your applications. Remember that the resource DLL needs to be in the **path** on Windows or in the **libpath** on OS/2.

Tool Bar Button Bitmaps

Now that you know how to make a resource DLL, you may want to make some real slick bitmaps for your tool bar buttons. There are a few details that are good to know when developing tool bar buttons for an application. Since tool bars are popular and very helpful, the next sections cover these details to help ensure your success.

Tool bar buttons are the unique size of 20 pixels by 17 pixels. This default size was picked more for aesthetics than for ease of programming. The OS/2 icon editor by default makes square icons which are 32 by 32 pixels. The Resource Workshop on Windows by default makes square bitmaps which are 64 by 64 pixels. For the best results in making tool bar icons, set the tool you are using so the bitmap size is 20 by 17 pixels.

You can assign bitmaps of different sizes to the tool bar button control, but at runtime the control uses an algorithm to adjust the bitmap to a size that fits the 20 by 17 pixel dimension and aspect radio of the tool bar button. This algorithm may not affect your icons if you use purely vertical and horizontal lines; but if your icons have diagonal lines, this algorithm will make the diagonal lines appear jagged like a lightning bolt.

Tool Bar Button Bitmap Size

There is a Visual Builder limitation that shows up when you use tool bar buttons. The size of tool bar buttons bitmaps is preset to 20 by 17 pixels. If you need to use bitmaps of a different size, 64 by 64 pixels in our example, you must change the **standardBitmapSize** value of the tool bar buttons. This can only be done before the bitmaps are applied to the buttons and presents a problem because you do not have direct control of the code generated by the Visual Builder. The code needs to be inserted at the appropriate place inside the constructor of the part which instantiates the tool bar control. There are two possible ways to get around this problem:

1. Edit the generated .CPP file and use the setStandarBitmapSize static member function of the IToolBarButton class, in the constructor code for the frame window which contains the tool bar. Do this before the tool bar is instantiated. See Code segment 61. This is not very good practice because, as you know, the .CPP file is replaced every time the Visual Builder generates the part code.

```
//————————————————————
// MainWnd :: MainWnd
//————————————————————
MainWnd::MainWnd(
      unsigned long id,
      IWindow* parent,
      IWindow* owner,
      const IRectangle& rect,
      const IFrameWindow::Style& style,
      const char* title)
            : IFrameWindow(id, parent, owner, rect,
style, title)
{
  iMainWndConnectionList = new IVBConnectionList;
  iCanvas = new ICanvas(
      IC_FRAME_CLIENT_ID,
      this,
      this,
      IRectangle());
IToolBarButton::setStandardBitmapSize(ISize(64,64));
iToolBar1 = new IToolBar(
id+WNDOFFSET_MainWnd_ToolBar1, this);
iToolBarButton = new IToolBarButton(
      id+WNDOFFSET_MainWnd_ToolBarButton,
      iToolBar1,
      iToolBar1,
      IRectangle(),
    IToolBarButton::defaultStyle() | IControl::group);
. . .
```

Code segment 61: Setting toolbar button bitmap size

2. Set the tool bar button size before the tool bar is constructed by using Visual Builder connections. This technique requires that you gain control of the application before the main window is constructed. This can be accomplished by creating a nonvisual part, which instantiates the main window of the application through a factory object. The **ready** event of the nonvisual part can be used to initiate two actions:

   ❑ set the standardBitmapSize value by using custom logic. See Figure 224.

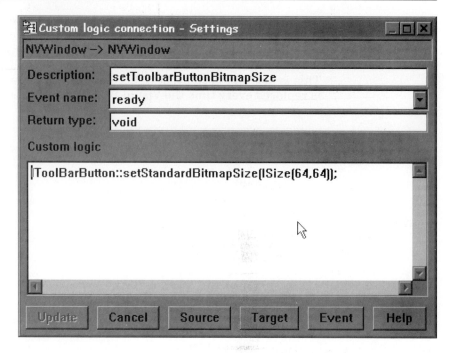

Figure 224: Custom logic to set tool bar button bitmap size

❏ create the main window of the application.

In Figure 225 you can see the two connections from the **ready** event:

❏ free-form surface (ready) → free-form surface custom logic(set-ToolBarButtonBitmapSize)

❏ free-form surface (ready) → mainWindowFactory(new)

The other two connections are:

❏ mainWindowFactory(newEvent) → mainWindow(this)

❏ mainWindowFactory(newEvent) → mainWindow(showModally)

In the Class Editor enter: **ITBARBUT.HPP** in the **Required include files** list.

The mainWindow part is a typical visual part which has IFrameWindow for its base class and also happens to have a tool bar attached to the frame window.

This is the preferred way to change the tool bar button bitmap size, as it does not require you alter the generated code.

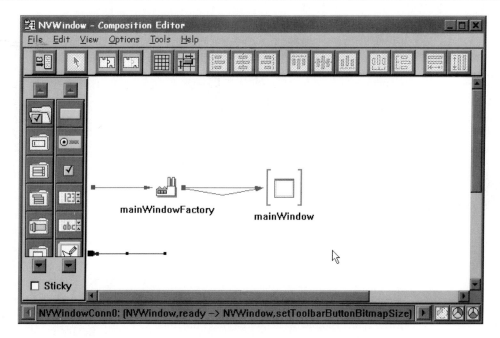

Figure 225: Dynamically Creating Main Window

In Figure 226 you see a test frame window with a tool bar with large (64×64 pixel) buttons. One button has a standard size (20×17 pixel) bitmap and the other has a full 64×64 pixel bitmap on it. As you can see all tool bar buttons are the same size regardless of the size of their bitmap.

One final point, no matter which of the two techniques you use you should be aware that the newly set tool bar button bitmap size will be in effect for all the tool bar buttons created by the application. If you create a secondary window, which also has a tool bar, its buttons will be set to the new **standardBitmapSize** value.

Bitmap Conversions

The bitmap file format and the resource file format are different in OS/2 and Windows. You can convert either the bitmap files or the .RC files to their target platform using utilities that come with VisualAge C++ for Windows. There are two conversion utilities for bitmaps and icons shipped with the VisualAge for C++ for Windows product:

❑ IBMPCNV.EXE (command line version)

❑ IBMPCNI.EXE (windowed version)

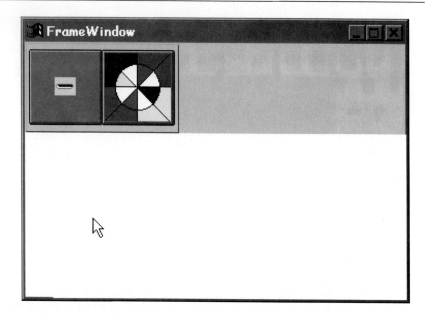

Figure 226: Toolbar with 64×64 pixel buttons

These utilities provide bi-directional conversion between OS/2 and Windows format bitmaps and icons.

The utility for converting resource files is called IRCCNV.EXE. It converts OS/2 resource files to the Windows format. All of these programs only run on Windows. There are many other commercially available utilities that convert bitmaps and icons from one format to another.

If you are developing in a multiplatform environment (using more than one operating system), you need to adopt some consistent naming conventions for the bitmap files to minimize confusion and errors. One technique is to put the bitmaps in subdirectories which indicate their type like, **x:\bitmapso** or **x:\bitmapsw**. This uses the last character to indicate the platform and makes it easy to keep the same file names for the bitmaps. Another technique is to use the platform suffix in the file name.

Other Uses for Bitmaps

There are other controls that use bitmaps in resource DLL files. If you want to display large bitmaps, use the **IBitmap** control. It is highly recommended that you use an **IViewPort** control under the **IBitmap** control in a canvas. This provides for vertical and horizontal scrolling with a large bitmap.

If you want a button to show action or movement, use the **IAnimatedButton** control. It uses a range of bitmaps in a resource DLL to get the effect of movement. The multimedia tool bar uses the IAnimatedButton for the play button. In the Visual Builder you specify the bitmap DLL and resources in the settings notebook of the IAnimatedButton, as shown in Figure 227.

You can also add bitmaps to IMenuItem, IGraphicPushButton, INotebook tabs, and the latched state for tool bar buttons. Unfortunately, INotebook tabs and the latched state for tool bar buttons do not have settings in the Visual Builder. Icons can also be used in the IContainer control in the tree view or in a container column.

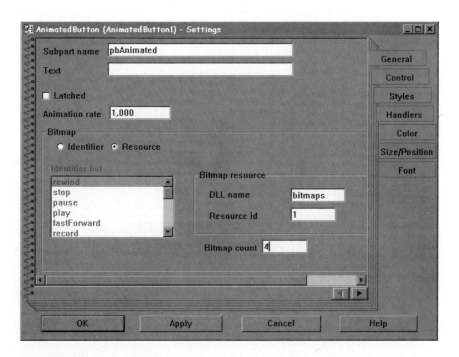

Figure 227: IAnimated bitmap settings

Externalizing Resource Strings

In all of the programs in this book the resource strings used by buttons, title bars, radio button text, static text, and so on, are directly compiled into the executable file. This is fine if you only plan to ship a single language version of the program and the people writing the program are the same people who decide what this text should be. Every time you change a word in any string the program needs to be recompiled.

The Visual Builder provides a facility to externalize the resource strings in a program in a separate resource file. This file contains all the strings and can be edited using a text editor by the people who translate the program or make the final wording decisions. This resource file is linked into the application by the make file. This method provides a less error prone and more convenient way to handle the text strings in an application.

As an exercise go back to the Adding Machine example in the **x:\VABOOK\ADDER** directory. Load the Open the **ADDER.VBB** file and load the **AdderView** part. Switch to the Class Editor.

In order to externalize the strings from a program, you must select the check box labeled **Starting resource id** in the Class Editor for the visual part. You must also supply the starting resource id number for the resources in that part. If you are working with an application that has multiple parts, you have to do this procedure for every part, taking care not to duplicate resource numbers, see Figure 228.

When you generate the part code and look in the DDERVIEW.RCI file, you see the string for the static text and push button strings, re-

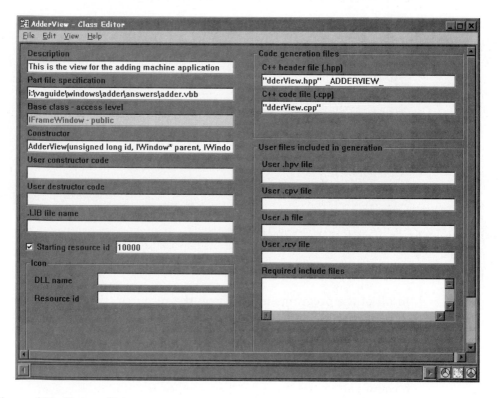

Figure 228: Externalizing resources

fer to Code segment 62. The text inside the quotes can be changed by anyone without the risk of accidentally adding bugs to your code. It is frustrating when a semicolon ";", parentheses "()", or brace "{}" is accidentally deleted from a program.

```
. . .
/*— Non-Window ID Related Resources —-*/
#ifndef AdderView_NONWINDOWRESOURCES_INCLUDED
#define AdderView_NONWINDOWRESOURCES_INCLUDED
STRINGTABLE
   BEGIN
      STRRC_AdderView_FrameWindow_title, "Adding Ma-
chine"
      STRRC_AdderView_txtNum1_text,   "First Number"
      STRRC_AdderView_txtNum2_text,   "Result"
      STRRC_AdderView_txtResult_text, "Second Number"
      STRRC_AdderView_pbAdd_text,   "A~dd"
      STRRC_AdderView_pbExit_text,  "E~xit"
   END
. . .
```

Code segment 62: Excerpt of DDERVIEW.RCI

Multiple Inheritance

Multiple inheritance is a very powerful feature in C++ which allows a subclass to inherit from more than one base class. Multiple inheritance is a little tricky because the subclass may inherit conflicting behavior from its base classes. In practice, most uses of multiple inheritance are rare and most use only two base classes. Other Object-Oriented languages like Smalltalk and Java do not support multiple inheritance.

The Visual Builder does not directly support multiple inheritance in the current release. When you select the Base class in the Visual Builder, you can only select one class. The documentation for the Open Class Library also recommends that you do not use multiple inheritance.

If you are determined to use multiple inherence, you can implement it in VisualAge C++. You need to edit the .HPP file to add the multiple inheritance to the declaration of the part. Using parts that have multiple inheritance in the Visual Builder is no different than using parts with single inheritance.

The WorkFrame IDE

VisualAge for C++ has an Integrated Development Environment, or IDE, called "WorkFrame". The WorkFrame can be customized for your environment, and the OS/2 version allows you to include other tools. The WorkFrame is very helpful for making compiler and build settings for applications.

The examples in this book do not require elaborate compiler settings, so the examples do not use the WorkFrame. A complete WorkFrame project and the detailed steps on how to use the WorkFrame are covered in the book *Object-Oriented Application Development with VisualAge for C++ for OS/2* by Marc Carrel-Billard.

Project Smarts

VisualAge for C++ includes a helpful set of functions called Projects Smarts which acts like wizards. Project Smarts helps you start creating applications and components for many of the commonly used types. There are samples for creating:

❏ C or C++ DLL

❏ Data Access application

❏ Direct to SOM application

❏ Distributed logic application

❏ Help as IPF format in OS/2and RTF format in Windows

❏ PM or Windows application

❏ UI Class Library application

❏ Visual Builder application

❏ Workplace Shell application

These samples provide good examples for different types of VisualAge for C++ applications. Unfortunately, the sample produced for a resource DLL does not include bitmaps. Use the sample provided in this chapter to make resource DLLs.

Making a Smart Window

Have you ever wished that applications remembered their window size and position when you close them? This would save the time it takes to adjust the windows every time you run the application. The **WindowSaver** part enables an application to save its window position and size when the application closes. When the application is run thereafter, the size and position are set from the previously saved values.

The WindowSaver part can be used with a minimum of three connections, as seen in Figure 229:

1. frame window(this) → windowSaver(theFrameWindow)

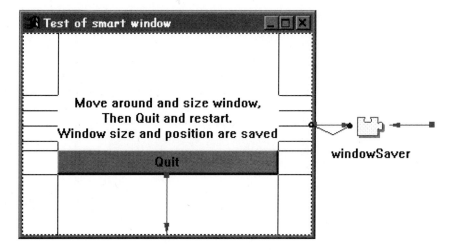

Figure 229: Minimum WindowSaver connections

   2. free-form surface(ready) → windowSaver(getWindowParms)

   3. frame window(closeEvent) → windowSaver(saveWindowParms)

By default, the information about the window position and size is saved in the Registry in Windows and in the **OS/2.INI** file in OS/2.

It is usually better for each application to have its own .INI file rather than storing the data in OS2.INI. One commonly used technique is to store the path where the application .INI file can be found in OS2.INI, query this path when the application starts, and then use the application .INI file to store any persistent data. If you already have an IProfile part in the application which saves other operating parameters or data, you can store the window position and size using the same profile. For example, you can add a WindowSaver part to the Reminder application. Connect the existing IProfile object to the windowSaver object as shown in Figure 230 with the following connection:

   ❑ yourIProfile(this) → windowSaver(theProfile)

The WindowSaver part uses an application name to store the window parameters in the profile. You can set this name by connecting:

   ❑ free-form surface (ready) → windowSaver(applicationName)

This connection needs a parameter which is the actual application name. Double-click on the connection, press the **Set parameters...** button, and enter the desired application name. If you use a different application name, make sure it is set before calling the **getWindow-Parms** actions. Do this by checking the order in the **Reorder Connections From** dialog on the free-form surface.

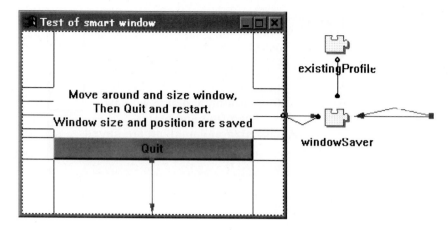

Figure 230: WindowSaver connected to IProfile

If the attribute **applicationName** is not set at the time the ready event occurs, an application name using the name of the executable file is appended with the string **:Window Parms**. For example, if the .EXE is called **WNDTEST**, then the application name in the profile is **WNDTEST:Window Parms**.

How It Works

The WindowSaver part works by asking the frame window its position and size when the window close event occurs. The **saveWindow-Parameters** member function can be seen in Code segment 63.

```
WindowSaver& WindowSaver::saveWindowParms()
{
  iTheProfile->addOrReplaceElementWithKey( "WIDTH",
    iTheFrameWindow->size().width(),
    this->applicationName()  );
  iTheProfile->addOrReplaceElementWithKey( HEIGHT",
    iTheFrameWindow->size().height(),
    this->applicationName() );
  iTheProfile->addOrReplaceElementWithKey( "XPOS",
    iTheFrameWindow->position().x(),
    this->applicationName()  );
  iTheProfile->addOrReplaceElementWithKey( "YPOS",
    iTheFrameWindow->position().y(),
    this->applicationName()  );
  return *this;
}
```

Code segment 63: WindowSaver saveWindowParms

The application initially starts in the default position, which is where it was placed on the Composition Editor free-form surface. When the application closes, its size and position are saved. When the application starts again, the **getWindowParams** member function reads the profile information and sets the window position and size using member functions of the IFrameWindow class as shown in Code segment 64.

```
WindowSaver& WindowSaver::getWindowParms()
{
  iTheFrameWindow->sizeTo(
    ISize( iTheProfile->integerWithKey( "WIDTH",
    this->applicationName()),
    iTheProfile->integerWithKey( "HEIGHT",
    this->applicationName()))));

  iTheFrameWindow->moveTo(
    IPoint( iTheProfile->integerWithKey( "XPOS",
    this->applicationName()),
    iTheProfile->integerWithKey( "YPOS",
    this->applicationName() )));

  return *this;
}
```

Code segment 64: WindowSaver getWindowParms

Notice that the four elements required, **XPOS**, **YPOS**, **WIDTH**, and **HEIGHT**, are stored individually as integers. When the values are retrieved they are paired into an **IPoint** and an **ISize** object, respectively, and used with the IFrameWindow member functions **moveTo** and **sizeTo** to restore the window. The **IPoint** and **ISize** classes are part of the Open Class Library; you can find more information about them in the on-line books.

The constructor for this class calls the private member function **setUpProfile**. This member function is used to set up the default IProfile object and defaultApplicationName in case none are provided, as shown in Code segment 65.

```
WindowSaver& WindowSaver::setupProfile ()
{
  IString appName = IApplication::current().argv( 0 );

  char path_buffer[_MAX_PATH];
  char drive[_MAX_DRIVE];
  char dir[_MAX_DIR];
  char fname[_MAX_FNAME];
  char ext[_MAX_EXT];
```

```
strcpy( path_buffer, appName );

splitpath(path_buffer, drive, dir, fname, ext);

   // Uses the system's user profile in OS/2: OS2.INI
   // In Windows = registry
iTheProfile = new IProfile (Profile::userProfile());

   // Use the file name of the Application+Window
   //Parms for the application name
IString temp = IString( fname ) +
    IString( ":Window Parms" );

setApplicationName( temp );

return *this;
}
```

Code segment 65: WindowSaver setupProfile

The complete files for this class are provided in the **x:\VABOOK\OTHER** directory.

Using the Class Hierarchy Browser

The **Browser** is a very helpful tool when you are working with C++ classes. Well designed C++ classes and class libraries take advantage of inheritance, which is a key aspect of objects. The Browser provides a way to view the hierarchy for a class library.

The Browser can load classes from the Open Class Library and your own classes. Files with an extension of .PDL are browser database files and the product includes .PDL files for:

❑ User Interface Classes

❑ Collection Classes

❑ I/O stream Classes

❑ Complex Math Classes

❑ Database Access Classes

❑ Application Support Classes

❑ OLE Framework Classes (only in Windows)

In order to browse your classes, you need to compile them with the /Fb or the /Fb* option and link with the /BROWSE flag. When you compile with these options the compiler generates a .PDB file, which can be loaded into the Browser. If you use WorkFrame you can use the

QuickBrowse feature, which does not require a compilation. The QuickBrowse uses a make file to scan the code for the browse information.

Let's browse the User Interface Class Library by following the steps below:

❑ First start the Browser by double-clicking the Browser icon.

❑ Then select File, Load, User Interface Classes.

The Browser loads the .PDL file and displays the list window with the classes, as seen in Figure 231.

Figure 231: Loading Classes in the Browser

❏ Display the class hierarchy by selecting **Actions**, **Show Inheritance Graph** from the menu bar.

The Browser tries to paint the entire User Interface class library in the window. It takes a little while and all you can see is a tangled web of lines. Let us examine the **IWindow** class. The Browser has a number of features to help you locate and narrow the scope of your interest. Follow these steps to zoom in on the IWindow class:

❏ Select **View**, **Max Zoom in**. You can also use the scroll bar on the left side to adjust the amount of zoom.

❏ Press Ctrl+F to display the Find dialog.

❏ In the Find dialog, enter **IWindow**, and the inheritance chart moves to the IWindow class.

❏ Press the right mouse button on top of IWindow and select **Graph All Base classes** from the pop-up menu. This shows the inheritance of IWindow, seen in Figure 232.

The Browser has the ability to combine classes in the hierarchy view. You can use the **File**, **Merge**, **Merge...** menu items to do this. You can load your classes into the Browser using either the **Load** or **Merge**

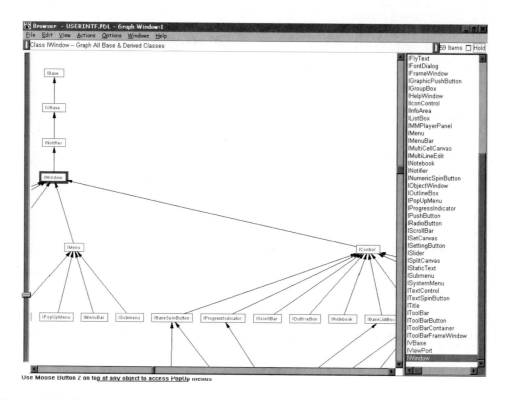

Figure 232: Browser view of IWindow

functions. Remember the Browser .PDB file produced from compiling the application? If you load your application, you can see it inherits from IFrameWindow.

Understanding the Error Log

Sometimes when you generate C++ code in the Visual Builder you get an error. A dialog displays the message Error occurred, see the ERROR.LOG file. This error happens when you do not have the required parts loaded for generation or are connecting to a deleted or renamed feature. This usually happens when you rename or unload parts while a Composition Editor is open. Figure 233 shows the error dialog.

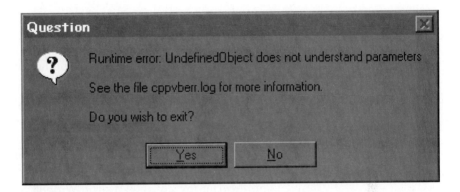

Figure 233: Runtime error

It is strongly recommended that you do not waste any time trying to read the *cppvberr.log* file. This file is provided as a diagnostic aid for the development team to aid problem detection if an error occurs in the Visual Builder when it is running. It is very unlikely that the contents of the error log file will make any sense to you. If it does make sense, you are probably qualified to assist the service and support team for the product.

Passing Parameters to a Program

The C and C++ languages use the variables **argv** and **argc** to pass parameters to programs when they are started. The IApplication class represents the current process or program. Two of its member functions can be used to access command line parameters, **argc()** and **argv()**. The argc() member function returns the number of arguments passed the application as parameters as seen in Code Segment 66:

```
int numOfParams = IApplication::current().argc();
```

Code segment 66: Number of command line arguments

Once you know how many parameters were passed, you can retrieve them using Code segment 67.

```
IString param1 = IApplication::current().argv(1);
```

Code segment 67: Retrieving command line arguments

The integer passed in the member function call in Code segment 67 should be less than the number returned in Code segment 66, as argc() returns a zero based number. Passing zero as a parameter to argv returns the fully qualified name of the program. This technique is used in the SmartWindow part in Code segment 65.

Running Applications on Windows 3.1

The examples in this book have covered developing applications in Windows NT, Windows 95 and OS/2. The Windows executable files (.EXE and DLL) are compatible between the different Windows platforms including Windows NT, Windows 95, and Windows V3.1. To run applications on Windows 3.1 you need to complete a few steps:

1. Install Win32S Version 1.30 with OLE on the Windows 3.1 system. There are three disk images included in the Win32s subdirectory which are installed with VisualAge for C++.

2. Copy the application executables to the Windows system including .EXEs and .DLLs.

3. Use **DLLRNAME** to determine which DLLs are needed for the application

4. Copy the necessary DLLs, located in the WIN32S subdirectory, to the Windows 3.1 system. You use these DLLs in place of the standard Open Class Library runtime DLLs.

That is all it takes, no recompiling is required. You only need to install the support software once. Additional applications can be copied right to the Windows system. Even the tool bar and the notebook control work fine. You need to be careful about the size of the applications, because most Windows 3.1 systems have less memory. And remember, Windows 3.1 is not a multitasking operating system!

Windows 3.1 Limitations

Some of the Open Class Library classes do not work on Windows 3.1, like the IThread class. Also, Windows 3.1 does not have the same amount of user interface styles as OS/2, Windows NT, and Windows 95, so these styles are ignored. Sometimes you may have problems using Win32s on some Windows machines. If you have problems running Win32s applications, you should look at the path statement in the system files. You can also test the application on a clean machine, one with only DOS, Windows, Win32s, the application, and the required DLLs.

If you are using the data access classes, you are limited to the ODBC support. DB2 CAE (Client Application Enabler) does not support Win32s, so you can not use the CLI (Call Level Interface) or the imbedded SQL.

Improving Application Performance

This book has covered a number of performance considerations throughout the different sample applications. The following list shows some of the things you can do to reduce the size of your applications and improve their performance:

❑ Be very careful with the depth of visual parts you layer. The Visual Builder makes it easy to put many layers of canvases and controls, often some of these layers are unnecessary.

❑ Only use the IMultiCellCanvas when needed for resizable controls. Windows that are not sizable should not use multicell canvases.

❑ Try to limit the number of connections. This may seem strange because the connections save coding, but each connection is a class. You can consolidate common functions in a nonvisual part and use one connection to start the functions.

❑ Your final program should be compiled with optimization on using compiler options /O+ or /Oc+. This takes a little longer to compile but is well worth it..

❑ Use the Performance Analyzer to find bottle necks and isolate resource intensive code.

❑ Use inline functions, but be careful because they cause code bloat.

❑ Use the most appropriate control. Becoming familiar with the Open Class Library will make this easier.

❑ Delete the **set** methods in your nonvisual parts for attributes which you only need to read.

These are some of the basic things that can be done to improve your VisualAge for C++ applications. There are also a number of things you can do in program design which will affect the application performance. Many program design trade-offs are specific to a certain application, so you need to rely on experience, intuition, experimentation, and a little luck to ensure success.

Reducing the Size of Runtime DLLs

Visual Builder applications use the Open Class Library runtime DLLs. You can create custom versions of the Open Class Library DLL by removing unused classes. The process for creating a custom DLL involves extracting the objects from the Open Class Library static DLLs included with the product. You can then delete any of the classes which you do not use (and not used by other classes), then re-link the DLLs. This entire process is documented in the on-line reference manual. This is a bit intricate, and it is only recommended for the more experienced developer.

Dynamic vs. Static Linking

When you prepare your application for distribution, you must consider whether you will be shipping all of the code in one executable file or shipping one executable file and one or more DLLs. There are pros and cons to both approaches. Shipping only one executable file involves statically linking the Open Class Libraries to your application. This greatly increases the executable file size as well as the time to start the application. The benefit of static linking is that the installation and packaging are fairly simple.

On the other hand, if you dynamically link the application with the class libraries, you will need to distribute the appropriate DLLs along with your program. Your program will also be dependent on the DLL levels which are distributed. To avoid conflicts with other applications that use the VisualAge for C++ runtime DLLs, you must rename the DLLs before shipping. The DLLRNAME utility that comes with VisualAge for C++ can change the executable file to use different DLL names. Use DLLRNAME to properly rename the Open Class Library DLLs in your .EXE files. Consult the "Open Class Library User Guide" for details on how and when to use the DLLRNAME utility.

All exercises in this book use the dynamic link process, this is the fastest way to develop an application because link times and swapper space are greatly reduced. You should consult the "Open Class Library User Guide" for details on compiler flags and different methods of distributing applications, and how to determine which class library DLLs you must distribute.

What Did Not Make It in This Book?

There are a number of more advanced topics which are not covered in this book. This section describes some of the programming topics which you may encounter when developing applications. Many of these topics have varying support in the Open Class Library and can be included in your applications with different amounts of hand coding. We have briefly covered some of these topics in the following sections.

Threads Support

The Visual Builder does not directly support developing applications that use multiple threads. There is an **IThread** class in the Open Class Library which can help you implement thread support in non-visual parts. Usually, tasks that are time consuming, such as reading a file or printing a report, should be performed in a separate thread, returning control to the user of the application immediately without tying up the user interface. There are many considerations when writing applications with multiple threads, mainly in the area of process synchronization and sharing resources.

Container Views

The DBViewer and DBAddRecord sample applications show how to use the details view of the container control. The IContainer also has a tree view and an icon view which can be very slick in some applications. These are not trivial to construct with the Visual Builder, but with a little code and practice you should be able to add these views to an application.

Container Direct Editing

There is a really useful feature you can implement with the **IContainer** control. When you display data in a container control, you can directly edit the data displayed on the container. The way to implement this requires a few steps:

1. In Windows you attach an IVBCnrEditHandler in the Handlers page of the container's settings notebook .

2. In OS/2 you must create your own class deriving from **ICnrEditHandler** and override the **endEdit** member function. A sample handler can be see in Code segment 68.

3. The container control and the container columns, if in details view, must have the style **readOnly** set to **off**.

```
class MyCnrEditHandler : public ICnrEditHandler
{
public:
  virtual Boolean endEdit (ICnrEndEditEvent& event)
  {
    ICnrEditHandler::endEdit(event);
    IVBContainerObject *cnrObj=(IVBContainerObject *)
      event.object();
    cnrObj->updateToObject();
    return false;
  }
};
```

Code segment 68: Container end edit handler

Directly editing containers which display objects from Data Access Builder parts require that an update to the database be made to finalize the changes.

Multimedia Support

VisualAge for C++ includes many multimedia classes which make it very easy to add some real dazzling features to applications. Using multimedia in your application requires that the target client machine support these features. For example, audio and video may require additional hardware and software that many commercial systems do not have and customers are unwilling to add.

To use the multimedia parts included with the Visual Builder, you must load the file VBMM.VBB. This file is in the **x:\IBMCPPW\IVB** directory in Windows or in the **x:\IBMCPP\DDE4VB** directory in OS/2.

DDE Support

The Open Class Library provides classes that support Dynamic Data Exchange (DDE). DDE has been around for a while, and it allows different processes to communicate using their own proprietary interface. You can use the DDE classes in nonvisual parts.

SOM Support

The current version of VisualAge for C++ supports the IBM System Object Model (SOM) Version 2.1. The Open Class Library classes are not SOM classes, but you can use them with your SOM classes. You can use SOM classes in the Visual Builder by creating an interface definition which makes SOM parts look like nonvisual parts.

OLE Support

The Windows version of the Open Class Library supports Compound Document Framework (CDF) classes. The CDF makes it easy to develop OLE containers and servers. This is a very powerful feature, and won VisualAge for C++ an award at the 1996 Object World show.

Drag and Drop Support

Simple drag and drop between entry fields and MLEs can be easily implemented in the Visual Builder by adding an **IVBDragDrop-Handler** to the Handlers page of the text control.

More complex drag-and-drop operations, for example between containers, is supported by the Open Class Library and requires hand coding of special handlers. This form of drag and drop is not simple to implement, especially the first time you code it, but it can add a lot of flexibility to an application.

User Defined Controls

There are many types of user defined controls. Simple attribute settings to controls can be saved and the parts can be added to the pallet. User defined controls with unique or different graphics can not be displayed in the Visual Builder. However, you can use these controls in VisualAge for C++ applications, and the Visual Builder indirectly supports these user defined controls. This feature is documented in the Windows version of *Building VisualAge C++ Parts for Fun and Profit* in the on-line books. The OS/2 documentation was available in FixPak CTV303.

The two types of parts are *userprimitive* and *usercomposer*. You can supply a bitmap resource which represents the user part in the part .vBE file. There is a limitation to these controls because they are represented by a bitmap. The bitmap can not be sized in the Visual Builder Composition Editor. You can, however, save and use customized versions of the Open Class Library primitive controls like IPushButton and IStaticText.

Team Programming

The current version of VisualAge for C++ is a single user, stand alone product. When developing in teams with multiple programmers you should use a configuration management and version control system or at least a library system. This helps store code and application files in different versions. It also provides the ability to share files between developers without endangering the integrity of the files. IBM markets two products that perform these functions, CMVC and TeamConnection. The most popular program for library control is called PVCS (Polytron Version Control System).

Chapter 14—Summary

This chapter covered a lot of small samples and tips that were not covered in the previous chapters. These helpful tips will make it easier for you to develop applications using VisualAge for C++. In this chapter you:

❑ Learned how to make a DLL

❑ Made a Resource DLL

❑ Use the Class Hierarchy Browser

❑ Learned how to pass parameters to a program

❑ Made a Smart Window

❑ Learned about some performance options

Conclusions for the Handbook

You have learned many of the basic concepts used to implement good Object-Oriented C++ PC applications. You have developed a number of well designed and functional sample applications which cover a broad range of user interface controls and nonvisual logic. You can solve many problems with software, given the right application development tools and sufficient hardware, time, and money to complete the programming.

Programming is still an art, and a good software professional should develop the best application possible under the constraints of the project. This means that experience and planning are key components to good software development. You need to budget time for iterating the design, testing, incorporating user feedback, adding error detection and correction, Help, and documentation. There is a lot more to application development than painting screens and making connections.

We hope you have enjoyed this book as much as we have enjoyed writing it.

M

main(), 35, 37, 45, 53, 127
make file, 127, 227, 289
marquee selection, 43
member function, 139
member functions, 130
memory, 3, 37, 356, 360
memory leaks, 360
message box, 359
mistake, 226
mnemonic, 41, 63, 107
modal, 359, 361
modeless, 359, 362
move
    connection, 288
multimedia, 402
multiplatform, 386
multiple inheritance, 389

N

naming conventions, 61, 386
nan, 158
new, 37, 356, 357, 358, 360
newEvent, 358, 359
nmake, 38, 152
Nonprimitive, 80
Nonvisual Parts, using, 88
notebook control, 294
notebook page, 296, 297
notification, 50, 53, 251, 286
notification framework, 130, 151
notifyObservers, 220, 251
NumDecOnlyKbdHandler, 115

O

ODBC, 321, 399
OLE, 402
Open Class Library, 12, 13
operating system, 3
options, 23
order connections, 278
out of sequence, 152

P

parameter, 120, 139, 287, 290
parsing, 281, 286
Part Interface Editor, 131
PARTCPPFLAGS, 152
Parts Interface Editor, 80
parts list, 73
Parts Selector, 22
paste, 170
PDB, 394
PDL, 394, 395
performance, 2, 82, 399
Performance Analyzer, 399
PIE. *See* Parts Interface Editor
platforms, 398
PM compatible, 335
pmCompatible, 336
pmprintf, 155
pointer, 313
pop-up menu, 124, 125
position, 390
pragma export, 376
pragma library, 377
precompiler, 331
Preferred connections, 44
Preferred list, 88, 119, 131
previousButton, 213
primitive part, 58
printf, 000
private variables, 273, 285
Program editor, 87
promote, 255, 266, 308
protection violations, 157
public interface, 130, 271, 273
pure virtual function, 368

Q

QuickBrowse, 395

R

radio button, 177
readOnly, 70, 239
ready event, 53, 123, 219, 224, 258, 288,
    313, 383

userName, 339
userprimitive, 403

V

valueAsDouble, 141
valueAsInt, 141
variable part, 313
VBB file, 22, 26, 333, 344
VBB files, 207
VBBASE.VBB, 22
VBDAX.VBB, 333
VBDEBUG, 152
VBE file, 206, 330, 332
VBE files, 205, 332
VBLOAD.DAT, 207, 208
Vertically in bounding box, 67

verticalSeparator
    container, 337
VGA, 4
viewport, 294, 301
virtual, 82
virtual function, 368
Visual Builder, 21

W

width, 241
Win32S, 399
Windows 3.1, 398
WorkFrame, 4
WorkFrame/2, 5
working directory, 60

LICENSE AGREEMENT AND LIMITED WARRANTY

READ THE FOLLOWING TERMS AND CONDITIONS CAREFULLY BEFORE OPENING THIS CD PACKAGE. THIS LEGAL DOCUMENT IS AN AGREEMENT BETWEEN YOU AND PRENTICE-HALL, INC. (THE "COMPANY"). BY OPENING THIS SEALED CD PACKAGE, YOU ARE AGREEING TO BE BOUND BY THESE TERMS AND CONDITIONS. IF YOU DO NOT AGREE WITH THESE TERMS AND CONDITIONS, DO NOT OPEN THE CD PACKAGE. PROMPTLY RETURN THE UNOPENED CD PACKAGE AND ALL ACCOMPANYING ITEMS TO THE PLACE YOU OBTAINED THEM FOR A FULL REFUND OF ANY SUMS YOU HAVE PAID.

1.   **GRANT OF LICENSE:** In consideration of your purchase of this book, and your agreement to abide by the terms and conditions of this Agreement, the Company grants to you a nonexclusive right to use and display the copy of the enclosed software program (hereinafter the "SOFTWARE") on a single computer (i.e., with a single CPU) at a single location so long as you comply with the terms of this Agreement. The Company reserves all rights not expressly granted to you under this Agreement.

2.   **OWNERSHIP OF SOFTWARE:** You own only the magnetic or physical media (the enclosed CD) on which the SOFTWARE is recorded or fixed, but the Company and the software developers retain all the rights, title, and ownership to the SOFTWARE recorded on the original CD copy(ies) and all subsequent copies of the SOFTWARE, regardless of the form or media on which the original or other copies may exist. This license is not a sale of the original SOFTWARE or any copy to you.

3.   **COPY RESTRICTIONS:** This SOFTWARE and the accompanying printed materials and user manual (the "Documentation") are the subject of copyright. The individual programs on the CD are copyrighted by the authors of each program. Some of the programs on the CD include separate licensing agreements. If you intend to use one of these programs, you must read and follow its accompanying license agreement. If you intend to use the trial version of Internet Chameleon, you must read and agree to the terms of the notice regarding fees on the back cover of this book. You may not copy the Documentation or the SOFTWARE, except that you may make a single copy of the SOFTWARE for backup or archival purposes only. You may be held legally responsible for any copying or copyright infringement which is caused or encouraged by your failure to abide by the terms of this restriction.

4.   **USE RESTRICTIONS:** You may not network the SOFTWARE or otherwise use it on more than one computer or computer terminal at the same time. You may physically transfer the SOFTWARE from one computer to another provided that the SOFTWARE is used on only one computer at a time. You may not distribute copies of the SOFTWARE or Documentation to others. You may not reverse engineer, disassemble, decompile, modify, adapt, translate, or create derivative works based on the SOFTWARE or the Documentation without the prior written consent of the Company.

5.   **TRANSFER RESTRICTIONS:** The enclosed SOFTWARE is licensed only to you and may not be transferred to any one else without the prior written consent of the Company. Any unauthorized transfer of the SOFTWARE shall result in the immediate termination of this Agreement.

6.   **TERMINATION:** This license is effective until terminated. This license will terminate automatically without notice from the Company and become null and void if you fail to comply with any provisions or limitations of this license. Upon termination, you shall destroy the Documentation and all copies of the SOFTWARE. All provisions of this Agreement as to warranties, limitation of liability, remedies or damages, and our ownership rights shall survive termination.

7.   **MISCELLANEOUS:** This Agreement shall be construed in accordance with the laws of the United States of America and the State of New York and shall benefit the Company, its affiliates, and assignees.

8. **LIMITED WARRANTY AND DISCLAIMER OF WARRANTY:** The Company warrants that the SOFTWARE, when properly used in accordance with the Documentation, will operate in substantial conformity with the description of the SOFTWARE set forth in the Documentation. The Company does not warrant that the SOFTWARE will meet your requirements or that the operation of the SOFTWARE will be uninterrupted or error-free. The Company warrants that the media on which the SOFTWARE is delivered shall be free from defects in materials and workmanship under normal use for a period of thirty (30) days from the date of your purchase. Your only remedy and the Company's only obligation under these limited warranties is, at the Company's option, return of the warranted item for a refund of any amounts paid by you or replacement of the item. Any replacement of SOFTWARE or media under the warranties shall not extend the original warranty period. The limited warranty set forth above shall not apply to any SOFTWARE which the Company determines in good faith has been subject to misuse, neglect, improper installation, repair, alteration, or damage by you. EXCEPT FOR THE EXPRESSED WARRANTIES SET FORTH ABOVE, THE COMPANY DISCLAIMS ALL WARRANTIES, EXPRESS OR IMPLIED, INCLUDING WITHOUT LIMITATION, THE IMPLIED WARRANTIES OF MERCHANTABILITY AND FITNESS FOR A PARTICULAR PURPOSE. EXCEPT FOR THE EXPRESS WARRANTY SET FORTH ABOVE, THE COMPANY DOES NOT WARRANT, GUARANTEE, OR MAKE ANY REPRESENTATION REGARDING THE USE OR THE RESULTS OF THE USE OF THE SOFTWARE IN TERMS OF ITS CORRECTNESS, ACCURACY, RELIABILITY, CURRENTNESS, OR OTHERWISE.

IN NO EVENT, SHALL THE COMPANY OR ITS EMPLOYEES, AGENTS, SUPPLIERS, OR CONTRACTORS BE LIABLE FOR ANY INCIDENTAL, INDIRECT, SPECIAL, OR CONSEQUENTIAL DAMAGES ARISING OUT OF OR IN CONNECTION WITH THE LICENSE GRANTED UNDER THIS AGREEMENT, OR FOR LOSS OF USE, LOSS OF DATA, LOSS OF INCOME OR PROFIT, OR OTHER LOSSES, SUSTAINED AS A RESULT OF INJURY TO ANY PERSON, OR LOSS OF OR DAMAGE TO PROPERTY, OR CLAIMS OF THIRD PARTIES, EVEN IF THE COMPANY OR AN AUTHORIZED REPRESENTATIVE OF THE COMPANY HAS BEEN ADVISED OF THE POSSIBILITY OF SUCH DAMAGES. IN NO EVENT SHALL LIABILITY OF THE COMPANY FOR DAMAGES WITH RESPECT TO THE SOFTWARE EXCEED THE AMOUNTS ACTUALLY PAID BY YOU, IF ANY, FOR THE SOFTWARE.

SOME JURISDICTIONS DO NOT ALLOW THE LIMITATION OF IMPLIED WARRANTIES OR LIABILITY FOR INCIDENTAL, INDIRECT, SPECIAL, OR CONSEQUENTIAL DAMAGES, SO THE ABOVE LIMITATIONS MAY NOT ALWAYS APPLY. THE WARRANTIES IN THIS AGREEMENT GIVE YOU SPECIFIC LEGAL RIGHTS AND YOU MAY ALSO HAVE OTHER RIGHTS WHICH VARY IN ACCORDANCE WITH LOCAL LAW.

ACKNOWLEDGMENT

YOU ACKNOWLEDGE THAT YOU HAVE READ THIS AGREEMENT, UNDERSTAND IT, AND AGREE TO BE BOUND BY ITS TERMS AND CONDITIONS. YOU ALSO AGREE THAT THIS AGREEMENT IS THE COMPLETE AND EXCLUSIVE STATEMENT OF THE AGREEMENT BETWEEN YOU AND THE COMPANY AND SUPERSEDES ALL PROPOSALS OR PRIOR AGREEMENTS, ORAL, OR WRITTEN, AND ANY OTHER COMMUNICATIONS BETWEEN YOU AND THE COMPANY OR ANY REPRESENTATIVE OF THE COMPANY RELATING TO THE SUBJECT MATTER OF THIS AGREEMENT.

Should you have any questions concerning this Agreement or if you wish to contact the Company for any reason, please contact in writing at the address below.

Robin Short
Prentice Hall PTR
One Lake Street
Upper Saddle River, New Jersey 07458

Index

A

aboveClient, 100
accelerator keys, 187
actions, 118, 214, 270
ADDER.VBB, 61
AdderView, 59
Adding Machine, 59
alignment buttons, 63
APPCPPFLAGS, 152
application icon, 122
argc, 397
argv, 397
ASCII, 233, 268
asString, 254
attributes, 120, 214, 268
Auto delete, 360

B

belowClient, 100
bind file, 343
bitmap, 99, 100, 375, 386, 387, 403
bitmapAndTextView, 125
bitmapView, 125
blank fields, 373
breakpoint, 161
breakpoints, 161, 162
Browse Part Features, 117
Browser, 394
bubble help, 27
bugs, 389
buttonClickEvent, 90, 119, 131
buttonView, 124, 125

C

C++ logic, 271
Calc, 59
Call Level Interface, 399
catch, 143
categories, 27

Class Editor, 83, 137, 141, 145, 388
class hierarchy, 394
Class Library, 12
clear, 117
CLI, 329
Client Application Enabler, 399
clipboard, 15, 117, 236, 237
close, 362
closeEvent, 167
code snippet, 82, 145
collection, 284, 285, 287
collectionPosition, 364
columns, 335
commandEvent, 124, 196
commit, 369, 370
Compiler, 4, 38, 49
compiler flag, 152
composite nonvisual parts, 303
composite parts, 58
Composition Editor, 26
Compound Document Framework, 402
configuration management, 403
connection, 114, 143, 146, 152, 289, 318, 399
connections, 43
constructor, 52, 141, 224, 259, 276
container column, 401
container control, 334
containers, 401
context sensitive help, 182
controls, 59, 403
convert
    bitmap, 385
    resource file, 386
copy, 196
copy parts, 95, 96
CSDs, 4
    service level, 4
currentButton, 213
custom logic, 143, 144, 145
cut, 196

D

data, 130
Data Access builder, 3, 5
Data entry, 64
datastoreName, 339
DB2, 5, 325
db2start, 331

deallocate
    memory, 360
debug, 152, 153, 159
Debugger, 2, 158
default button, 69
default length, 70
delete, 360
depth, 399
destroy, 345, 361
destructor, 52, 141, 362
detailsViewSplit, 355
dialogBorder, 126
directly edit, 41
directly editing, 31. *See* direct editing
Distribute, 67
DLLRNAME, 398
Documentation, 10
drag, 110
drop down menu, 187
duplicate definitions, 86
Dynamic Data Exchange, 402

E

endOfFile, 278
environment variable, 362
eof, 278
error, 158, 386, 388, 397
error message, 101, 137
error window, 359
errors, 129, x, 146, 228
ESC
    escape, 103
events, 120, 214, 258, 270
exception handling, 139, 000, 000
exceptionOccured, 366
exceptionOcurred, 147, 277
executable file, 376, 377, 392, 398, 400
expandable, 265
export, 376
export file, 205
exporting a feature, 376
externalize, 387

F

factory, 358
FAT, 23

FAT files, 279
feature generation, 136
Feature source..., 86
features, 308
file position, 275
file size, 400
Fixpak, 361, 362
FixPak CTV, 403
FixPaks, 5
flat file, 233
Floating title, 100
floating tool bar, 110
fly over help, 108, 109
focus, 359
font, 33
Frame Extensions, 98
free-form surface, 29, 124

G

general protection fault (GPF), 157
Generate All, 86
get member function, 133
Group, 70

H

handler, 205, 206
hardware, 1, 3
header file, 15
header files, 49
Help, 11
help id, 182
HexOnlyKbdHandler, 115
horizontalSeparator
    container, 337
hot spot, 177
hover help, 108
HPFS, 23

I

IAnimatedButton, 387
IApplication, 397
IBitmap, 386
ICanvas, 30, 39, 170, 171, 173, 301

LICENSE INFORMATION FOR DB2 Trial Version

The products on this CD-ROM are licensed under the International Program License Agreement (IPLA) terms and conditions.

The following products entitle one person to use the product:

- DB2 for Windows 95 & Windows NT Single-User,
- DB2 Software Developer's Kit for Windows 95 & Windows NT
- DDCS for Windows NT Single-User.

The DB2 Server product and the DDCS Multi-User Gateway product entitle up to five concurrent users. If more than five people need to use these products concurrently, you must purchase Entitlements for Additional Users. These Entitlements are available for 1, 5, 10, or 50 additional users.

This program has one or more features that are designed for use on machines other than the machine on which the Program is used. You ma make copies of the feature(s) and documentation in support of your authorized use of the Program. Persons using a machine outside of your Enterprise may use the copy only to access the associated Program.

You can install and try any of the DB2 or DDCS products (other than the product that you bought) for a period of 60 days or until July 31, 1998 whichever comes first. After the trial period expires, the products become inactive until a license key is entered into the nodelock file. If you decide you want to buy a product you tried, contact your IBM software reseller or the IBM office nearest you.

When you purchase one of the DB2 or DDCS CD-ROM products, you receive a label which contains a license key. These labels are not transferable and should be kept in a secure place. To permanently install the product, you enter the license key in the nodelock file on the machine where the product is installed. You can enter the license key at installation time or you can install the product and enter the key in the nodelock file at a later time.

If you buy a product after the trial period has ended, you do not need to re-install the product. Instead, you would edit the nodelock file and add the license key that you received in the product box to reactivate the product.

LICENCE AGREEMENT FOR VisualAge for C++ for Windows Trial Version

This is a no charge Evaluation License ("License") between you and International Business Machines Corporation ("IBM") for the evaluation of IBM's software and related documentation. ("Program")

IBM grants you a non-exclusive, non-transferable license to the Program only to enable you to evaluate the potential usefulness of the Program to you. You may not use the Program for any other purpose and you may not distribute any part of it, either alone or with any of your software products.

IBM retains ownership of the Program and any copies you make of it. You may use the Program on one (1) machine only.

You may not decompile, disassemble or otherwise attempt to translate or seek to gain access to the Program's source code.

The term of your License will be from the date of first installation of the Program, and will terminate 60 days later, unless otherwise specified. THE PROGRAM WILL STOP FUNCTIONING WHEN THE LICENSE TERM EXPIRES. You should therefore take precautions to avoid any loss of data that might result. You must destroy and/or delete all copies you have made of the Program within ten (10) days of the expiry of your License.

If you are interested in continuing to use the Program after the end of your License, you must place an order for a full license to the Program and pay the applicable license fee. In that event, your use of the Program will be governed by the provisions of the applicable IBM license for the Program.

IBM accepts no liability for damages you may suffer as a result of your use of the Program. In no event will IBM be liable for any indirect, special or consequential damages, even if IBM has been advised of the possibility of their occurrence.

YOU UNDERSTAND THAT THE PROGRAM IS BEING PROVIDED TO YOU "AS IS," WITHOUT ANY WARRANTIES (EXPRESS OR IMPLIED) WHATSOEVER, INCLUDING BUT NOT LIMITED TO ANY IMPLIED WARRANTIES OF MERCHANTABILITY, QUALITY, PERFORMANCE OR FITNESS FOR ANY PARTICULAR PURPOSE. Some jurisdictions do not allow the exclusion or limitation of warranties or consequential or incidental damages, so the above may not apply to you.

IBM may terminate your License at any time if you are in breach of any of its terms.

This License will be governed by and interpreted in accordance with the laws of the State of New York.

This License is the only understanding and agreement we have for your use of the Program. It supersedes all other communications, understandings or agreements we may have had prior to this License.

VisualAge for C++ for Windows

Hardware Requirements

- Processor:

    80386 minimum
    80486 or higher strongly recommended
- Display:

    VGA minimum
    SVGA recommended
- Mouse or pointing device
- CD-ROM drive required\
- Memory requirements for Win95 (add 4 MB for Win NT):

    C development: 8 MB minimum, 12 MB recommended
    C++ development: 12 MB minimum, 16 MB recommended
    C++ visual development: 16 MB minimum, 24 MB recommended
- Disk space requirements:

    Minimal when running product from the CD-ROM

Custom install of the following is also available:

    285 MB for all tools and toolkits
    60 MB for samples and tutorials
    25 MB for all documentation
    40 MB swap space minimum

Software Requirements

- Development environment:

    Windows NT 3.51 or higher
    Windows 95

- Execution environment:

    Windows 3.1
    Windows NT 3.51 or higher
    Windows 95

Prereq products

- For Data Access Builder

    DB2 for Windows NT Version 2.1 and higher, or

    Oracle 7 and higher, or

    Sysbase SQL Server 10 and higher.

DB2 for Windows NT and Windows 95

Hardware requirements

Intel 486 or higher processor
For Clients, at least 1 MB of memory in addition to the OS requirements
For Servers, 10 MB or more RAM.
Hard disk space requirements:
    DB2 CAE: 9 MB
    DB2 SDK: 17 MB

Software Requirements

Windows NT 3.51 or higher
Windows 95

Communications Protocols

IPX/SPX or NetBIOS or TCP/IP or APPC or local IPC